THE
MEXICAN
RIGHT

THE
MEXICAN
RIGHT

The End of Revolutionary
Reform, 1929–1940

John W. Sherman

Westport, Connecticut
London

Library of Congress Cataloging-in-Publication Data

Sherman, John W.
   The Mexican right : the end of revolutionary reform, 1929–1940 /
John W. Sherman.
      p.   cm.
   Includes bibliographical references (p.   ) and index.
   ISBN 0–275–95736–5 (alk. paper)
   1. Mexico—Politics and government—1910–1946. 2. Conservatism—
Mexico—History. I. Title.
   F1234.S53   1997
   972.08′2—dc20   96–22015

British Library Cataloguing in Publication Data is available.

Library of Congress Catalog Card Number: 96–22015
ISBN: 0–275–95736–5

First published in 1997

Praeger Publishers, 88 Post Road West, Westport, CT 06881
An imprint of Greenwood Publishing Group, Inc.

Printed in the United States of America

The paper used in this book complies with the
Permanent Paper Standard issued by the National
Information Standards Organization (Z39.48–1984).

10 9 8 7 6 5 4 3 2 1

To the victims of *los tecos*, paramilitaries recruited at the
Autonomous University of Guadalajara.

Contents

Acknowledgments

Like any author, I am indebted to far more persons than I have opportunity to mention. While I take responsibility for the shortcomings of this work, many friends and colleagues deserve some credit for its merits. Since this is a revised version of my 1994 University of Arizona dissertation I am, not surprisingly, particularly indebted to the Latin Americanists teaching there. Michael C. Meyer, now Emeritus, Donna Guy, and Kevin Gosner read the manuscript with care. I am also grateful to Bert Barickman, Oscar Martínez, and student-colleagues, including Rob Buffington, who swatted mammoth mosquitos with me at our *pensión* in Mexico City. Thanks also to Juan García, Michael Schaller, the Latin America Area Center and Graduate School for research support, staff at the various archives, Praeger, and my sister-in-law, Jean, who aided in the final stages of manuscript preparation.

Introduction

For historians of Latin America, the political Right has become an important topic of inquiry.[1] Several scholars in other disciplines analyzed the military regimes that seized power in the 1960s and 1970s, but only recently have historians begun to delve into Latin American archives in order to uncover the roots of Latin America's Right. The Left has stolen the spotlight throughout the breadth of twentieth-century world political history, and for young Latin Americanists in particular, the substantial and growing interest in the Right contrasts with the focus of a previous generation of scholars.[2] Working in the context of the Cold War and shaken by the dramatic unfolding of the Cuban Revolution in 1959, academics in the 1960s were preoccupied with the nature and possibilities of the Latin American Left. In an era of worldwide social and political upheaval, it seemed as though the whole region south of the U.S. border might erupt in revolution. Instead, to the surprise of many, Ché Guevara's plans of exporting peasant insurrection from Cuba fizzled, and by the mid-seventies most of Latin America was under the control of rightist military regimes. Bureaucratic authoritarianism snuffed out vestiges of populism in the southern cone; coups in Brazil (1964), Argentina (1966), and Chile (1973) pointed to a failure of a developmentalist model that had predicted democracy, political stability, and the rise of an economically vibrant middle class.

Where did these rightist regimes come from? Historians, who had focused so predominantly on the Left, have been slow to give answers. Nonscholarly explanations attributing the resurgence of the Right to exogenous forces, such as the machinations of the United States, fall far short of offering adequate explanation. In the past three decades, when antidevelopmentalist theoreticians such as Guillermo O'Donnell analyzed military dictatorships in Latin America, they did so largely without the help of historians.

Not all Latin Americans lived under military rule, however. Mexico in particular remained remarkably stable until the 1990s. For Mexican scholars, many pertinent questions have hinged on why the nation was in fact *not* undergoing massive political instability like that which took place in South America. Despite the 1968 chaos in Mexico City, which included the massacre of hundreds of antigovernment demonstrators at the Plaza of Tlatelolco, and despite nascent guerrilla movements in the early seventies, Mexico's Partido Revolucionario Institucional [PRI] retained political power with little difficulty. Though many scholars, particularly Mexicans themselves, began to define the PRI as authoritarian, the roots of the regime's stability, rather than its authoritarian or rightist origins, have long attracted scholarly attention. Political scientists have been in the forefront of explaining the PRI's longevity, emphasizing its ability to absorb dissent and co-opt its opponents, while employing a number of concepts such as clientilism, corporatism, and patronage in explaining the durability of Mexico's government.[3]

Although able to retain power, the Mexican regime has changed over time. Convulsed by a decade of profound social revolution beginning in late 1910, Mexico has been governed by its "Revolutionary" establishment and party ever since. Yet a revolutionary heritage notwithstanding, the political leadership has tracked a decidedly conservative course, especially since 1940. In fact, historians have long used the 1940 presidential elections as a point of demarcation between an era of "institutionalized" revolutionary reform and an evolving developmentalist state.[4] The 1934–1940 presidency of Lázaro Cárdenas has been viewed as the apogee of institutionalized revolution, when the "mandates" of the 1910–1920 social convulsion—such as land and labor reform—were fulfilled. After revving up the revolutionary engine of reform, so the argument goes, prudent political leaders "cooled" the system down for a few years, presumably before revving it up again.

Yet although some presidential administrations, such as that of Adolfo López Mateos (1958–1964), have been more progressive than others, an honest assessment of Mexico's history should lead to the conclusion that the "engine of reform" has not even been kept in idle since the 1930s, and that—beginning with Miguel de la Madrid (1982–1988)—it has in fact been turned off. The revolutionary discourse spewed forth by Mexico's government and official press, as aptly noted by Illene O'Malley in an underappreciated 1986 book, cloaks the real nature of Mexican political life—sometimes even from Mexicans. The PRI has "usurped the lexicon of socialist revolution," positioned itself as an alternative to "reaction," and effectively undercut real revolutionary possibilities in Mexico.[5]

It is time, then, that we reevaluate the political dynamics of 1930s Mexico. Were the goals of the Cárdenas government (the Cardenista project) in the mainstream of Mexican political culture? Were they driven by consensus politics and an authentic mandate for reform? If the reform impetus is genuine in Mexico, then it follows that the PRI's subsequent endurance may be a product of repression and an inherently authoritarian nature. If, however, the Cárdenas reform agenda was largely out of step with the sentiments of the bulk of the Mexican people, the fundamentally conservative nature of a regime that has successfully endured is more comprehensible.

In order to answer these questions and more fully grasp the nature of cardenismo, we must obviously study the political Right. Multifaceted and sophisticated, the 1930s Right transcended class lines and consisted of a series of disconnected groups. Among its components were the "Gold Shirts," an organization influenced by the international surge of fascism and especially by the Spanish Falange. A Catholic Right included the dissolving peasant guerrilla fighters known as Cristeros, as well as groups resisting the expansion of secular education. Added to this were the "White Guards," paramilitary forces employed by great landowners to terrorize peasants seeking land reform. Small businessmen and sizable portions of the urban middle class also supported the Right in its call for electoral reform and pro-business economic policies, while rural middle sectors, such as northern *rancheros* who owned modest tracks of land, joined in order to resist what they perceived to be radical agrarian reform. Much of the army, battling the government's attempts to control it, aligned with the Right as well.

Despite its importance for understanding both cardenismo and contemporary Mexico, the 1930s right has been neglected. Earlier works, however, have examined particular facets of the Right, especially its most colorful and controversial components. In 1976 Hugh Campbell published his *La derecha radical en México, 1929–1949*, an edited version of a 1967 dissertation. Using Seymour M. Lipset's conceptualization of radicalism and class as a model, Campbell divides the extreme Right into secular and religious branches.[6] As the title suggests, he focuses on the "radical" groups, especially the Gold Shirts and Sinarquistas. Today, with new sources such as the Presidential Papers in Mexico's Archivo General de la Nación available, a more complete examination of the broader 1930s Right is possible. A richer historiography of the 1930s now exists as well, facilitating the study of the Right's role on multiple fronts.

In contrast to the 1930s Right, scholars have thoroughly investigated the preceding Cristero rebellion of 1926–1929.[7] Not only did 1929 see the end of this rural Catholic insurrection, it also witnessed the failed presidential bid of José Vasconselos, an independent candidate who garnered support from conservatives. Thus 1929 is the best point of departure for an examination of the Mexican right, one that bridges the critical gap in its history from its apparent demise to pivotal election year of 1940.

NOMENCLATURE: WHAT IS MEANT BY THE "RIGHT"

This work focuses on the Mexican political Right, but what is meant by the Right? The term, though widely used, is slippery. Some scholars such as Sandra

McGee Deutsch, the leading scholar on the South American Right, have avoided it because it is "broad and vague." Deutsch opts instead to use counterrevolution as her defining term, and multiple studies of the Right in modern European history use the term *fascism*, another oft-debated label that, for purposes of this study, will be applied in a narrow context.

The political significance of "Right" and "Left" began with the French Revolution. When the Third Estate withdrew from the Estates General and convened the National Assembly in June 1789, radicals (the Jacobins) positioned themselves to the left of the speaker's podium, while defenders of the king were on the opposite side of the chamber and to the right. Comprised primarily of aristocrats, including nobles and prelates, the right featured spokesmen such as Duval d'Eprémesuil, Abbé Maury, and royalist army officer Cazalés. These aristocrats were monarchists who defended the notion of royal prerogative and "moved to the right in their determination to halt the progress of the revolution." Just to the left of the monarchists, but still on the right side of the chamber, were bourgeois delegates who sought political power for themselves under a constitutional monarchy.[8]

As the French Revolution took an increasingly radical course, the Right sharpened and stiffened ideologically. Emigrés, aristocrats, and refractory priests united by mid-1790 in their opposition to the revolutionary government and in their desire for counterrevolution. The priests became particularly important in wooing part of the rural masses into the counterrevolutionary camp; devotion to the church evolved into a means of demonstrating one's opposition to the revolution.[9] Thus the practical alliance of the religious establishment with forces on the political Right had begun, a natural ideological positioning given the anticlericalism of major Enlightenment thinkers such as Voltaire.

Still, as suggested by this background, the early Right was defined not so much by what it was as by what it was not: the Right rejected the Enlightenment and the French Revolution. It was antiliberal, opposed to Jean Jacques Rosseau's "natural righteousness," John Locke's egalitarian political notions that focused on the individual, and Adam Smith's laissez-faire economics.[10] A more affirmative definition evolved during the nineteenth century, aided by the articulation of conservatism.

Not only did opposition to the French Revolution foment from within, but increasingly it fomented from without. The foremost intellectual voice disparaging the revolution was British thinker Edmund Burke, author of *Reflections on the Revolution in France*. The work became a cornerstone of conservatism and is essential to defining the Right. Burke viewed society as organic, resting on pillars of tradition and hierarchy, yet he did not oppose change. On the contrary, he granted the need for reform. Instead of "destroying the foundation," however, Burke chided the French: "You might have repaired those walls, you might have built on those old foundations . . . You had all the advantages in your ancient state, but you chose to act as if you had never been molded into a civil society and had everything to begin anew." Burke acknowledged that the

Ancien Régime was "full of abuses" acquired over time, but he argued that reform was the solution, not sweeping revolution.[11] This feature of organic growth, allowing for reform, distinguishes the Right from simple reaction.

The term counterrevolution, by its very nature, implies reaction or a restorationist agenda. One might expect it to most aptly fit the Mexican situation, since Mexico had a revolution, but because most components of the Right were not simply seeking to "turn back the clock," use of another term is preferable. Further, counterrevolution is itself a contested word.[12] A leading scholar of twentieth-century Mexico, Oxford University's Alan Knight, uses it to define the 1913–1915 Mexican government of Victoriano Huerta. According to Knight, who argues that revolution and counterrevolution can exist at the same time, Huerta's regime was counterrevolutionary because it suppressed populism. Thus we may deduce that Knight equates the term with extreme conservatism rather than with a restorationist agenda. A useful definition is that of Deutsch, who defines the "counterrevolutionary tendency in politics" as that which seeks "to promote stability . . . by strengthening family, morality, religion, authority, property, ethnic loyalties, and nationalism."[13]

Beyond distinguishing between the concepts of the Right, conservatism, and counterrevolution, it is necessary to briefly clarify what is meant by fascism and nationalism. Some Mexican rightist organizations such as the Gold Shirts and Sinarquistas readily evoke use of the adjective "fascist." Yet like other concepts, fascism is hotly contested. One scholar, Gilbert Allardyce, points to the failure of academics to explain it adequately, concluding that fascism does not even exist!

The so-called fascist parties are too mixed, diverse, and exceptional to be collected into such a general typology. It is not enough, therefore, to replace the German and Italian prototypes with a conservative international model. Instead, it is necessary to declassify fascism altogether as a generic concept.[14]

This skepticism notwithstanding, use of the term continues, and several scholars have tendered viable definitions. A practical one is proffered by Deutsch, who states that fascism "narrowly designates the most extreme groups of the right, whose opposition to modernism and egalitarianism assumes a radical, antibourgeois character appealing to the masses." Seymour Lipset, in his influential 1960s work *Political Man*, scrutinized election data and determined that fascism constitutes the "extremism of the liberal center." More abstract in his definition, Ernest Nolte has attracted considerable attention with his notion that fascism is the process of the middle class betraying their own revolution by siding with the ruling class against the rising proletariat. To Nolte, "fascism has at its command forces which are born of the emancipation process and then turn against their own origin."[15]

Despite debate, some degree of consensus has emerged with regard to the nature of fascism. Nearly all theoreticians agree that it is rooted in mass appeal, tapped by way of media propaganda directed primarily at the lower middle class. In this sense, while counterrevolution comes from above, fascism springs forth from below. While traditional dictatorships intimidate a populace into passivity, fascism elicits the active participation of a people in reaching state-defined goals. This embrace of mass politics and the primacy of the state speaks to fascism's unusual intellectual roots, a strange mixture of "reactionary and revolutionary impulses [that] collide dialectically." Fascism is corporatist, using vertical hierarchies and institutions to build preeminent allegiance to the state. It is also a social dynamic of resistance to modernization and industrialization. Consequently, some scholars like Nolte hold that fascism was unique to a specific period of time, while others such as Lipset do not restrict its existence to one particular epoch.[16]

Interestingly, nearly all these consensus components could be applied to the Right, and hence do not sufficiently delineate it from fascism. Despite the extensive literature on European fascism, and the sizable number of books and articles attempting to define the term, it seems that, as much as anything, we associate fascism with certain images: distinctive uniforms and insignias, displays of highly disciplined military units, expressions of sadism, and extreme racial and religious (especially anti-Semitic) hatred. Because of these mental associations derived primarily from European fascism, this work uses the term sparingly—only with regard to organizations and activities that conjure up these same images.

Fascists are often fierce nationalists, and nationalism is often associated with the Right. Nationalism denotes a devotion to the modern nation-state, both culturally and politically, that prompts adherents to seek to enhance their nation's power and international standing. Traditionally, historians have looked to the French Revolution for the roots of nationalism, when the French embraced a communal identity after 1789, mobilizing as a modern state for the task of world war. More recently Benedict Anderson has argued that the origins of nationalism more properly lie in Latin America, where "creole pioneers" wooed non-Spanish speaking masses into independence movements with nationalistic rhetoric.[17]

A frequent component of nationalism is a hostile reaction to foreigners that results when natives feel culturally, economically, or politically threatened. This hostility generally leads to the curtailment of civil rights and the rejection of liberal notions of individual freedom in favor of communal integrity, thus making hypernationalism more of a progeny of the Right than of the Left. Previous studies of Mexican nationalism have pointed to xenophobia as a crucial contributor in its evolution.[18] David Brading, in his study of Mexican nationalism's origins, finds that early patriotism evolved into nationalist rhetoric in the writings of Fray Servando Teresa de Mier and Carlos María de Bustamante. White-skinned Mexican descendants of the Spanish, known as *criollos*, resented foreigners (particularly Spaniards who came to Mexico and dominated colonial political offices). As a consequence, they began to extol the Aztecs and disparage the Spanish Conquest, cultural themes echoed a century later in post-revolutionary *indigenismo*.[19] This xenophobic tendency is evident in the 1930s nationalism of the Right.

TOWARD A NEW POLITICAL HISTORY: POPULAR VALUES AND CULTURE

Finally, a word about the wider historiographical and theoretical contours of this work is in order. Since the triumph of French *Annaliste* thought in the historical profession over the past several decades, we have been blessed with innumerable incisive studies of social and cultural history (and some less-than-incisive, imitative works as well). What does that mean for those of us who continue to write political history?

It should mean that if not engaging in a quest for a "new" political history, we must at least pay attention to the social dynamics and the political culture (or political *mentalité*) of an age. Top-down, state-oriented, institutional political history runs the risk of misinterpreting the strengths and weaknesses of any given regime, because a powerful centralist state with a modicum of autonomy can take aggressive steps in the shortterm and look impressive on paper. Take, for example, cardenismo, which featured the reorganization of the official party into corporate blocs that have supported the PRI into the 1990s. By noting this and by observing its ambitious reform programs, statistics on the scope of land distribution and labor mobilization (especially if we take those figures at face value), and by recalling the image of cheering throngs in the Zócalo when Cárdenas expropriated American oil company properties, we can conclude that cardenismo was a success. As one recent dissertation posits, after examining the stated goals and convention decrees of the cardenista Confederación Nacional Campesina, "the Revolution mobilized peasants, the [official party] united the mobilized peasants, and . . . the peasants recognized Cárdenas' achievements and worshiped him."[20]

In truth, millions of Mexican peasants despised Cárdenas, and the broader goals of the Cardenista project, as evidenced by the decisive and lasting shift in the ideological direction of the Mexican government, did not endure. In order to understand the brevity, limitations, and failures of cardenismo, we must incorporate an understanding of the political culture. The term "political culture" was first widely used and thoroughly defined by a generation of political scientists in the early 1960s. Lucian Pye, Gabriel Almond, and Sidney Verba pioneered the concept, followed by others such as Donald Devine and Walter Rosenbaum. They noted that politics invariably shows up "in the daily thinking and activity of people," and offered a plentitude of subordinate terms to distinguish various elements of political culture, such as regime orientation and political efficacy.[21] Their methodology for evaluating political culture was rather dry, usually consisting of examining polling data regarding politics and related social and cultural values. For the historian lacking scientific polling data, the task is to deduce those same values in the past by grappling with the literary appeals and political discourse employed by both the government and the opposition.

Certain segments of this examination of the Mexican Right attempt to take the reader, ever so modestly, in this direction. The advent of gender analysis and women's history is helpful in this task, since examining the conceptualization and role of gender involves, by its nature, wrestling with values. For Mexicans, family and ideas about the meaning of family are an essential element of life and culture. Contemporary polls repeatedly show that "family" is what Mexicans value most, and political leaders invariably engage the familial discourse accordingly.[22] By the 1930s Mexicans routinely spoke of "the Revolutionary family," and today the family is at the heart of Mexican political appeals: in the 1994 presidential campaign of Ernesto Zedillo, for example, the PRI's official slogan was "for the well-being of the family."

The primary thesis of this study, that the Cardenista project was fraught with fragility and severe limitations in the political culture, is tentative. Such an argument, as already implicitly stated, stands opposite some of the conclusions of an older, traditional historiography.[23] The scope of this work, the Mexican Right, is only one aspect of 1930s Mexico (albeit a crucial one) that must be examined in order for scholars to test this hypothesis adequately. As historians and interdisciplinary colleagues continue to approach the Mexican past in innovative ways, the concomitant advent of what historian Gilbert Joseph and anthropologist Daniel Nugent call "a more adequate political history" that may prompt some reperiodization and revision of political history may well be forthcoming.[24]

NOTES

1. Examples of the surge in recent studies include Douglas Chalmers, Maria do Carmo Campello, and Atilio Boron, eds., *The Right and Democracy in Latin America* (New York: Praeger, 1992), and scholarship by country such as Orazio Ciccarelli, "Fascism and Politics in Peru during the Benavides Regime, 1933–39," *Hispanic American Historical Review* 70:3 (August 1990): 405–32, and Sandra McGee Deutsch and Ronald Dolkart, eds., *The Argentine Right: Its History and Intellectual Origins, 1910 to the Present* (Wilmington, Del.: Scholarly Resources, 1993).

2. Eugen Weber, "The Right: An Introduction," in Hans Rogger and Eugen Weber, eds., *The European Right: A Historical Profile* (Berkeley: University of California Press, 1965), p. 2; Sandra McGee Deutsch, *Counterrevolution in Argentina, 1900–1932: The Argentine Patriotic League* (Lincoln: University of Nebraska Press, 1986), p. 2.

3. Viviane Brachet-Márquez, "Explaining Sociopolitical Change in Latin America: The Case of Mexico," *Latin American Research Review* 27:3 (Fall 1992): 91. The best recent synopsis of the traditional political science explanation is Roderic Camp, *Politics in Mexico* (New York: Oxford University Press, 1993).

4. Regarding the significance of 1940 see, among others, select essays in Stanley Ross, ed., *Is the Mexican Revolution Dead?* (Philadelphia: Temple University Press, 1966), and Howard Cline, *Mexico: Revolution to Evolution, 1940–1960* (New York: Oxford University Press, 1963).

5. Illene O'Malley, *The Myth of the Revolution: Hero Cults and the Institutionalization of the Mexican State, 1920–1940* (Westport, Conn.: Greenwood Press, 1986), pp. 7, 117.

6. Hugh Campbell, *La derecha radical en México, 1929–1949*, trans. Pilar Martínez Negrete (Mexico City: Editorial Jus, 1976). Campbell's book is an abridged version of a 1968 UCLA dissertation. Lipset argued that the three classes of society have natural political preferences: the working class tends to the left, the middle class to the center, and the ruling class to the right. Each class has the possibility of extremism, with the middle prone to fascism. See Seymour Martin Lipset, *Political Man: The Social Bases of Politics* (Garden City, N.Y.: Doubleday, 1963). Some have asked whether or not Latin American societies lacking strong middle sectors can be fascist. On this question see Alistair Hennessy, "Fascism and Populism in Latin America," in Walter Laqueur, ed., *Fascism, a Reader's Guide: Analyses, Interpretations, Bibliography* (Berkeley: University of California Press, 1976), pp. 255–60.

7. Jean Meyer's study of Sinarquismo appeared in Spanish as *El sinarquismo: ¿Un fascismo mexicano? 1937–1947* (Mexico City: Editorial Joaquín Mortiz, 1979). It came on the heels of Meyer's authoritative study of the Cristeros, *La Cristiada* 3 vols. (Mexico City: Siglo Veintiuno Editores, 1973–1974). See also David Bailey, *Viva Cristo Rey: The Cristero Rebellion and the Church-State Conflict in Mexico* (Austin: University of Texas Press, 1974).

8. Deutsch, *Counterrevolution in Argentina*, p. 2; Albert Soboul, *The French Revolution, 1787–1799: From the Storming of the Bastille to Napoleon*, trans. Alan Forrest and Colin Jones (New York: Random House, 1974), p. 164.

9. Soboul, *French Revolution*, pp. 211–12; D.M.G. Sutherland, *France 1789–1815: Revolution to Counterrevolution* (London: Fontana Paperbacks and William Collins, 1985), pp. 116–17.

10. David Rock, "Antecedents of the Argentine Right," in Deutsch and Dolkart, eds., *The Argentine Right*, p. 3.

11. Edmund Burke, *Reflections on the Revolution in France*, ed. Oskar Piest and Thomas H. D. Mahoney (New York: Liberal Arts Press, 1955), p. 40.

12. For further commentary on the implications of the term counterrevolution, see Arno J. Mayer, *Dynamics of Counterrevolution in Europe, 1870–1956: An Analytic Framework* (New York: Harper & Row, 1971), pp. 1–5.

13. Alan Knight, *The Mexican Revolution: Counter-revolution and Reconstruction*, vol. 2 (Cambridge: Cambridge University Press, 1986), pp. 99–102; Deutsch, *Counterrevolution in Argentina*, p. 1.

14. Gilbert Allardyce, "What Fascism Is Not: Thoughts on the Deflation of a Concept," *American Historical Review* 85 (April 1979): 368, 378–79.

15. Deutsch, *Counterrevolution in Argentina*, pp. 4–5; Wolfgang Sauer, "National Socialism: Totalitarianism or Fascism?" *American Historical Review* 73 (December 1967): 409–10; Ernst Nolte, *Three Faces of Fascism: Action Française, Italian Fascism, National Socialism*, trans. Leila Vennewitz (New York: Holt, Rinehart & Winston, 1966), pp. 5, 453.

16. Deutsch, *Counterrevolution in Argentina*, p. 232; Sauer, "National Socialism," pp. 413–17, 420–21. Sauer points out that, although the middle class serves as the base, fascism can receive support from big business and the aristocracy. The argument of active participation is articulated by Jackson Spielvogel in *Hitler and Nazi Germany: A History* (Englewood Cliffs, N.J.: Prentice-Hall, 1988); Rock, "Antecedents of the Right," p. 3.

17. Benedict Anderson, *Imagined Communities: Reflections on the Origin and Spread of Nationalism* (London: Verso, 1991), pp. 47–50.

18. Weber, "The Right," pp. 9–10; see Frederick C. Turner, *The Dynamic of Mexican Nationalism* (Chapel Hill: University of North Carolina Press, 1968), pp. 22–53, 202–48.

19. David Brading, *Los orígenes del nacionalismo mexicano*, trans. Soledad Loaeza Grave (Mexico City: Secretaría de Educación Pública, 1973), pp. 10, 13–14.

20. Allan Spencer, "The Mexican Revolution under Lázaro Cárdenas: Strategies of Institutionalization" (Ph.D. dissertation, University of Pittsburgh, 1990), pp. 284, 286.

21. Walter Rosenbaum, *Political Culture* (New York: Praeger, 1975), pp. 5–9. Rather than "Regime Orientation," I prefer to speak of perceptions regarding the government's legitimacy. "Political Efficacy" is the degree to which a populace believes that they can effect meaningful political change under a given system.

22. Camp, *Politics in Mexico*, pp. 56–57.

23. Weakness and a rightward shift on the part of Cárdenas has long been identified, however. See in particular Albert Michaels, "The Crisis of Cardenismo," *Journal of Latin American Studies* 2 (1970): 51–79, and Alan Knight, "The Rise and Fall of Cardenismo," in Leslie Bethell, ed., *Mexico since Independence* (Cambridge: Cambridge University Press, 1991). Knight notes the exceedingly limited and uneven nature of its political power in "Weapons and Arches in the Mexican Revolutionary Landscape," in Gilbert Joseph and Daniel Nugent, eds., *Everyday Forms of State Formation: Revolution and the Negotiation of Rule in Modern Mexico* (Durham: Duke University Press, 1994), p. 51.

24. Gilbert Joseph and Daniel Nugent, "Popular Culture and State Formation in Revolutionary Mexico," in *Everyday Forms of State Formation*, p. 23.

Acronyms

ACF	Acción Cívica Femenina
ACJM	Asociación Católica de la Juventud Mexicana
ACM	Acción Católica Mexicana
ACN	Acción Cívica Nacional
AEACAJ	Asociación Española Anti-Comunista y Anti-Judía
ARM	Acción Revolucionaria Mexicana
CCC	Confederación de Cámaras de Comercio
CCM	Confederación de la Clase Media
CNA	Cámara Nacional de Agricultura
CNC	Confederación Nacional Campesina
CNE	Confederación Nacional de Estudiantes
CNOP	Confederación Nacional de Organizaciones Populares
CNPI	Confederación Nacional de Partidos Independientes
COPARMEX	Confederación Patronal de la República Mexicana
CROM	Confederación Regional Obrera Mexicana
CRPI	Confederación Revolucionaria de Partidos Independientes
CRRN	Comité Revolucionario de Reconstrucción Nacional
CTC	Confederación de Transportes y Comunicaciones
CTM	Confederación de Trabajadores de México
FCDM	Frente Constitucional Democrático Mexicano
FEU	Federación Estudiantil Universitaria

FNPI	Frente Nacional de Profesionistas e Intelectuales
FROC	Federación Revolucionaria de Obreros y Campesinos
JCFM	Juventud Católica Femenina Mexicana
LNDL	Liga Nacional Defensora de la Libertad
LNDLR	Liga Nacional Defensora de la Libertad Religiosa
PAN	Partido Acción Nacional
PCM	Partido Comunista Mexicana
PCN	Partido Católico Nacional
PNA	Partido Nacional Antireeleccionista
PNR	Partido Nacional Revolucionario
PNSP	Partido Nacional de Salvación Pública
PRAC	Partido Revolucionario Anti-Comunista
PRI	Partido Revolucionario Institucional
PRM	Partido de la Revolución Mexicana
PROC	Partido Revolucionario Obrero Campesino
PRUN	Partido Revolucionario de Unificación Nacional
PSD	Partido Social Democrático
PSDM	Partido Social Demócrata Mexicano
STERM	Sindicato de Trabajadores de la Enseñanza de la República Mexicana
STFRM	Sindicato de Trabajadores Ferrocarrileros de la República Mexicana
STPRM	Sindicato de Trabajadores Petroleros de la República Mexicana
UCM	Unión de Católicos Mexicanos
UDC	Unión de Damas Católicas
UFCM	Unión Femenina Católica Mexicana
UN	Unión Nacionalista
UNEC	Unión Nacional de Estudiantes Católicos
UNPF	Unión Nacional de Padres de Familia
UNS	Unión Sinarquista Nacional
UNVR	Unión Nacional de Veteranos de la Revolución
UPP	Unión de Pequeños Propietarios
VMN	Vanguardia Mexicana Nacional

1

ANTECEDENTS OF THE MEXICAN RIGHT TO 1929

The simple and tidy political meanings of Right and Left, begun with the seating arrangement at the National Assembly in revolutionary France in the summer 1789, are nearly lost in the chaos of early national Mexican political history. A light thread of conservative ideology can be detected in nineteenth-century Mexico, though often ill defined and elusive. Ideological distinctions sharpened during the long dictatorship of Porfirio Díaz (1876–1910), matured further in the upheaval of the great Revolution (1910–1920), and fomented in its aftermath, primarily with the Cristero Rebellion (1926–1929).

With the advent of Independence in 1821, Mexico's mercantile economic elite displaced their political rivals, the Spaniards, only to find themselves divided ostensibly along ideological lines. Liberals, influenced by the writings of French Enlightenment thinkers such as Benjamin Constant, gathered in the York Masonic Lodge and received guidance from the U.S. minister to Mexico, Joel Poinsett. Conservatives gravitated toward Scottish Rite Masonry, conferring frequently with British Minister H. G. Ward. Whereas liberals like Lorenzo de Zavala and José María Luis Mora admired North American federalism and proclaimed their faith in constitutionalism, conservatives such as Lucas Alamán extolled the young nation's colonial heritage and a tradition of strong central government. Predictably, conservatives enjoyed the support of the army and the church, as they defended privileges such as *fueros*, which exempted priests and army officers from civil trial.

With political cliques defined by ideology, one would expect to encounter an easily identifiable Mexican Right. But although traditional political historians have long emphasized the schism between liberals and conservatives—a phenomenon present throughout early national Latin America—the ideological boundaries are not nearly so sharp as they appear. Most political figures were pragmatic, and ideology often proved secondary in their governance. Alamán, for example, a Scottish Rite conservative, revived Mexico's textile industry by employing state intervention and establishing a federal bank. He criticized the ecclesiastical tithe as damaging to agriculture. Fray Servando Teresa de Mier, a monarchist, found fault in Emperor Augustín Iturbide's centralism (1822–1823), while by the 1850s liberals had embraced in practice the centralism they had so long disparaged. Antonio López de Santa Anna, the most famous Mexican political figure of the age, overthrew a conservative government in 1832, only to oust the liberals in a second coup in 1834. Subsequently, he used the clout of liberals as a counterforce with which to blackmail the church.[1] Hence early Mexican politicians were far more pragmatic and opportunistic in practice than ideologically driven.

Beyond the limited importance of ideology, the roots of the Right are marginal in early Mexican national history because of the dominance of liberalism. From the collapse of a brief Mexican empire in the wake of Independence (1821–1823) until a period of civil war and reform (1855–1862), liberalism held the upper hand. A more accurate division of the early Mexican body politic, in fact, is by liberal factionalism, for many Scottish Rite Masons became *moderados*, or moderate liberals, by the 1850s, and only in the late 1840s had Alamán and the conservatives organized openly. And since the contours of conservatism are faint, it is not surprising that nationalism, so often allied to the ideology of the Right, is "most conspicuous by its absence" in early Mexico.[2]

While conservatism remained ill defined, Mexican liberalism evolved in the decades following Independence, shifting its foundation from the imitation of foreign constitutional models onto the firmer ground of tenets formulated, at least in part, by the analysis of Mexican historical experience. Foremost among these was anticlericalism, which, coupled with a willingness to assault unmerited privilege in general, increasingly motivated liberal thinkers. The church and the army, two institutions that respectively wielded vast economic and political power, drew the ire of liberals determined to instill the Enlightenment notions of equality and individuality into Mexican society. Inspired by the writings of José María Luis Mora, ultraliberals, known as *puros*, decried the *fueros* and assaulted the vestiges of clerical power and privilege.[3]

During the Reform (1855–1862) a new generation of statesmen led by Benito Juárez implemented an agenda that brought the liberal-conservative conflict to a breaking point. In a series of laws incorporated into the Constitution of 1857, Juárez and his *puro* compatriots undermined the economic resources of the church. The army, which had reached enormous proportions under Santa Anna's last reign (1853–1855), also came under attack. In 1855 a law named after its author, *Ley Juárez*, abolished military and clerical *fueros* and restricted ecclesiastical court jurisdiction to church affairs. Within two years *Ley Lerdo* forced the sale of property not actively involved in religious ministry, while *Ley Iglesias* regulated clerical fees charged for a variety of services and sacraments such as baptism and burial, adjusting them downward to pre-Independence levels.

Motives for such reform legislation were complex, but rested on liberal faith in private property, suspicion of clerical power, and the conviction that stagnant church wealth was retarding Mexico's economic growth.

Convinced that compliance with *puro* reforms would effectively crucify the church on an economic cross, clerics resisted. With little modification, *puros* incorporated their laws into a new 1857 constitution, complementing it with a Bill of Rights granting universal male suffrage, freedom of the press, freedom of assembly and speech, and the right to bear arms. Within short order conservatives embraced the last of these rights, for with the cry of "religión y fueros" officers and priests sparked reactionary revolts, the first of which erupted in the orthodox bastion of Puebla even before the constitution was ratified. Fortunately for the conservative cause, one critical modification of *Ley Lerdo* in the new constitution effectively removed *ejidos*, or Indian communal lands, from exemption from forced sale or confiscation. The subsequent civil war, or War of the Reform (1858–1860), then, actually saw myriad Indians enlist on the side of conservatism. The rural elite, delighted at the prospect of buying church properties at reduced prices, generally supported the liberals.

Historians agree that the biggest loser of the War of the Reform was the church. Pillaged by *puros* who gleefully seized (and often desecrated) its properties, the wealthiest institution in Mexico suffered deprivation at the hands of its conservative allies as well. For although conservative General Félix Zuloaga voided *Ley Lerdo*, he extracted forced loans from the church, backed by the value of properties held behind conservative lines. Yet liberals often sold these very same church properties in absentia, using their value as collateral against their own European bank loans.

The tide of battle eventually swung in favor of the liberals, bringing the army of Jesús González Ortega into Mexico City on New Year's Day 1861. The triumph of *puro* liberalism in the War of the Reform should have doomed Mexican conservatism, but the Right received a brief respite with the arrival of French troops and a European crown prince, Maximilian, in 1862. Despite an elaborate coronation in Mexico City's cathedral, Maximilian eventually disappointed his allies. Determined to curry the favor of liberals led by Juárez, he recognized the sale of church properties, decreed a series of liberal reforms, and even legally abolished debt peonage in 1865. Yet all was for naught. Unbending *puros* under Juárez and González Ortega co-opted nationalism as they led a successful guerrilla war against the French, culminating in Maximilian's death at the hands of a firing squad in midsummer 1867. For the right, the French Intervention was a disaster: not only did Maximilian betray it in the short term, but its association with the foreign imposition tossed the banner of nationalism into the hands of the liberals, laying to rest forever the Right's monarchist aspirations and tainting it with treason.

The departure of the French also terminated the Right's tentative outward organization. The conservative party founded by Alamán dissolved, and the "disastrous defeat" of the conservative-French coalition "had a chastening effect on the clergy's political activities."[4] The army, too, was weakened as Juárez regained power. Dramatically reduced in size, its officers found themselves subject to trial in civil courts. "The old Conservative army, so prone to insubordination and revolt, had been dissolved for good."[5]

Fortunately for the church, Benito Juárez provided space for a modest continuity of Catholic activity. During his tenure from 1867 to his sudden death in 1872, he eased punishments on conservatives, allowing exiles to return, restoring their political rights, and ultimately issuing an amnesty decree. Though politically impotent, Catholic conservatives took advantage of this space to form the Sociedad Católica de México in 1868. This organization, joined by a parallel women's group in 1869, promulgated conservative social values in its press organ, *La Voz de México*, from 1870 to 1875. The brief tolerance under Juárez ended with the administration of Sebastián Lerdo de Tejada (1872–1876), however, fraying the conservative camp and bringing it into renewed crisis. One faction accepted the triumph of secularism and the Constitution of 1857, acknowledging the supremacy of the state in political matters. Another faction, involved in the Sociedad, refused to surrender social and political ground.[6]

Conservatism had largely pivoted on questions regarding the role of the church ever since anticlericalism had become the hallmark of Mexican liberalism in the days of Luis Mora. In 1876 it divided and began to redefine itself as Porfirio Díaz rebelled. Díaz, a man of impeccable liberal credentials, initiated his successful revolt under the Plan de Tuxtepec (1876). Aggravated church-state tensions under Lerdo contributed to the rise of Díaz, who was able to garner support from conservatives sympathetic to his pleas for national reconciliation. In contrast, belligerent conservatives such as those active in the Sociedad engaged in politics, motivated by the calls of *La Voz de México* to return to the political arena, establish public morality, and bring order to society. In early 1877 regional political associations formed, including the "Díaz and Chacón" society in Morelia (named for conservative Michoacanese governor Felipe Chacón) and the Junta Central Conservadora in Guadalajara. Simultaneously, the conservative press revived, part of a resurgence that alarmed liberals, who feared that the Reform and its triumphs may have been in vain.

Conservative revival posed such an apparent threat to Mexican liberalism at the outset of 1877 that Díaz himself had to reaffirm his commitment to the Reform and the constitution. Yet in the 1877 elections for governors, congressional deputies, and Supreme Court justices, the opposition was roundly defeated. Conservatism could not capture popular support because of its previous associations with the discredited 1853–1855 Santa Anna regime and the French. The Catholic Right would not reenter the political arena until 1911.[7]

With the defeat of the stalwart Catholics, a well-known modus vivendi between the Porfirian government and the church emerged. Acceptance of the secularized state led to ceremonial contacts between the high clerics and Porfirian officials. The church kept a low profile, and tensions eased as Díaz declined to implement the anticlerical legislation and constitutional provisions descended from the Reform.[8] Yet the peace was deceptive. The threat of implementation hung over the brow of the church. Similarly, the process of increased state control over the army continued from the days of Juárez, as Díaz professionalized the officers' corps and weakened its access to power. Troops in the field received better instruction and equipment. Other policing forces such as the *Rurales* (Rural Police), operating in the countryside, multiplied under Díaz, counterbalancing the influence of the conservative army that had revolted so many times in the past.[9]

Intellectually the clash of liberalism and conservatism persisted. Outward manifestations of political peace masked ideological tensions. Indeed, during the Porfiriato, Catholic thinkers planted the intellectual seedlings of the modern Mexican Right. The basis of Catholic thought was the rejection of the modern secular state, and as early as 1878 Juan Donoso Cortés presented the framework. In an essay comparing Catholicism with liberalism and socialism, Donoso Cortés portrayed society as a collection of corporate entities distributed among classes and resting on one foundation—the family. Other intellectuals embraced his model. They contended that attacks on civil marriage (such as an 1859 Reform law that made marriage a civil contract) weakened the base, as did any secularization of education. They projected the familial model onto the political structure of society. God the Father, they held, could alone remain the source of political authority. Writers like José Ignacio de Anievas rejected the Enlightenment concept of popular sovereignty as the basis of government. The rise of the secular state was a symptom of man's rebellion against God, for separation of church and state denied divine prerogative.[10]

The God to which these Catholic thinkers referred was, of course, the Christian god. Rival faiths, particularly Judaism, were suspect. "Three hundred years of Spanish domination, under the most militant Catholic European nation, left Mexico a heritage of hatred and suspicion of Jews." During the course of the colonial era, Jews were equated to heretics, and many, prohibited from the New World, were persecuted by the Holy Office of the Inquisition. During the nineteenth century there was hardly a trace of Judaism in Mexico, but by the close of the Porfiriato a small community would begin to emerge in Mexico City, augmented by immigration in the 1920s.[11]

Juxtaposed with liberalism, and just as fully rejected by the Catholic thinkers as Judaism, was positivism, the specific intellectual foundation of the Díaz regime. Descended from the teachings of French philosopher Auguste Comte and carried to Mexico by Gabino Barreda, positivism espoused scientific solutions to social problems. The positivists viewed society as an organism not unlike the human body, subject to empirical analysis and rational rules of behavior. Consequently, Catholic attacks on positivism were mostly theological in nature. Cleric Rafael Carlos criticized the positivist faith in science as atheistic and socialistic, and the First Ecumenical Congress of 1906 again linked it with atheism. Positivism yielded dangerous by-products because of its imbedded materialism and Jacobin liberalism, argued Catholic author Francisco Zavala, who pointed specifically to the seizure of church property, criminality, and nihilism. In an interesting twist of analysis that bespoke conservative nationalism, he also tied positivism to imperialism, adding the consequences of foreign debt and loss of independence to his list. Mexico City's Catholic press contended that rampant prostitution came in part from positivist thinking, coupled with an alarming rise in alcoholism that, by 1886, reputedly made Mexico City a greater consumer of alcohol than the much larger city of London.[12]

The conservative assault on positivism reflected the church's ongoing battle against the tide of secularization that slowly transformed western society in the wake of the Enlightenment and French Revolution. Yet fundamental changes in social and economic relations, occurring in the context of the second industrial revolution, could not be denied by conservatism, which in the Burkian tradition accepted organic reform. In 1891 Pope Leo XIII addressed social needs in the encyclical *Rerum Novarum*, in which he acknowledged tensions between workers and capitalists and rejected socialism as a solution. The encyclical called for both groups to seek social justice. The wealthy were to respect worker dignity and pay fair wages—wages that provided sufficient support for the worker's family and allowed savings "with which, little by little, he would be able to accumulate a small amount of capital."

Rerum Novarum would eventually rouse the social conscience of Mexican Catholics, inviting the church to address problems such as immigration to the United States, concentration of land in the hands of a few (a process termed *latifundia*), and child labor.[13] There was no immediate impact of the encyclical in Mexico, however, given the delicate nature of church-state relations. It was not until the turn of the century that an emerging new generation of Catholic leaders, including Archbishop Próspero María Alarcón, even began to grapple with what the church termed the *cuestión social*.[14]

The most important forum for this new social conscience was a series of Catholic congresses, which constituted the first stepping stones of Catholic social action in Mexico. The congresses grew steadily. Thirty-nine clerics and lay leaders met in Puebla in 1903, one hundred met at Morelia a year later, and nearly two hundred met at Guadalajara in 1906 and Oaxaca in 1909. The complexity with which issues were discussed and debated increased with each meeting as well. Central themes included education, alcoholism, workers' rights, and Indian affairs. The first two congresses pressed for free Catholic primary schools, especially for the purpose of "civilizing the indigenous race." Inspired in part by Protestant abstinence campaigns in Mexico and overseas, Catholics railed against alcoholism. In Morelia, delegates urged priests to preach frequently on the dangers of liquor, while in Guadalajara some argued for lobbying to make drunkenness a felony. Catholic Workers' Clubs emerged from the congresses, encouraging "sobriety and thrift" among workers and establishing mutual aid funds. The Oaxaca delegates resolved that workers should be taught to avoid communistic propaganda and understand that strikes hurt their cause more than they could help. The Oaxaca meeting also saw great effort expended on how to address Indian problems such as adultery, illiteracy, and hygiene.[15]

Yet calls for modest reform, addressing profound social and economic questions of the day, fell far short of the liberal indictment of the Díaz regime. Young professionals in San Luis Potosí, led by Camilo Arriaga and offended by the government's *modus vivendi* with the Catholic Church, organized Liberal Clubs in the early years of the twentieth century and began to criticize the regime. In the face of repression, these malcontents sharpened their rhetoric, which ultimately addressed the need for sweeping economic and social change in Porfirian Mexico. With publication of insurrectionist literature in the United States, unrest festered on the border. Seeing the need for change, political schism unfolded among Mexico's elite. Francisco I. Madero, aspirant for president in the 1910 elections, became the unlikely head of a revolution that engulfed Mexico. With it the line between church and state was again challenged, and Catholics slowly prepared to reenter the political sphere.

THE RIGHT IN REVOLUTIONARY MEXICO, 1910–1929

The Mexican Revolution began in November 1910, when Madero, easily defeated in a fraud-ridden election, called his countrymen to arms. Madero was an unlikely revolutionary. The son of a wealthy northern landowner, he had studied in Paris and at Berkeley before returning to his family's estates, having become an adherent of spiritualism in France (he spent long nights in séances) and having acquired an admiration for democracy in the United States. In a culture cognizant of the manliness of its leaders, he was hardly the image of Mexican *machismo*, standing five foot three, with a shrill, high-pitched voice and a childless marriage as well. Yet he opposed the Díaz regime on grounds of continual reelection, believing that democracy must take root in Mexico, and this brave stand endeared him to millions of Mexicans. As revolutionaries defeated small columns of Federal soldiers in the mountains of western Chihuahua in spring 1911, support for the aged dictator quickly ebbed. In May 1911 Díaz fled the country.

At the outset of the Revolution, Catholics agreed with many of the ideas of maderismo, such as the need for liberty, social justice, and some type of land reform. Madero's own agenda was more limited than his rhetoric, however, hinging primarily on his conviction that political reform and democratic processes would solve Mexico's profound economic and social problems. After assuming the presidency in November 1911, he opened the political process, facilitating rapid growth in grassroots organizations. Although the four Catholic congresses in the previous decade of 1900 had applied *Rerum Novarum* to the Mexican situation in resolutions, only "the fall of the Díaz dictatorship signalled the real beginning of the Catholic Social Action program."[16] Multiple social action groups emerged, foremost among them a new political party, the Partido Católico Nacional [PCN].

Founded in 1911 with the motto of "God, Fatherland, and Liberty," the PCN was a precursor of the 1930s Mexican Right, ostensibly allying itself with Madero, a man later glorified in the official hagiography of the Revolution. It nominated him for the presidency (along with Madero's own political organization, the Partido Progresista) and received the praise of the new president. Though embracing the democracy of the immensely popular Madero, the PCN was fundamentally conservative. Liberals charged that it was the reborn Conservative Party of Alamán, an unfair label, given the PCN's rejection of monarchy and acceptance of separation of church and state. Yet Catholics addressing the "social question" of inequities in Mexican society were largely driven by fears of socialism and revolutionary radicalism, and did not stray from the conservative reform ideology of Edmund Burke.[17]

The PCN fared well in the 1912 gubernatorial and congressional elections, winning four governorships and holding twenty-nine seats in the Chamber of Deputies. Unfortunately for the budding "Party of God," Mexico's experiment in democracy under Madero came to an abrupt end.[18] In February 1913, during the *Decena Trágica*, or Tragic Ten Days, the reform-minded president was removed and killed in a coup by General Victoriano Huerta. The Huerta dictatorship, which lasted from February 1913 to July 1914, degenerated into a desperate struggle simply to remain in power. Huerta militarized Mexico, imposing a hated conscription, the *leva*, on lower classes, and ended the nascent experiment in free elections and a free press. Huerta's government was so clearly an imposition that even most of the Right opposed it; the best the general could do with the church was sustain a relationship that "was proper but cool." The church delivered a loan to the Huerta government shortly after it came to power, but it was at least partially coerced, with near-mutinous troops threatening to sack Mexico City.[19]

Though the church was wrongly accused of alliance with Huerta's government, its image as traitor to the Revolution persisted in the eyes of the ultimate victors, the Constitutionalist forces led by Coahuila Governor Venustiano Carranza. A coalition under Carranza ousted Huerta in July 1914, only to splinter into internecine civil war until a Carranza comeback three years later. Once militarily secure, Carranza authorized the drafting of a new constitution for Mexico, with delegates meeting in the historic colonial city of Querétaro. Though nearly all the participants were anticlerical in the liberal tradition, a more radical segment of the delegates, led by Francisco Múgica and known as the Jacobins, gained control of the convention. They produced a document of social reform that went beyond the limits of nineteenth-century liberalism and allowed for active state intervention in a quest to solve Mexico's social and economic ills.

The final draft of the Constitution of 1917 contained several provisions that shaped the liberal-conservative struggles in the 1930s and demonstrated that "rampant anticlericalism had won the day at Querétaro." The first and most heated debate of the meeting, in which Múgica and the Jacobins triumphed, centered on the nature of primary education. The delegates ultimately turned back attempts to revise the section and allow for parochial schooling, so that Article 3 of the Constitution provided for free and obligatory secular primary schools in Mexico.[20] Other anticlerical provisions were scattered throughout the lengthy final document, including measures that decreed marriage as a civil ceremony, restricted worship to church buildings, and required that priests be Mexican-born, abstain from politics, and register with the government. Article 27 addressed land reform, undercutting the position of the landed Porfirian elite, while Article 123 mandated labor reforms, including the eight-hour workday, nondiscrimination on the basis of nationality, and the right of unions to organize and collectively bargain.

Carranza's constitutional reforms were matched by legal changes affecting the status of women and the family. While the Querétaro convention declined to enfranchise women, the Revolution began the process of the legal liberation of Mexican women. In 1914 Carranza legalized divorce by decree—for the first time in Mexican history—and gave women greater rights regarding property ownership. In April 1917 the Law of Family Relations codified the decree, granting married women guardianship and custody rights equal to that of their husbands, while sanctioning paternity suits. The law viewed marriage as a breakable contract, yet sought to mitigate injury to children. These changes, although still marred by double standards, began a process of liberalization and presaged the importance of the family in political discourse in the 1930s.[21]

Major constitutional articles and the activism of the new Revolutionary state alarmed Mexican conservatives. The church continued as the focal point of ideological tensions, with passage of the Constitution of 1917 fueling the growth of the Right. Resistance coalesced by 1918 in the Asociación Católica de la Juventud Mexicana [ACJM], which replaced the defunct PCN as the keystone of Catholic opposition. Founded by Jesuit Father Bernard Bergoend, the ACJM emerged out of similar youth organizations such as the Centro de Estudiantes Católicos and the Liga Nacional de Estudiantes, adopting the goal of "restoring Christian social order in our fatherland." After slow growth in the 1913–1918 period, the ACJM expanded rapidly at the end of the decade. It spearheaded Catholic resistance in Jalisco in 1918, where anticlerical governor Manuel Bouquet cracked down on clerical activities and allowed "leftist agitators" to run rampant.[22]

Although the governments of Carranza and his successor, Alvaro Obregón (1920–1924), pursued conciliatory policies toward the church, grassroots organizations continued to emerge and work for "the implantation of the temporal reign of Christ." Women gathered in the Unión de Damas Católicas [UDC], begun in 1920 and organized into its first national congress in 1922. The UDC published *La Dama Católica* and grew substantially by the mid-1920s, with as many as eight hundred members in Guadalajara alone. Early on the Damas served primarily as a charity organization, with members visiting hospitals and orphanages and distributing aid to the poor. Yet in their quest to reassert the "influence of Catholic women in the family and society," they played a political role. At their first congress the UDC condemned Article 3 of the constitution, arguing that only parents had the right to determine the nature of their children's education. Yet "while the church recognized the source of strength it possessed in its women and the important role they would play in its social action programs, it felt that a woman's place was still in the home, where they were to instill Christian principles in their children."[23] Hence the Damas faced limits on their political activities, though they cooperated with the ACJM and several lesser organizations, such as the Caballeros de Colón (Knights of Columbus), in seeking to resist social changes wrought by the Revolution.

With the ascension of Plutarco Elías Calles to the presidency in 1924, anticlericalism became the hallmark of the Mexican state. Calles ordered his subordinates to enforce the anticlerical provisions of the constitution with vigor, and men such as Tabascan governor Tomás Garrido Canabal gladly complied. In Mexico City, pro-government priests tried to take over La Solidad parish and stage a schism, prompting clashes with Catholic militants. In response to the crisis at La Solidad in early 1925, while ACJM members warily guarded Mexico's reknowned Shrine of the Virgin of Guadalupe, a new defense organization rose from among Catholic lay leaders: the Liga Nacional Defensora de la Libertad Religiosa [LNDLR or Liga]. It had middle-class origins and was led by an executive committee headed by René Capistrán Garza, with a deliberate lack of direct linkage to the church hierarchy. The goal, as stated in its program, was "to reestablish religious liberty," which meant the repeal of provisions in the constitution restricting the church. Thus the Catholic Right had set its face squarely against the advance of the Revolution. Not surprisingly, the government quickly condemned the Liga as "extralegal and seditious." Yet the LNDLR grew with remarkable speed, plugging into the multiple layers of lay organizations already in existence. It reported a membership of thirty-six thousand within three months, and hundreds of thousands of members one year later, quickly surpassing the ACJM as the center of the Catholic opposition.[24]

The presence of the Liga encouraged the church hierarchy to stiffen its resolve as it faced a quickening pace of anticlerical measures. By early 1926 two hundred foreign-born priests had been expelled and scores of monasteries, convents, and schools had been closed. The persecution was uneven, with certain local and regional officials more zealous than others, but on a national scale the crisis drew steadily to a climax. In July 1926 the government publicly issued the Calles Law, a presidential decree ordering strict enforcement of the anticlerical provisions of the constitution. Mexican bishops were particularly annoyed that the decree required registration of priests, which would enable the government to divide the clergy and utilize those willing to cooperate with it. When the Liga staged massive demonstrations in response to the Calles Law, the impressed but divided bishops found the courage to retaliate, ordering the suspension of masses throughout Mexico.[25]

In the fall of 1926 the Liga reinforced the episcopal counteroffensive by organizing a nationwide boycott. Inspired by the dazzling success of an ACJM-organized boycott in Guadalajara during the 1918–1919 Jalisco crisis, and perhaps by the tactics of Mohatma Ghandi in India, the Liga called on Catholics not to pay taxes and to abstain from unnecessary consumption. The Damas Católicas played an active role in promoting the boycott in the face of increasing government repression.[26] All Mexico was not like fervently religious Guadalajara, however, and the boycott had mixed success. It did not cause Calles to blink, and civil war resulted.

For three years, from August 1926 to September 1929, devout Catholics waged guerrilla warfare against the Revolutionary regime. Known as Cristeros because of their battle slogan, "Viva Cristo Rey," they concentrated in Los Altos, the highlands of westcentral Mexico, a geographic area known as the Bajío. Scholars disagree on the size of the insurrection, but at a peak the Cristeros may have numbered fifty thousand.[27] The leadership was haphazard. Three groups that one might expect to have played leadership roles defaulted: the church hierarchy wavered from the start in its support for armed rebellion, its rural priests overwhelmingly flocked to the cities in order to avoid the bloodshed, and wealthy Catholics sided with the government. The latter group, which included entrepreneurs like Manuel Gómez Morín, had been alienated by the boycott of their businesses. Hence, ostensibly Capistrán Garza and the Liga assumed leadership of the Cristeros. In truth, the LNDLR's leadership was "invisible," as *La Cristiada* was a rural, spontaneous revolt. In places like San José de Gracia, Michoacán, the people increased their religious fervor when the churches closed, with a hatred of Calles growing as locals fondly remembered their priests; some Cristeros found motivation in personal grudges against local politicians as well.[28]

Despite facing overwhelming odds, the Cristeros were able to fight the Federal army to a stalemate into 1927. It was soon clear that the guerrillas would have no hope of spreading their rebellion beyond the Bajío and toppling Calles, however, while at the same time the Federals—hampered by high desertion rates and Cristero hit-and-run tactics—could do little more than contain the rebellion. Both sides carried out brutal excesses, with little regard for the rules of war. Few prisoners survived. Though the Damas officially withdrew from the insurrection in 1927 in order to remain apolitical, women actively supported the Cristeros in the field, delivering supplies and serving as spies and nurses in hideaway camps. As such, they became targets of rape.[29]

With the arrival of Dwight Morrow as the new U.S. ambassador to Mexico in October 1927, a long and tedious process of negotiation began. By assisting in establishing communication between the church hierarchy and Calles, Morrow slowly worked to defuse the crisis. In June 1929 the institutional conflict ended as the *Arreglos* (Arrangements) were announced. The government agreed to refrain from enforcing the Calles Law (although it remained legally valid) and issued a rather nebulous statement that it had never intended "to destroy the identity" of the church, while the bishops resumed services and ordered the disarming of the Cristeros.

The *Arreglos*, if not tantamount to surrender, certainly demonstrated the weakness of the postrevolutionary Mexican church. The rise of the modern state meant that the Right would have to adapt to new forms of expression and resistance beyond the older institutional avenues of church and army. If fact, if the church was in decline, the conservative Mexican military was nonexistent. The Federal army that sought to vanquish the Cristeros was not the same force that had been tamed by Juárez and Díaz. The "weak and decrepit" prerevolutionary army had been defeated by a new juggernaut beholden to the Mexican Revolutionary state. It would not serve the Right, although its loyalty to the regime was also always tenuous—endemic corruption made it similar to a lion that, if hungry, might turn on its master. Alvaro Obregón faced several uprisings in the early 1920s, when the army suffered a regional orientation and fierce command rivalries. Yet as difficult as it might be to manage, the army was slowly integrated into the power structure of the new regime. Though factions of the army would support conservative causes in the 1930s, the institution itself was restructured and kept under government control.[30]

The rise of a powerful "new capitalist state" was perhaps the most important consequence of Mexico's 1910 Revolution. In the 1920s and 1930s the state sought to consolidate its hold on the Mexican countryside, foster national unity, promote political and economic modernization, and validate its claim to the emerging Revolutionary hagiography by propaganda that employed nationalism and even Christian imagery.[31] But if the state was transformed by the Revolution, so too was the Mexican Right. The Right had been largely defined, from Independence until the demise of the Cristeros, by the ongoing debate over the role of the Catholic Church in Mexican society. The Porfirian social ills that gave rise to revolution also awakened the Catholic social conscience, however, and with the papal encyclical *Rerum Novarum* the Catholic Right began to reengage in politics in the Burkian reform tradition after a long, uneven hiatus. This process, expressed in Catholic congresses and the PCN, was cut short by the Huerta dictatorship and by the Constitutionalist triumph that produced the anticlerical 1917 constitution.

With the constitution in their hands, triumphant revolutionaries sparred with the church, leading to civil war under the Calles regime. The Cristero revolt—what historian Jean Meyer has termed "the last insurrection of the masses"—failed militarily, yet this defeat did not portend the demise of the Right.[32] On the contrary, it had come to an important crossroads: one in which it had to begin to redefine itself in both ideology and action. New, diverse factions emerged in the 1929–1934 period, at the very time when Plutarco Calles was seeking to consolidate national political power. The state-building project, which sought validation through popular elections, encountered stubborn rightist resistance; a grassroots Catholic and moralist Right was also fomenting from below.

NOTES

1. Jan Bazant, "From Independence to the Liberal Republic, 1821–1867," in Leslie Bethell, ed., *Mexico since Independence*, pp. 13, 21, 35.

2. Brading, *Orígenes del nacionalismo*, pp. 157, 172; Turner, *Mexican Nationalism*, p. 22.

3. Charles Hale, *Mexican Liberalism in the Age of Mora* (New Haven, Conn.: Yale University Press, 1968), pp. 124–25, 133, 141.

4. Bazant, "Independence to Republic," pp. 29–36, 43–47; Robert Case, "Resurgimiento de los conservadores en México, 1876–1877," *Historia Mexicana* 25:2 (October–December 1975): 204.

5. Bazant, "Independence to Republic," pp. 49–51.

6. Adame Goddard, *El pensamiento político y social de los católicos mexicanos, 1867–1914* (Mexico City: Universidad Nacional Autónoma de México, Instituto de Investigaciones Historicas, 1981), pp. 16–21, 27–29.

7. Karl Schmitt, "Catholic Adjustment to the Secular State: The Case of Mexico, 1867–1911," *Catholic Historical Review* 18 (July 1962): 183; Case, "Resurgimiento," pp. 208–12, 217–30; Goddard, *Pensamiento de los católicos*, pp. 97–99.

8. Schmitt, "Catholic Adjustment," p. 189; W. Dirk Raat, "The Antipositivist Movement in Prerevolutionary Mexico, 1892–1911," *Journal of Inter-American Studies and World Affairs* 19:1 (February 1977): 84, 92.

9. Jesús García Gutiérrez, *Acción anticatólica en México* (Mexico City: Editorial Campeador, 1956), p. 152; Bazant, "Independence to Republic," p. 85.

10. Goddard, *Pensamiento de los católicos*, pp. 45, 51–58.

11. Corinne Krause, *Los judíos en México* (Mexico City: Universidad Iberoamericana, 1987), pp. 31–32, 175.

12. Raat, "Antipositivist Movement," pp. 93–95; Moises González Navarro, *La vida social*, in Daniel Cosío Villegas, ed., *Historia moderna de México*, vol. 4 (Mexico City: El Colegio de México, 1958), pp. 413, 416.

13. Goddard, *Pensamiento de los católicos*, pp. 145–49; Jean Meyer, "Le catholicisme social au Mexique jusqu'en 1913," *Revue historique* 260 (July–September 1978): 148–49.

14. Alicia Olivera Sedano, *Aspectos del conflicto religioso de 1926 a 1929: sus antecedentes y consecuencias* (Mexico City: Instituto Nacional de Antropología e Historia, 1966), pp. 31, 34–37; Goddard, *Pensamiento de los católicos*, pp. 127–28.

15. Wilfrid H. Callcott, *Liberalism in Mexico, 1857–1929* (Hamden, Conn.: Archon Books, 1965), 178–80; Paul V. Murray, *The Catholic Church in Mexico: Historical Essays for the General Reader*, vol. 1 (Mexico City: Editorial E.P.M., 1965), pp. 336–64.

16. Olivera Sedano, *Aspectos del conflicto*, p. 57; Robert Quirk, *The Mexican Revolution and the Catholic Church, 1910–1929* (Bloomington: Indiana University Press, 1973), p. 25.

17. Jean Meyer, "Le catholicisme social," p. 158; Olivera Sedano, *Aspectos del Conflicto*, p. 46; O'Malley, *The Myth of the Revolution*, p. 7; Quirk, *Revolution and the Church*, pp. 28–31.

18. Antonio Rius Facius, *La juventud católica y la revolución mejicana, 1910–1925* (Mexico City: Editorial Jus, 1963), pp. 22, 30.

19. Michael C. Meyer, *Huerta: A Political Portrait* (Lincoln: University of Nebraska Press, 1972), pp. 156, 167–69; Olivera Sedano, *Aspectos del conflicto*, pp. 58–59.

20. Quirk, *Revolution and the Church*, pp. 89–94.

21. Shirlene Soto, *Emergence of the Modern Mexican Woman: Her Participation in Revolution and Struggle for Equality, 1910–1940* (Denver: Arden Press, 1990), pp. 56–59; Lillian Fisher, "The Influence of the Present Mexican Revolution upon the Status of Mexican Women," *Hispanic American Historical Review* 22 (February 1942): 212–13.

22. Rius Facius, *Juventud católica*, pp. 35, 42–45, 66, 125.

23. Barbara Miller, "The Role of Women in the Mexican Cristero Rebellion: Las Señoras y las Religiosas," *The Americas* 40:3 (January 1984): 304–5; Olivera Sedano, *Aspectos del conflicto*, pp. 88–89; Bailey, *Viva Cristo Rey*, pp. 39–40.

24. Rius Facius, *Juventud católica*, p. 279; Bailey, *Viva Cristo Rey*, pp. 54–56; Olivera Sedano, *Aspectos del conflicto*, pp. 110–13.

25. Bailey, *Viva Cristo Rey*, pp. 65–66, 75; Jean Meyer, *The Cristero Rebellion: The Mexican People between Church and State, 1926–1929*, trans. Richard Southern (Cambridge: Cambridge University Press, 1976), p. 43.

26. Olivera Sedano, *Aspectos del conflicto*, pp. 126–28; Miller, "Women in Cristero Rebellion," p. 310.

27. Jean Meyer, *Cristero Rebellion*, pp. 84–85. Meyer's work on the Cristeros is most convincing, incorporating statistical analysis to show how population patterns, rather than topography, favored Los Altos as the center of the revolt.

28. Jean Meyer, *Cristero Rebellion*, pp. 75, 80; Luis González, *Pueblo en vilo: Una microhistoria de San José de Gracia* (Mexico City: Colegio de México, 1968), pp. 201, 205–8.

29. Bailey, *Viva Cristo Rey*, pp. 135–36; Miller, "Women in Cristero Rebellion," pp. 312–16; Jean Meyer, *Cristero Rebellion*, p. 79.

30. Edwin Lieuwen, *Mexican Militarism: The Political Rise and Fall of the Revolutionary Army* (Albuquerque: University of New Mexico Press, 1968), pp. 11, 37–38. Article 13 of the Constitution extended the Reform's *Ley Juárez*, which prohibited the *fuero militar*, but Lieuwen notes that attempts to terminate all military courts failed.

31. Jean Meyer, "Revolution and Reconstruction in the 1920s," in Bethell, ed., *Mexico since Independence*, pp. 202–4; O'Malley, *Myth of the Revolution*, p. 113.

32. Jean Meyer, *Cristero Rebellion*, pp. 215–16.

PART I

THE MAXIMATO, 1929–1935

2

THE POLITICAL OPPOSITION

Students of Mexican history face a dilemma when studying the period from 1929 to 1934. On the one hand, Mexico was ruled by a Revolutionary regime espousing leftist rhetoric, yet in practical matters this same regime often governed like a capitalistic and conservative dictatorship. This paradox prompted one of the foremost early historians of Revolutionary Mexico, Frank Tannenbaum, to label the period "most perplexing." To Tannenbaum, who knew Mexico and many of its political power brokers firsthand, it appeared that Mexico's leaders had "repudiated their commitments" to the Revolution. Most of these men, products of the impoverished countryside and thrown into positions of great power by the tumult of the Revolution, succumbed to temptations because they lacked "moral fortitude."[1]

Given the disorienting nature of this six-year period, or *sexenio*, it is perhaps not surprising that the Mexican Right was also adrift ideologically. While pockets of the Right steadfastly opposed the Revolutionary government, other segments cooperated with it. For Catholic rightists, the relentless persecution of the church continued, making the decision between opposition or cooperation easy. For other groups, the decision was not so obvious.

As the 1928 presidential elections approached, the entire Right—including church supporters, landowners, foreign investors, and business executives— "saw in the coming election a possible turning point in their fortunes."[2] The leftist presidency of Plutarco Elías Calles was coming to a close, and the momentum of the social revolution, in terms of such projects as agrarian reform, seemed to be on the wane. For those who valued a political opening and an end to reelection, or *continuismo*, however, the 1928 election was to be disillusioning. Alvaro Obregón, president from 1920 to 1924 and original head of the "Sonoran clique," ran for president and won easily in the manipulated July 1 elections. Seventeen days later he was dead, the victim of assassin José de León Toral.

Toral was a twenty-six-year-old fanatic greatly troubled by the Mexican government's anticlericalism and the increasingly bloody Cristero war. Active in the Liga Nacional Defensora de la Libertad Religiosa in Mexico City, he had become involved with a small band of Catholic urban terrorists who took refuge in the home of María Concepción Acevedo y de la Llata, better known as Madre Conchita. Inspired by these contacts, Toral stalked Obregón, and when opportunity presented itself, shot him.[3]

Obregón's sudden departure from the political arena left an awkward power gap, filled only by the continued dominance of the other Sonoran luminary, Plutarco Calles. Calles, known as the Maximum Chief (*jefe máximo*) of the Revolution, appointed the cooperative Emilio Portes Gil as provisional president. Portes Gil, the first of three executives subject to considerable control on the part of Calles, led Mexico into the era termed the Maximato. Thus the irony of Toral's action was that it kept the anticlerical Calles in charge. When similar would-be assassins, also apparently linked to the Cristero rebellion, attempted to kill the provisional president by blowing up his train in February 1929, they were making the same mistake.[4] Calles was the power behind the throne.

1929: THE PNR, ESCOBAR REVOLT, AND VASCONCELISMO

In 1929 Plutarco Calles was continuing the decade-old work of the Sonoran clique—the consolidation of national power. Historian Jean Meyer has posited that this process, which involved vesting both economic and political control in Mexico City at the expense of local and regional political bosses, or *caudillos*, gave birth to "a modern nation-state." The 1926–1929 Cristero war, then, can be viewed as a clash between traditional Mexico and the intrusive modern state. The Right viewed the rise of such a powerful secular bureaucratic machine with alarm. *La Palabra* (The word), a Catholic magazine, noted the ominous rise of the state:

Influenced by the most wicked and absurd ideas, based on the ideological mindlessness of greed, converted into an instrument without reason—into a brutal army of antireligious and antipatriotic sectarianism, the Revolutionary state has renounced the noble goals of natural law and has become an absolute and threatening entity, before which the family and the church must stand in defense in order to avoid being absorbed and destroyed.[5]

For purposes of consolidating political control, Calles created the Partido Nacional Revolucionario [PNR]. Ironically, while the Mexican Right feared the new statism, outside observers condemned the PNR as fascistic. North American Carleton Beals, writing in *The Nation* and presaging later condemnation of the official party, observed that "the PNR is the government and the government is the PNR." He concluded that the party, "imposed from above," existed for the purpose of "keeping the government in power through effectively destroying all opposition." Another contemporary observer from the United States compared the PNR to Benito Mussolini's Fascist Party in Italy.[6]

At first glance the early 1929 founding of the PNR looks like a true point of departure for modern Mexico. Calles himself had declared the "end of caudillos" (an apparent reference to the death of Obregón and a statement that enraged Obregonistas).[7] Yet in reality, Calles persisted in the best tradition of caudillismo. Marked by the same personalism evident in previous decades, Maximato politics revolved around pro-Calles and anti-Calles loyalties more than around ideology, making the course of the Mexican Right sometimes difficult to detect. As PNR delegates haggled over details in historic Querétaro, however, they still worked within the framework of the Revolution's leftism. They committed the party to the principle of no reelection and to "the perfecting of our democracy."[8] Delegates subsequently nominated an obscure politician, Pascual Ortiz Rubio, for president instead of the assumed frontrunner, moderate businessman Aarón Sáenz, a politician who enjoyed the support of the Obregonistas.

Political opposition to Calles and his PNR surfaced during the special 1929 presidential elections and within the military. The presence of the Right, though not sharply pronounced, was evident in both movements. Popular opposition came with the candidacy of José Vasconcelos; military resistance unfolded in a revolt under General Gonzalo Escobar. Vasconcelismo marked the beginning of the Right's earnest electoral challenge to the Revolutionary regime, a challenge that resurfaced gently in 1934, robustly in 1940, and continues under the auspices of the Partido Acción Nacional today.

If Vasconcelismo denoted a beginning, in many ways the Escobar revolt signaled an end. As historian Edwin Lieuwen aptly notes, it was a closing chapter in the long history of Mexican military intervention in national politics. For the Right, it was a final effort to overthrow the government by force of arms. The Escobar insurgency began, as has been the longstanding tradition in Mexico, under the auspices of a pronouncement, the Plan de Hermosillo. Drafted by opposition leader, Sonoran lawyer, and former Minister of Gobernación Gilberto Valenzuela, the Plan de Hermosillo denounced Calles as a dictator and berated him as "the supreme administrator of this wicked market of moral values, the diabolical inspirer of inhuman and savage persecutions . . . [the] Judas of the Mexican Revolution." The references to low morals and "savage persecutions" were designed to woo Cristeros to the cause, and labels such as the "Judas" and also "Jew" of the Revolution appealed to the Cristero anti-Semitic impulse.[9]

Military insurrection supporting the plan began in the state of Veracruz, where General Jesús Aguirre accused leftist agrarian governor Adalberto Tejeda of committing "seditious acts" and attempted to deceive Mexico City into believing that it was Tejeda who was in revolt. Soon, however, it was unmistakable that a clique of Obregonista generals, joined by a variety of rightist opposition figures, were orchestrating nationwide upheaval. In the north, Raúl

Madero, General Francisco Manzo, and Antonio I. Villarreal joined Valenzuela and Escobar in the efforts, while in Sinaloa, Ramón F. Iturbe—who would later become a prominent right-wing opponent of Lázaro Cárdenas—helped General Roberto Cruz open a third front with an assault on Mazatlán.

Though many opposition leaders were in favor of the Escobar revolt, José Vasconcelos, the most important of them, instructed his followers not to participate. He interpreted the matter as largely a feud between Obregonistas and Callistas rather than a battle based on principle or ideology.[10] To a large extent, he was right. Though the Portes Gil government joined the Mexican Left in condemning the insurrection as "reactionary," frequently personalism tainted the not-so-pure motives of many rebel adherents. Escobar led a force fashioned as the *Ejército Renovador*, but as historian José C. Valadés astutely points out, "the real renovation consisted of exterminating Calles and the callismo that had dominated the country for four years."[11]

The Escobar rebellion was quickly checked by the authorities in Mexico City. Ex-president Calles became minister of war and oversaw military operations after Joaquín Amaro was incapacitated at the critical hour by a facial injury he received in a polo game.[12] The government crushed the revolt with the help of the United States, and by mobilizing labor and agrarian forces (as well as loyal army troops), though these facts do not necessarily reflect strong ideological underpinnings to the conflict. Many of the agrarians were led by avowed conservatives themselves, such as San Luis Potosí's Saturnino Cedillo, who mustered five thousand troops. Juan Andreu Almazán, a conservative destined to become the Right's flag bearer in the 1940 presidential elections, played the pivotal role in defeating the insurrection with a crushing defeat of Escobar at the Battle of Jiménez. The rebels failed to take Mazatlán in Sinaloa, and Tejeda recovered and routed Aguirre's insurgents in Veracruz.

Aid from the United States enhanced the Mexican government's capacity to snuff the revolt out quickly. U.S.-Mexican tensions had eased dramatically during the tenureship of Ambassador Dwight Morrow, and the Escobar insurrection provided Washington with yet another opportunity to improve relations, avoid chaos along the border, and ostensibly "promote democracy" abroad. The embassy was in consultation with the Mexican government before the anticipated revolt even began. Morrow received a warning telegram from the Foreign Ministry as early as February 14 advising him that Escobar contingents would likely include Sonoran governor Fausto Topete and endanger border regions. When this prediction came true, the United States was ready. Aircraft and infantry vigilantly patrolled the frontier as Topete's forces laid siege to the border town of Naco, threatening intervention and forcing the rebels to retire after a few shells landed on the American side. The extent of U.S. support for the government forces went beyond the bounds of international law elsewhere along the border as well. In March nearly the entire garrison at Ciudad Juárez, totaling three hundred men, received refuge at Fort Bliss, along with their arms and ammunition. When rebels fled into the United States at Sasabe, Arizona in

April, however, they were arrested and delivered into the vengeful hands of Mexican authorities at Nogales. Washington turned away the rebel diplomatic mission of Gilberto Valenzuela in March, siding decisively with the Portes Gil government as it quashed the insurrection.[13] With the demise of Escobar it was increasingly clear that, in the wake of the Revolution, direct military intervention in government had become anathema to the vast majority of Mexicans, no matter their ideological leanings.

Far more serious than the Escobar revolt in its challenge to the Revolutionary government was the 1929 Vasconcelos presidential campaign. Former secretary of public education under Obregón, José Vasconcelos had earned a national reputation through his promotion of free public schools, contacts with workers and intellectuals, prolific authorship, and promotion of the mestizo "cosmic race." When he traveled in Europe and the United States in the mid-twenties, newspapers such as *El Universal* kept him in the Mexican public mind.[14] With this name recognition and bases of support, Vasconcelos plotted a return to Mexico and to politics in 1928. His efforts actually first took root north of the border among a receptive immigrant population. The largest number of Mexican immigrants to the United States in the late 1920s were from the Bajío, many of them fleeing the terrors of the Cristero war. They welcomed Vasconcelos's calls for an end to government repression in the Bajío countryside.[15]

Other features of Vasconcelos's campaign appealed to those disenchanted with the institutionalized Revolution. Political outcasts on both the Right and the Left heralded the candidate's theme of replacing corrupt dictatorship with honest civil government. Calls for constitutional rule attracted many anti-Callista factions, including old Madero partisans who viewed *continuismo* as the ultimate mockery of the Revolution. Vasconcelos decried the out-of-touch Mexico City bureaucracy, opposed the centralization of power in the Federal government, and argued for the strengthening of local government through the *municipio libre*. Not surprisingly, he made considerable inroads among the populace in outlying areas of northern Mexico.[16]

Indeed, in vasconcelismo there was something for everyone. Labor liked the campaign's commitment to labor reform and the right of unions to organize; an overwhelming number of railroad workers supported the candidate because of his promise to keep the rail and telegraph lines government-owned. Antimilitarists favored the idea of a "democratic army" used in public works. Agrarians delighted to hear of Vasconcelos's support for more land reform. Women embraced the platform's call for their suffrage, which drew an "anonymous multitude" of them into the campaign. Many communists joined the work, too. Knowledge of these facets of support has caused some analysts to conclude that Vasconcelos's popularity was a product of the political Left.[17]

The Revolutionary establishment, however, labeled it "reactionary." This adjective was part of a political vocabulary understood by the general populace. In postrevolutionary Mexico, "reactionary" translated into "against the Revolution," which in turn implied "pro-Porfirio Díaz, pro-Victoriano Huerta, pro-foreign interests." In short, reactionary meant "unpatriotic."[18] There is much evidence attesting to the acceptance, as early as the mid-1920s, of the myths of the Revolution as a historical experience. The pantheon of Revolutionary heroes and villains had been defined in the popular imagination: Madero was noble and pure, Huerta the betrayer, likened to Judas. Vasconcelos attempted to prove on the campaign trail that his PNR opponent, Ortiz Rubio, and other government officials, had been Huertistas.

In truth, vasconcelismo was, in some ways, reactionary. Many components of the fragmented Mexican Right aligned themselves with this opposition candidate, and Vasconcelos sought them out with rightist rhetoric. He courted devout Catholics. Vasconcelos himself "was always religious. He was anticlerical, but profoundly religious." He targeted the *Arreglos*—the June 1929 arrangement that settled the Cristero war—for criticism, and he blamed the government for the murder of Cristero leader Enrique Gorostieta.[19] Before the *Arreglos* he had repeatedly called for an end to Calles's relentless anticlericalism, quipping in speeches that he, as president, would "combat fanaticism with books instead of machine guns." Vasconcelos also took aim at the high-profile Callista governor of Tabasco, the fervently anticlerical Tomás Garrido Canabal, whom he referred to as "un caníbal."[20] He attacked both Mexican and North American bankers as "usurers"—an anti-Semitic code word for Jew. The Catholic Right rallied to Vasconcelos's cause, with delegates from myriad Catholic grassroots organizations in attendance at the Partido Nacional Antireeleccionista [PNA] convention that nominated him. The LNDLR endorsed Vasconcelos, and he enjoyed his strongest support in the Bajío, where Cristeros "were hoping that his election to the presidency would permit them to live and pray in peace."[21]

In addition to Catholics, Vasconcelos attracted segments of the Mexican Right through his nationalism. The focal point of his ire was the U.S. ambassador to Mexico, Dwight Morrow, whom Vasconcelos repeatedly criticized in his speeches. He identified Morrow as a romanesque "proconsul," a shadowy figure behind the scenes who ran the government. He compared the ambassador to Joel Poinsett, the first U.S. minister to Mexico, who boldly interfered in domestic affairs and who had won the ire of an earlier generation of Mexican conservatives for his efforts. He charged that Morrow had arranged for the United States to assist the government in order to crush the Escobar revolt, a charge that held considerable merit.[22] Lastly, Vasconcelos held some attraction for conservative businessmen. The candidate disparaged Luis Morones, leader of the government-sponsored umbrella union, the Confederación Regional de Obrera Mexicana [CROM], as a tool of great industrialists seeking to snuff out small businesses. He also roused interest among the conservative urban middle classes, especially devout Catholics, with promises to restore clean government in Mexico.[23]

José Vasconcelos reentered Mexico at Nogales, Sonora on November 28, 1928 and trekked southward through the Bajío to the PNA's convention in Mexico City. The PNA, revitalized in 1927–1928 as Obregón prepared to return to the presidency, traced its roots to Madero and his patriotic movement that brought down the Díaz government in 1911. This attempt to echo the glorified past, reflected in the slogan "with Madero yesterday, with Vasconcelos today," rested largely on the party's name and opposition to *continuismo* (a principle that, technically, Calles and his PNR did not violate). In the 1929 effort, Vito Alessio Robles steered the party, though he had noteworthy differences with Vasconcelos. The six hundred delegates to the convention had significant differences among themselves, too, as reflected in the heated platform debates, especially regarding the issue of woman's suffrage.[24] Rejection of Plutarco Calles and his government united the forces behind Vasconcelos's candidacy, not ideology.

After the convention of July 1929, Vasconcelos again toured the country. Despite a shoestring budget, he enjoyed considerable "spontaneous popular support." Fearing an alliance between this movement and the Cristeros, the government had made peace with the latter in June; it employed repression to slow the opposition's electoral machine, and fraud to assure Ortiz Rubio's victory by an unbelievable margin of 1,826,000 votes to 106,000. After the November balloting Vasconcelos himself fled the country, awaiting an insurrection that did not come.[25]

Vasconcelos's campaign attracted segments of the Mexican Right and a number of young idealists who would later become worthy opponents of the Revolutionary government on their own terms. Manuel Gómez Morín, founder of the Partido Acción Nacional in 1939, for example, contributed financially and handled campaign funds.[26] Though José Vasconcelos rode the support of ideologically divergent groups, his failure in 1929 served to disillusion much of the Right with the electoral process.

LAZARO CARDENAS AND THE 1934
ELECTORAL OPPOSITION

This disillusionment accounts for the relative weakness of the Right in the next presidential contest five years later, coupled with the assumption that nothing could prevent the Maximum Chief from continuing his domination of Mexican political life through puppet presidents and use of electoral fraud. Of course, from the perspective of rightists some presidential aspirants within the PNR were better than others, the power of Calles notwithstanding. All Mexicans watched the internal PNR jockeying for power with interest. It was no secret, as the 1934 contest approached, that conservatives loathed the prospect of Lázaro Cárdenas becoming even a puppet president, for the former Michoacanese governor had a proven track record of reform and leftist sympathies.

Cárdenas actively sought the PNR's presidential nomination. His chief rival, the more conservative Manuel Pérez Treviño, held considerable sway within the party structure itself, but garnered only a minority of support in other political forums such as congress. As a brigadier general and governor of Coahuila,

Pérez Treviño had not attained the stature of Cárdenas, who was a general of the highest ranking, that of *divisionario*. Historians debate whether or not Cárdenas received the nomination solely by the will of Plutarco Calles, or if the strong-man favored him with an eye toward popular and political pressures. Even if the latter were true, few would doubt at the time that Cárdenas would serve as a willing puppet. There was nothing in his past to suggest otherwise, and, perhaps as a precaution, Cárdenas's successor in Michoacán, Benigno Serratos, was quickly dismantling the worker-peasant base the governor had enjoyed.[27]

In June 1933 Pérez Treviño accepted the inevitable, telegraphing Calles and announcing to the press that his pre-candidacy was at an end. The Maximum Chief responded by calling the renunciation "patriotic," explaining that it would "serve as an example for the future" and by promising his friend a warm *abrazo*. The potentially dangerous ongoing rift between Cárdenas and Pérez Treviño loyalists further defused two months later, as the pre-candidacy Cárdenas campaign wound down and Pérez Treviño resigned from his position as president of the PNR.[28]

The election itself raised difficult questions for the Mexican Right. Operating outside the PNR, the Right could not contest the nomination; now, however, it struggled anew with the merits of waging electoral opposition in the face of almost certain ballot box fraud. José Vasconcelos, the Right's flag bearer in the election of 1929, did not hesitate in his evaluation of the matter. From self-imposed exile abroad, he advised his followers to abstain from the election so as not to legitimize the official party and its regime. As early as July 1933, in a letter to his close friend Alfonso Taracena, Vasconcelos warned that extensive corruption would prohibit an effective movement in Mexico; the following January he dismissed the elections as "ridiculous," a charade that he completely rejected.[29]

Despite the position taken by Vasconcelos, a segment of the Mexican Right mobilized to contest the presidency in 1934. This mobilization, haphazard and feeble in comparison to the undertaking in 1929, reveals the ideological and tactical struggles of the Right in the face of advancing cardenismo.[30] The opposition, frayed by the lack of coherent organization, had difficulty mustering a platform, selecting a candidate, and mounting a campaign. In 1933 several opposition groups existed in Mexico, foremost of which were the Partido Nacional Antireeleccionista, which had orchestrated the Vasconcelos effort in 1929, and the Confederación Revolucionaria de Partidos Independientes [CRPI]. The CRPI emerged from a mix of lesser political clubs and parties, with three figures vying for leadership: Aurelio Manrique, Antonio Díaz Soto y Gama, and Antonio Villarreal. These men were joined together more by their opposition to Calles than by ideological leanings; all had been Alvaro Obregón loyalists at one time or another, and Villarreal had backed the failed 1929 rebellion of Pablo Escobar. Another participant in the Escobar rebellion, still in self-imposed exile in El Paso, was Gilberto Valenzuela, leader of the small Partido Social Democrático [PSD]. Adalberto Tejeda, the leftist governor of

Veracruz, weighed in against the Callista political machine with his Partido Socialista de las Izquierdas. Opposition activities began in the winter of 1933, when the PNA openly criticized the PNR's policy of deducting party contributions from the wages of government workers. The party sent petitions protesting the forced contributions and consulted with the Mexican Lawyers Union about the constitutionality of the practice, though it declined to contest the matter in court.[31]

The opposition could readily agree that the line between the Revolutionary government and the PNR should be clearly drawn, yet it sputtered on the question of a candidate with which to oppose the political establishment. The PNA debunked Vasconcelos as its potential candidate at an early party meeting in July 1933, a move encouraged by the embittered 1929 campaign manager, Vito Alessio Robles.[32] Early favorites for the nomination were Luis Cabrera, a former finance minister under Carranza, and longtime revolutionary Antonio I. Villarreal. Cabrera was the clear favorite by November 1933, when the PNA joined the CRPI and other opposition factions for a convention in Mexico City's Politeama Theater.

The Politeama meeting was a colorful affair that reflected the difficulties of unifying a diverse political opposition. Opening the convention on November 19, in honor of the start of the 1910 Revolution, the meeting ended unceremoniously when police broke it up with arrests, gunfire, and tear gas. Before the police raid, delegates had an opportunity to listen to speeches by Manrique, Soto y Gama, Villarreal, and Diego Arenas Guzmán, editor of the rightist newspaper *El Hombre Libre*. These orators praised Luis Cabrera, the potential opposition candidate, and denounced government corruption. Villarreal took aim at the excesses of the "Revolutionary family," scolding them for "an offensive lifestyle of grand automobiles, beloved luxuries, dogs riding in your cars, all of which insult the Revolution." The Revolutionary leaders, he said, had become multimillionaires and despots. In reference to the government's widely publicized highway construction program, Villarreal cynically remarked that, without graft, "these small stretches of highways . . . would have cost the nation less if they had been covered with sheets of silver." A volatile mixture of disgruntled Obregonistas, conservatives, and agrarians, segments of the Politeama crowd readily contended with the speakers. When Soto y Gama, a Zapatista who moved toward the right of the political spectrum with age, explained that between Lenin and Christ he would choose Christ, a man in the crowd jeered that he wanted Lenin. Shouts of "down with Calles" were sprinkled in with all the speeches, reflecting the personalism of Maximato politics.[33]

The police raid that ended the rally followed a pattern of repression and condemnation on the part of the government. After his arrest and an interview with Mexico City police chief Juan José Méndez, Aurelio Manrique went to Monterrey, where another opposition meeting was broken up. On November 24 police in Puebla disbanded a PNA rally with plain-cloths officers, who arrested the featured speaker, party leader Vito Alessio Robles. Meanwhile, in Mexico

City, members of the Chamber of Deputies charged that the opposition parties were instruments of the clergy, and the press attacked the movement.[34] *El Nacional*, in an editorial entitled "The Opposition," reasoned that

The present regime can not be so terrible, when all the offenders in the Politeama Theater last Sunday are enjoying absolute freedom and all manner of guarantees. The opposition claims as its model the opposition of 1910, but that opposition was pure and inspired by the highest ideals, reminding one of the Christians of the catacombs.[35]

Government attacks and the divisive nature of the opposition took its toll. Another joint convention to name a candidate had to be postponed twice in early 1934, and efforts to recruit Luis Cabrera as the nominee failed due to conflicting loyalties. Cabrera, a former Carranza partisan, enjoyed the open support of the PNA, but had lingering Obregonista enemies in the ranks of the CRPI. Pressured to declare his intentions in public, he summarily declined to accept leadership of the opposition in January 1934, explaining that he saw no purpose in the elections when Calles controlled the bureaucracy and the army. This position prompted criticism from opposition leaders, including Soto y Gama; Cabrera, in turn, labeled Soto y Gama an Obregonista and a hypocrite, who, "if Obregón had not died . . . would doubtless be running the PNR or assisting Calles as a candidate to succeed General Obregón again."[36]

This dispute over the Cabrera candidacy created a division between the PNA and CRPI, causing the two groups to hold separate conventions in March and April. A faction of former Obregón supporters dominated the CRPI. Its president, Aurelio Manrique, had served under Obregón in the Revolution and blamed Calles for his mentor's murder. Known for his exceptional oratorical skills, Manrique successfully urged the convention to nominate Villarreal. The PNA, now aligned with three minor groups operating under an umbrella organization called the Consejo Nacional de la Oposición, backed Gilberto Valenzuela for president. Valenzuela was practicing law in El Paso, a refugee from the potential wrath of Calles for his role in the Escobar rebellion. Even across the border he did not feel safe: in early 1933 he alleged that there was a plot to kidnap him and transport him to Mexico for assassination, a charge Ciudad Juárez officials dismissed as "absurd." Yet by remaining outside the country Valenzuela had invalidated his candidacy, since the constitution required one year of immediate residency for a presidential candidate. Subsequently, the PNA turned to his running mate, Román Badillo, whose efforts on the campaign trail faltered badly.[37]

With the effective demise of the PNA, Villarreal became the leading candidate of the opposition. At fifty-four years of age, he had begun his career as a critic, along with Ricardo Flores Magón, of Porfirio Díaz. After the Revolution he served as minister of agriculture under Obregón, supported the Escobar insurgents in 1929, and had remained in the United States during most of the Maximato. On the campaign trail he harped on unimaginative and ideologically ambiguous themes—a testimony to the divergent nature of the coalition he led—the most common of which was government corruption, the topic he had engaged at the Politeama Theater six months earlier.

The unwillingness of the 1934 opposition to position itself sharply along ideological lines, while reflecting the personalism of Maximato politics, does not mean that the Right was not present in its ranks. Like the Vasconcelos campaign five years earlier, the 1934 opposition included a large contingent of rightists and produced considerable rightwing rhetoric. Though Vasconcelos failed to endorse him, many of his 1929 followers supported the candidacy of Villarreal, as did countless Catholics and ex-cristeros.[38] Opposition figures routinely appealed to the right in their stump speeches. Manrique, for example, denounced anticlerical policies before a crowd of two thousand persons in Nuevo Laredo. Yet predictably, in the wake of the agreement with the government, the church hierarchy distanced itself from the opposition movement. "The ecclesiastical authorities do not approve the organization or existence of any political party as Catholic," explained Archbishop Pascual Díaz in an April 1, 1934 statement. The archbishop was particularly anxious to make his point because of the presence of the small Partido Acción Nacional [PAN, also known as Acción Nacionalista], one of three parties that had comprised the Consejo Nacional de la Oposición and later supported Villarreal. After meeting with representatives of the party, including its president, Octavio Elizalde, Díaz explained that PAN was not a Catholic party and had "no connection whatsoever with the ecclesiastical authorities."[39]

Despite the position of the church hierarchy, many clerics participated in opposition efforts, not infrequently evoking the name of José Vasconcelos.[40] And good Catholics could find much that pleased them in the official publication of the opposition, a newsletter edited by Filomeno Mata entitled *Nuevo Régimen*. "The opposition is fighting," explained the newsletter, "against shameful immorality, disgraceful nepotism, and infamous persecutions." Targets of the publication's ire included the rabid anticlerical Tabasco governor, Tomás Garrido Canabal, and Narciso Bassols's plans for sex education.[41]

The Right could also appreciate the nationalism embraced by the opposition movement, which revolved around a *cause célèbre* in 1933—the Chamizal border dispute with the United States. Chamizal had been a part of Mexico until the mid-nineteenth century, when the Río Grande suddenly changed course and placed this valuable parcel of land, urbanized as part of the city of El Paso, north of the border. In late 1932 the Abelardo Rodríguez administration had reopened talks with Washington aimed at breaking this diplomatic impasse, only to reject a proposed scheme that amounted to financial compensation for Mexico. Rightist nationalists rallied around Chamizal; at the PNA nominating convention, for example, the most conspicuous banner was one demanding Chamizal be returned to Mexico. The Catholic news magazine *La Palabra* repeatedly called for its return, noting that the tract of land was "still under the domination of the imperialistic Yankee." *Nuevo Régimen* joined the chorus, too, demanding a more aggressive foreign policy.[42]

The belligerent nationalism of the Right was not far removed from an impulse evident across the political spectrum. Cárdenas himself appealed to Mexican nationalism with the expropriation of foreign oil interests in 1938—the one time he enjoyed widespread political support which even came from some of his rightist critics. Mexico had emerged from its Revolution with a strong sense of sovereignty. By the 1930s the 1910 Revolution itself was well on its way to becoming a national legend, and it is a testimony to the depth of emotion and conviction surrounding the great upheaval that the opposition and *Nuevo Régimen* treated it as sacrosanct. Even rightists among their ranks would never condemn the Revolution, viewing themselves as heirs to the antireelection efforts of Francisco I. Madero. It was "His Majesty Calles," according to *Nuevo Régimen*, who sought to establish a new imperial dynasty in Mexico and betray the Revolution.

Lázaro Cárdenas received little attention from the opposition because it perceived him as only an agent of the Maximum Chief and the "corrupt" Revolutionary regime. Cárdenas, though certainly never questioning his pending electoral victory, undertook an ambitious tour of the country. Traveling more than 16,000 miles and visiting all twenty-eight states, the PNR's energetic candidate urged worker unity in his campaign speeches and rarely acknowledged the opposition. The results of the July 1 election were a foregone conclusion. Although the "Opposition Hymn" excitedly proclaimed

a las urnas vayamos unidos!
a votar, a votar, camaradas!

the schismatic antigovernment forces mobilized a feeble turnout. Of just over 2.3 million votes cast, official returns showed Cárdenas the winner with 2,268,507 votes to Villarreal's 24,690. The left-leaning Tejeda garnered 15,765 votes, according to the government, while communist Hernán Laborde followed with 1,188.[43] Unofficially, Tómas Garrido Canabal got at least one vote: Lázaro Cárdenas, still on the campaign trail on election day, cast his ballot for the Tabasco governor in the city of Durango. Though the 1934 opposition was much weaker than that undertaken in 1929, and though the Rodríguez government proclaimed its commitment to democracy and free elections, there can be little doubt that the Cárdenas vote was inflated and the Villarreal vote diminished by use of fraud. On July 3, *La Palabra* expressed amazement that the anticlerical Cárdenas won a 91.7 percent majority in a Catholic nation.[44] The only armed movement in the wake of the election returns appears to have been a minor affair on the Sonora-Arizona border. On July 14, authorities apprehended two Villarrealistas 10 miles southwest of Agua Prieta. One was Marcial Gallegos, an ex-colonel who had fought under Francisco "Pancho" Villa in the Revolution. Gallegos, distraught by the apparent election fraud, issued circulars that criticized the PNR and called Sonorans to revolt in the face of continued "brutal tyranny." His call went largely unheeded, though rumors of pending insurrection swept the border region and 250 Mexican troops moved into northern Sonora in an effort to avert any problems.[45]

One reason why few Mexicans enthusiastically participated in the election was the fact that, in the eyes of most, there was little hope for real change. Lázaro Cárdenas ascended into the presidency, but the power behind him remained the ever-present Plutarco Calles, whose allies controlled the PNR, bureaucracy, army, state governments, congress, and Cárdenas's cabinet. Even the Communist party distanced itself from the outwardly leftist new president, assuming him to be the fourth Calles puppet. Though triumphant in the PNR and in the election, Cárdenas would not have genuine political power unless he successfully broke from Calles. Yet neither he nor Calles could evoke anything but disdain from the opposition Right. Electoral fraud, destined to become a standard feature of the modern Mexican state, bred a new cynicism among Mexicans, who increasingly looked for other avenues of resistance. Although political opposition from the Right sputtered as the Maximato wore on, Catholic mobilization persisted after the demise of the Cristeros in new and lively forums.

NOTES

1. Frank Tannenbaum, *Mexico: The Struggle for Peace and Bread* (New York: Alfred A. Knopf, 1956), pp. 69–70.

2. Tannenbaum, *Mexico*, p. 68.

3. John W. F. Dulles, *Yesterday in Mexico: A Chronicle of the Revolution, 1919– 1936* (Austin: University of Texas Press, 1961), pp. 362–67. The Catholic Right in the 1930s extolled Toral as a martyr.

4. Dulles, *Yesterday in Mexico*, p. 425.

5. Jean Meyer, "Revolution and Reconstruction in the 1920s," in Leslie Bethell, ed., *Mexico since Independence*, pp. 202, 239; "El culto al estado," *La Palabra* 2:73 (November 29, 1931): 5.

6. Carleton Beals, "Mexico Turns to Fascist Tactics," *The Nation* 82 (January 28, 1931): 110–12; Frank Hanighen, "Mexico Moves to the Right," *The Commonweal* 14:11 (July 15, 1931): 280.

7. Salvador Azuela, *La aventura vasconcelista, 1929* (Mexico City: Editorial Diana, 1980), p. 63.

8. Dulles, *Yesterday in Mexico*, pp. 427–28; PNR, "Declaración de principios," March 4, 1929, p. 37, Archivos Plutarco Elías Calles y Fernando Torreblanca, Archivo Plutarco Elías Calles [hereafter APEC], Fondo Manuel Pérez Treviño, 4468/125.0.0 [numbers indicate fondo, expediente, legajo, and foja, with zeroes reflecting only one legajo and no document number].

9. Lieuwen, *Mexican Militarism*, p. 104; Dulles, *Yesterday in Mexico*, pp. 415, 438. Calles was particularly vulnerable to anti-Semitic attack because of his Hebraic middle name, Elías, which caused some to wrongly conclude that he was Jewish.

10. Emilio Portes Gil, *Quince años de política mexicana* (Mexico City: Ediciones Botas, 1941), pp. 171, 415, 438; José Vasconcelos, *El Proconsulado* (Mexico City: Ediciones Botas, 1939), p. 136.

11. José C. Valadés, *Historia general de la revolución mexicana*, vol. 8 (Mexico City: Editor Quesada Brandi, 1967), p. 200. Typical was the career of Ramón F. Iturbe, who as an Obregonista had fallen into disfavor with the Revolutionary family by joining the failed de la Huerta rebellion in 1923. See Carlos Tresguerras, "Quién es quién en la Revolución: Ramón F. Iturbe, El Petrolero," *La Prensa*, May 16, 1939.

12. Dulles notes Amaro's unimpressive exit in *Yesterday in Mexico*, p. 441. Amaro sought medical attention at the Mayo Clinic in Rochester, Minnesota, a common procedure for the Revolutionary elite in the 1920s—Juan Almazán recuperated there for several weeks in 1928.

13. "Relations between the U.S. and Mexico during the Administration of President Hoover," memo on Escobar revolt, no date, pp. 1–2, 39–40, Herbert Hoover Presidential Library, Presidential Papers, Cabinet Offices: Secretary of State, Latin American Affairs, box 49, folder 12. Regarding Almazán's role and the government's masterful use of air power, see Untitled Report to War Department, April 10, 1929, APEC, Fondo Juan Andreu Almazán, 192/192.2.0; Lorenzo Meyer, *Los inicios de la institucionalización: La política del Maximato* (Mexico City: El Colegio de México, 1978), p. 206.

14. John Skirius, *José Vasconcelos y la cruzada de 1929* (Mexico City: Siglo Veintiuno Editores, 1978), pp. 17–28; Javier Garciadiego Dantan, "Duelo de Gigantes," *Boletín de los Archivos Calles y Torreblanca* 11 (September 1992): 9–10.

15. Azuela, *Aventura vasconcelista*, p. 81; Skirius, *Cruzada*, pp. 53–57.

16. Interview with Manuel Gómez Morín in James and Edna Wilkie, *México visto en el siglo XX* (Mexico City: Instituto Mexicano de Investigaciones Económicas, 1969), p. 157; Skirius, *Cruzada*, pp. 43, 69, 79; Azuela, *Aventura vasconcelista*, pp. 130–31.

17. Skirius, *Cruzada*, pp. 68–72, 77, 88; Azuela, *Aventura vasconcelista*, p. 104. Dulles identifies the movement as leftist and depreciates it, see *Yesterday in Mexico*, pp. 469–80.

18. Antonieta Rivas Mercado, *La campaña de Vasconcelos* (Mexico City: Editorial Oasis, 1981), p. 81. The use of "reactionary" by Mexico's predominant political establishment appears to have been similar to the Republican Party's use of "liberal" in the United States during the 1980s. Without regard to the true meaning of the word, one side defined it so well in the public imagination that no one readily adopted it as a label.

19. Dulles, *Yesterday in Mexico*, pp. 472–73; Gómez Morín in Wilkie, *Visto en siglo XX*, p. 170.

20. Mauricio Magdaleno, *Las palabras perdidas* (Mexico City: Manuel Porrúa, 1956), p. 62; Azuela, *Aventura vasconcelista*, p. 133.

21. Vasconcelos, *El Proconsulado*, p. 225. For an example of his charge that Calles had sold Mexico out to greedy foreign bankers, see same source, pp. 697–99. Vasconcelos became fiercely anti-Semitic by 1940, when he launched the pro-Nazi newsletter *El Timón*. Skirius, *Cruzada*, p. 85.

22. Azuela, *Aventura vasconcelista*, pp. 83, 138–39; Portes Gil, *Quince años*, p. 189; Lorenzo Meyer, *Política del Maximato*, pp. 206–8.

23. Skirius, *Cruzada*, pp. 76–77, 86; Meyer, *Política del Maximato*, p. 100.

24. Azuela, *Aventura vasconcelista*, pp. 61–62, 125–27; Magdaleno, *Palabras*, p. 72. For Alessio Robles's view of the campaign, not always kind to Vasconcelos, see *Mis andanzas con nuestro Ulises* (Mexico City: Editorial Botas, 1938).

25. Azuela, *Aventura vasconcelista*, pp. 156–57. Dulles implies that the popular support was not so widespread or spontaneous. Jean Meyer, "Revolution and Reconstruction," pp. 214–16. Not surprisingly, Portes Gil claims that his government combatted harassment of Vasconcelistas by local authorities; see *Quince años*, pp. 180–83.

26. Vasconcelos, *El Proconsulado*, p. 229; Gómez Morín in Wilkie, *Visto en siglo XX*, p. 158. Some rightwing opponents of cardenismo, such as Gómez Morín, were perhaps not so conservative in their earlier days; see same source, p. 169.

27. Lorenzo Meyer, *Política del Maximato*, pp. 274–80, 284–85. Cárdenas also served briefly as president of the PNR in the fall 1930, unwavering in his allegiance to Calles. Governor Serratos was a supporter of Pérez Treviño, which might explain his zealousness in uprooting the state's Cardenistas.

28. Manuel Pérez Treviño to Calles, telegram, June 8, 1933, and Calles to Pérez Treviño, telegram, June 8, 1933, both in APEC, Fondo Pérez Treviño, 4468/125.0; Lorenzo Meyer, *Política del Maximato*, p. 289.

29. "El Licenciado Vasconcelos Señala un Rumbo," *El Universal*, April 9, 1940; Vasconcelos to Alfonso Taracena, July 18, 1933, and Vasconcelos as quoted in *Crítica* (Buenos Aires), January 8, 1934, both in Alfonso Taracena, ed., *Cartas políticas de José Vasconcelos* (Mexico City: Editora Librera, 1959), pp. 128–33.

30. In sharp contrast to the myriad accounts on vasconcelismo in 1929, the 1934 opposition has received scant attention. The only noteworthy discussion, though charged with personal opinion, is that found in Luis Cabrera's (given name, Blas Urrea) *Veinte años después* (Mexico City: Ediciones Botas, 1938), pp. 133–64. This neglect of the opposition is partly because it was overshadowed by Lázaro Cárdenas and his ambitious campaigning.

31. "La convención oposicionista aplazado," *El Universal*, March 9, 1933; Stanley Hawks to Secretary of State [SS], March 21, 1933, United States Department of State, Records Relating to the Internal Affairs of Mexico [USDS], 812.00/29833, microflim reel 2; "Los antireeleccionistas consultan la abogacía," *La Palabra*, April 16, 1933.

32. Cabrera, *Veinte años después*, pp. 141–43; Dulles, *Yesterday in Mexico*, p. 579. The tensions between Alessio Robles and Vasconcelos were visible in 1929, and also appear in Robles's *Mis andanzas con nuestro Ulises*. The PNA's rebuff of Vasconcelos, who was in Spain at the time and still claiming the presidency by fraud, perhaps explains his subsequent condemnation of the 1934 opposition.

33. "Presidenciables del antirreeleccionismo," *La Palabra* 3:183 (January 8, 1933): 1; Cabrera, *Veinte años después*, p. 144; Dulles, *Yesterday in Mexico*, pp. 581–82; speeches from PNA-CRPI meeting, November 19, 1933, APEC, Fondo Partidos Varios 4334/11.577 pp. 580–81. Guzmán's speech appears in *El Hombre Libre*, November 22, 1933.

34. Josephus Daniels, ambassador, to SS, November 24, 1933, USDS 812.00/29959; Daniels to SS, November 28, 1933, USDS 812.00/29961; "Sesión de los Independientes," *Excelsior*, November 23, 1933. The CRPI met on November 22 and protested the charges of the deputies.

35. "La oposición," *El Nacional*, November 24, 1933. This is a fascinating quote. The first part obviously neglects to consider that the police broke up the Politeama meeting! The second part reveals the deep reverence for the 1910 Revolution in the political discourse of the 1930s, ironically employing Christian tradition in its veneration of the 1910 participants.

36. Cabrera, *Veinte años después*, pp. 147–49; Luis Cabrera, "Las puertas de corrupción en 1920," *La Palabra* 185 (February 1, 1934): 1. Cabrera also wrote a letter in response to Soto y Gama, reprinted in *Veinte años después*, pp. 167–73.

37. Roderic Camp, *Memoirs of a Mexican Politician* (Albuquerque: University of New Mexico Press, 1988), p. 226; Dulles, *Yesterday in Mexico*, pp. 583–85; "No se ha tratado jamás de secuestrar a Valenzuela," *La Palabra* 189 (March 29, 1933): 1. Valenzuela's failed candidacy was noted by the U.S. embassy, which advised Washington that he was "well-informed" and "most friendly to Americans." See Daniels to SS, March 20, 1934, USDS 812.00/30020.

38. "Vasconcelos señala un rumbo," *El Universal*, April 9, 1940; José Alvarado, "¿La oposición es siempre reaccionaria?" *Excelsior*, May 8, 1958.

39. Romeyn Wormuth, Consul in Nuevo Laredo, to SS, November 29, 1933 USDS 812.00/29963; Daniels to SS, April 6, 1934 USDS 812.00/ 30031. Acción Nacionalista should not be confused with the present-day PAN, founded in 1939. The PAN begun in 1934 was minuscule.

40. Vasconcelos to Taracena, March 3, 1934, in Taracena, ed., *Cartas políticas*, p. 299. By mid-1934 Vasconcelos condemned the Villarrealistas with disgust, contending that they were "as corrupt as the government" and giving the Revolutionary regime legitimacy. See Vasconcelos to Taracena, undated, same source, pp. 244–45.

41. See Filomeno Mata, "Otra vez en la lucha"; K. Ojito, "Puntos de fuego"; and no author, "El plan sexual," all in *Nuevo Régimen* 1 (January 12, 1934): 1–4.

42. Daniels to SS, March 25, 1934, USDS 812.00/30026; "La zona de Chamizal debe ser entregada a México," *La Palabra* 185 (January 15, 1933): 1; "Panamericanismo," *Nuevo Régimen* 2 (January 19, 1934): 4. For details regarding Chamizal and the Rodríguez administration, see Francisco Gaxiola, Jr., *El President Rodríguez* (Mexico City: Editorial Cultura, 1938), pp. 211–23.

43. "El tercer imperio" and "Himno oposicionista," both in *Nuevo Régimen* 1 (January 12, 1934): 3–4; Nathaniel and Sylvia Weyl, *The Reconquest of Mexico: The Years of Lázaro Cárdenas* (New York: Oxford University Press, 1939), pp. 125–27.

44. Lázaro Cárdenas, *Obras: Apuntes, 1913–1940*, vol. 1 (Mexico City: Universidad Nacional Autónoma de México, 1986), p. 289; Gaxiola, *Presidente Rodríguez*, pp. 190–93; "Cárdenas contra la nación," *La Palabra* 215 (July 3, 1934): 1.

45. Lewis Boyle, consul in Agua Prieta, to embassy, July 15, 1934, USDS 812.00/30082; "Revolt in Mexico Is Only Rumor," *Douglas Daily Dispatch*, July 15, 1934. Gallegos escaped punishment and reportedly lived in Tombstone, Arizona during the fall of 1934, with the U.S. Immigration Service and Justice Department tracking him. See Boyle to embassy, September 10, 1934, USDS, 812.00/30100.

3

THE CATHOLIC OPPOSITION

If the Vasconcelos experience left many rightists wondering about the useful-ness of opposing the Revolutionary regime through the ballot box at the outset of the Maximato, the demise of the Cristeros similarly dropped the curtain on ideas of victory through armed rebellion. Spring 1929 found the Catholic guerrillas short on ammunition and facing ever-increasing numbers of Federal troops in Los Altos. On June 21, just three weeks after the death of their field commander, Enrique Gorostieta, the Cristero position was undermined by the *Arreglos*, coordinated statements by Portes Gil and the Catholic hierarchy that effectively ended the rebellion. The government gave up very little, stating simply that it did not intend to destroy the church or interfere in spiritual matters; the bishops agreed to resume masses and abide by the laws in force. The *Arreglos* constituted a settlement at the top which bypassed both the LNDLR and the Cristeros.[1]

Reaction to the *Arreglos* was mixed: the hierarchy tried to clamp down quickly on any dissent, but the bishops themselves were divided—though they kept silence in public. Cristero fighters laid down their arms but viewed the compromise as tantamount to surrender, while the LNDLR, which indirectly led the revolt, endorsed peace even though, in reality, it was already "reduced to absolute impotence."[2] It had been lay organizations, primarily the LNDLR and the Asociación Católica de la Juventud Mexicana, that had provided the impetus for rebellion in the first place. Hence, in its quest for peace the hierarchy immediately moved to control lay Catholics and their organizations. Pascual Díaz, named Mexico's archbishop as he concluded the *Arreglos*, appointed a commission that recommended the restructuring of lay organizations under an umbrella group, Acción Católica Mexicana [ACM].

One purpose of ACM, established in December 1929, was to monitor radical Catholics opposed to the *Arreglos* at the parish level and to bring "lay Catholic activities under ecclesiastical control." A small number resisted, especially LNDLR leaders and unbending Cristeros.[3] A motive for their resistance, besides a sense of betrayal on the part of the church, was the persecution they encountered after June 1929. For them the *modus vivendi* turned into a *modus moriendi*, as the army carried out a "systematic and premeditated murder of all the Cristero leaders." The long list of victims included forty-one ex-Cristeros who suffered mass execution in a Jalisco village in February 1930. In fall 1931 *La Palabra* reported assassinations throughout the Jalisco countryside, with former fighters disappearing and their tortured bodies turning up days or weeks later. Those who escaped the death squads did so by fleeing their homes and finding refuge in the United States, large cities, or Governor Saturnino Cedillo's state of San Luis Potosí.

By 1932 many Cristeros were rearming in the countryside as church-state relations began to deteriorate anew. Efforts by most of the church prelates and President Pascual Ortiz Rubio to smooth relations in the 1929–1931 period had been slowly undermined by intransigent Callistas.[4] Tensions increased greatly in December 1931, when the church celebrated the four hundred-year anniversary of the apparition of the Virgin of Guadalupe by rededicating the renovated basilica on the outskirts of Mexico City. Coinciding with the celebrations was a six-day meeting of ACM delegates, called together by the archbishop in order to study "ways of promulgating devotion to the Virgin," as well as means of saving the church "from the great dangers threatening the faith."

The government interpreted these activities as belligerent and took steps in retaliation. *El Nacional*, the PNR press organ, criticized the celebrations, the Chamber of Deputies investigated its radio broadcast, and Minister of War Calles punished a military band that had imprudently participated.[5] Far more serious, however, was the subsequent spread of laws and decrees limiting the number of priests and closing churches. Some of these measures, generally passed at the local or state level, had taken effect before the celebrations. Most notable had been the June 1931 anticlerical law in Adalberto Tejeda's Veracruz, which limited the number of priests to one per hundred thousand persons, and Querétaro's Law Number 25—passed on the eve of the Guadalupe extravaganza—which both limited the number of priests and required the remainder to register.

After the early December celebrations, many state governments throughout Mexico followed these examples. Tamaulipas passed a law restricting the number of priests, while Morelos imposed a 300-peso tax on clergy before the first of the year. Lázaro Cárdenas, governor of Michoacán, advised Calles of his spring 1932 measures restricting and registering priests.[6] Other states like Chihuahua and Sonora, which had already limited the number of priests in 1931, lowered their numbers. Sonoran governor Rodolfo Calles, son of the former president, accelerated a "defanatization" campaign that featured closed churches and clerical deportations. Sonoran priests had their ranks further reduced, faced registration procedures, and watched as the governor closed churches like Hermosillo's cathedral by decree. Not to be outdone, Tabasco's Garrido Canabal, arguably the most anticlerical of all, organized the Bloque de Jóvenes Revolucionarios, or Red Shirts, who gained notoriety by burning religious images and terrorizing the devout.[7]

Anticlerical measures also accelerated at the national level. In mid-December the Mexican congress slapped a limit of one priest per fifty thousand persons on the church in Mexico City and Baja California (a territory under national jurisdiction), allowing only twenty-four priests to minister to the capital's more than 1.2 million population. Beginning in the same month, a wide variety of churches, from small parishes to major cathedrals, were shut down by presidential decree. During the remainder of the Maximato, 264 churches had their doors closed in this manner throughout Mexico.[8] The church hierarchy responded rather timidly to the quickening pace of anticlerical measures in late 1931 and early 1932. Archbishop Díaz called for nonviolent opposition in the Federal District, including the filing of *juicios de amparo*. Díaz reasoned that the new laws limiting the number of priests violated Articles 24 and 130 of the 1917 Constitution, which guaranteed liberty to practice the Catholic faith. Since a lack of priests would impair the ability of the faithful to practice their faith, *juicios de amparo* appealing for the protection of individual rights from the law seemed justified.[9]

The church hierarchy's tepid response to increased persecution reflected a lack of instructions from Rome. The Vatican broke its silence in September 1932, however, when Pope Pius XI, in the encyclical *Acerba Animi*, addressed his Mexican flock "so long harassed by grievous persecutions." The pope took a hard line. He chided the government, which had previously "frustrated every attempt to arrive at an understanding," and charged it with violating the spirit of the *Arreglos*. Perturbed by recent anticlerical laws, the pontiff concluded that

since any restriction whatever on the number of priests is a grave violation of divine rights, it will be necessary for the bishops, the clergy and the Catholic laity to continue to protest with all their energy against such violation, using every legitimate means.

Legitimate means did not include renewing rebellion, though, and the encyclical ended with an admonition for the laity to seek "the closest union with the church and the hierarchy." The pope clearly did not want restless radicals to break ranks.

The Revolutionary government did not respond well to papal criticism. The PNR's press organ, *El Nacional*, labeled *Acerba Animi* "violent" and "nonapostolic," and again reminded Mexicans of reputed clerical involvement in Obregón's assassination. President Abelardo Rodríguez (Ortiz Rubio had been forced out of office by Calles a month earlier) took note of the "insolent and defiant" attitude of the encyclical, and appealed to Mexican nationalism with a stern warning that the government "will not tolerate dominion of any outside power."[10] Not only was Mexico City's response to Pius XI unconciliatory, but Catholic extremists rejected Rome's instructions to submit to the moderate hierarchy. Some Cristeros regrouped in the countryside, striking targets soon after the encyclical. In October, terrorists placed bombs on the railroad tracks outside of Guadalajara, a tactic reminiscent of *La Cristiada*, and on the eleventh a train in Puebla was derailed. On October 17 Guadalajara police raided a house, killing two Cristeros in a gun battle and capturing a printing press and religious literature. One week later, three soldiers suffered injuries in a skirmish with Cristeros at Romita, Michoacán.[11] These sporadic incidents attest to the sharpening tensions in late 1932, though the number of Cristeros appears to have been small, and would remain so until 1934–1935.[12]

Just as the Cristeros revived modestly in late 1931 and 1932, worsening church-state relations gave renewed life to lay Catholic grassroots political efforts. The near-complete absence of Cristero resistance during the 1929–1931 period was not matched in terms of grassroots activities: the 1929 establishment of ACM preserved some continuity. Yet with the hierarchy-controlled ACM came restructuring, the incorporation of the once-powerful ACJM, and the emasculation of the radical LNDLR. ACM was an umbrella to four subgroups: the Rama Masculina was comprised of the Unión de Católicos Mexicanos [UCM], for married men and bachelors thirty-five and older, and the "new" ACJM for single males fifteen to thirty-five; the Rama Femenina consisted of the Unión Femenina Católica Mexicana [UFCM] for married women and single women over thirty-five, and the Juventud Católica Femenina Mexicana [JCFM] for single women fifteen to thirty-five. The UFCM absorbed the Unión de Damas Católicas of the 1920s, and the extremist wing of organized Catholic women—which had formed the Feminine Brigades that had actively participated in insurrection—disappeared.[13]

The four associations sought to fulfill the objectives of ACM as identified in its General Statutes:

1. To again place Jesus Christ in the middle of the family, school, and society.
2. To combat by all just and legal means anti-christian civilization.
3. To repair by the same means the grave disorders in our society.
4. To reestablish the principle that human authority is representative of that of God.[14]

These goals were clearly ambiguous in terms of political content. On the whole, ACM activities were more restricted, less overtly political, and much more closely monitored by the church hierarchy than those of predecessor groups in the 1920s. The bishops instructed ACM to avoid direct political participation except in matters where moral or religious issues were concerned. During most of the Maximato, membership was low and projects minimal. Work picked up, predictably, as the church underwent new persecution and the pope issued *Acerba Animi*. Although the size and scope of work increased in the mid-1930s, ACM paled in comparison to the former LNDLR, which in its heyday had been tightly run and boasted hundreds of thousands of members.

The LNDLR itself survived into the 1930s, though "survival" is almost too strong a word to describe the group's condition as it underwent rapid decay. Leaders dropped "religiosa" from the organization's name in an effort to save it from being abolished by the bishops. With a legacy of radicalism in an era of appeasement, the demise of the Cristeros which it had fostered, and hierarchical sympathy-now-turned-hostility, the LNDL collapsed. In 1931–1932 it mustered a few protests against the new anticlerical measures on its way down the road to irrelevance.[15]

Grassroots political action among lay Catholics took other forms beyond those of the organizations. When Governor Tejada restricted the number of priests in Veracruz, for example, *La Palabra* raised funds for expelled clerics and delivered the money to the bishop of Veracruz. Also, spontaneous protests and demonstrations supplemented those planned by groups such as the LNDL. In February 1933, Tapatíos stoned police who were trying to arrest a priest, and firemen with hoses had to disperse the crowd.[16]

All modes of Catholic resistance to the Revolutionary regime, from rearmed Cristeros to ACM activities to spontaneous protests and unrest, intensified during the heightened anticlericalism of late 1931–1932 and continued to intensify as the Maximato drew to a close. The additional catalyst for rightist efforts in the late Maximato was the government's aggressive promotion of sexual and socialist education, begun under Secretary of Public Education Narciso Bassols. Bassols, a law professor at the University of Mexico, was a committed Marxist when he assumed his government post in 1931 at age thirty-five. Intellectually gifted, energetic and outspoken, as an atheist and materialist he recited Karl Marx's maxim that religion is an "opium of the masses," which quickly won him the ire of the Catholic Right.

Even before Bassols began his tenure in office, the stage had been set for church-state conflict over education. Pope Pius XI had issued an encyclical in 1930 entitled "The Christian Education of Youth," in which he argued that the church was superior to the state in educational matters. In Mexico, Catholic schools had flourished in the 1920s, relatively free of government harassment even under Calles, in part due to the moderating influence of then education secretary J. M. Puig Casauranc. Yet as Bassols came into the cabinet the Catholic Right sounded the alarm: *La Palabra* warned its readers that the Revolutionary state "has invaded the territory of the family, snatching the young minds of children and fixing them on an educational course that leads to the abyss of complete atheism."[17]

New government measures regarding education followed the Guadalupe celebrations of December 1931, in sync with the crackdown on Mexican priests. On December 29 congress passed a law, largely crafted by Bassols, that extended state control over schools affiliated, or "incorporated," into the Federal system. The law restricted the role of the church in these schools, prohibiting clergy from teaching and outlawing the display of religious symbols. It did not close church schools, require them to affiliate, or block the establishment of new religious schools. Church-run schools could not, however, incorporate into the system. Most damning for devout Catholics in the middle class was a provision that made diplomas from nonaffiliated schools invalid for admission into state-run universities. Catholic secondary schools served as de facto preparatory schools, so this change created a hardship for college-bound Catholic youth. The small Unión Nacional de Padres de Familia [UNPF] petitioned against this step, but to no avail. Indeed, the December legislation generated minimal furor. Some church schools made the necessary changes and incorporated, while occasional public outcry came as affiliated schools pulled clerics from the classroom and religious symbols from the walls. In Monterrey the local press dramatized the removal of an image of the "Heart of Jesus" from the hallway of the Colegio Elizondo.[18]

Tensions over education increased with an April 1932 amendment to previous legislation that prohibited clergy from teaching in all primary schools. Article 3 of the 1917 Constitution required purely secular education, and Bassols therefore reasoned that clergy could not teach anywhere since they would, by their nature, influence young children with their religious presumptions. An additional law in mid-1932 required student health inspections, a step the UNPF opposed with inflammatory propaganda claiming that the inspectors might perform immoral acts with school children.

Despite the gradual tightening of restrictions under Bassols, 1932 was, with regard to education, a comparatively quiet year. In 1933 and 1934 the education secretary sparked a firestorm of reaction. In the spring he received the recommendations of a commission regarding sexual education in a report that ended up in the Mexico City press; the controversy heightened as Bassols released an instruction manual entitled *Educación sexual*. The right responded in several localities. Opponents gathered five thousand petition signatures in Morelia, for example, denouncing "pornography in the schools."[19] Sexual education initiatives were followed by discussion of socialist education in 1933, sparking widespread opposition.

The socialist education debate first took hold in the sphere of higher education. Its proponents were often Marxists, and at the heart of the debate was academic freedom. Leading the fight for a socialist curriculum at the University of Mexico in mid-1933 was Vicente Lombardo Toledano, an articulate faculty member supported by the student Left. Lombardo's agenda disturbed some of his colleagues, who feared a loss of intellectual freedom; a group of law professors threatened to resign if the university imposed Marxist dogma. In October, student opponents staged a strike, which prompted fist fights and spread unrest to other universities throughout the country. The University of Mexico settled down by month's end, when Rector Manuel Gómez Morín expelled Lombardo and the government granted the campus full autonomy.

As Mexico City's main campus quieted, the University of Guadalajara erupted. Students upset at the rector's declaration of their school as "a Marxist university" demanded the same full autonomy and occupied buildings, only to be forcefully expelled by police, who injured one hundred protesters and arrested two hundred.[20] The drama attracted national attention. On the floor of congress, deputies such as José Santo Alonso and Fernando Moctezuma blamed the unrest on clergy, while Deputy Alberto Coria posited that the reactionary protesters sought to bring a "Mussolini-type regime to Mexico." Two large student groups involved with the unrest rejected both accusations. The Federación Estudiantil Universitaria [FEU] and the Confederación Nacional de Estudiantes [CNE] had undergone ideological power struggles early in the Maximato, with conservative factions triumphing in the former while a mixture of moderates guided the later. In the context of events in Guadalajara, these organizations contended that they desired only "the improvement of the cultural institutions of the country."[21] Their defense was seconded by the UNPF, which expressed surprise that the government viewed unruly students as "reactionary," and offered to mediate. A smaller student organization also involved in mobilizing students at Guadalajara and in Durango was the Unión Nacional de Estudiantes Católicos [UNEC], founded by Jesuits and operating remarkably free of hierarchical or ACM control. The UNEC's efforts spread university unrest briefly to two small campuses in Durango, though by early December all demonstrations had fizzled.[22]

In December 1933 the PNR adopted a Six Year Plan that included socalist education, thus assuring that in 1934 the controversy would persist. Additionally, in the last two years of the Maximato the government cracked down more vigorously on primary and secondary schools in violation of Bassols-inspired legislation. Tensions in spring 1934 led to a UNPF-sponsored boycott of public schools in the Federal District, a strike so successful that it prompted the resignation of Bassols in May. But the Right could hardly savor this victory. Calles himself, the power behind the presidency, called for stricter state influence in shaping the minds of Mexican children in his July 20 "Grito de Guadalajara" speech, and in October the legislature reformed Article 3 of the 1917 Constitution to provide a tighter legal framework for the secularizing of schools.[23]

The Right was not well organized nationally as it faced increasing state intervention in education. Opposition was often local and spontaneous in nature, triggered when authorities moved against neighborhood schools. In the conservative city of Puebla, for example, riots broke out when officials closed the Colegio Teresiano, a secondary school in violation of Bassols's measures. Though city officials had turned away a committee of women seeking a rally permit, three thousand persons gathered in protest near the city's main plaza. Agitated police fired warning shots into the air, and then into the crowd, injuring several demonstrators and killing one. The FEU and CNE attempted to turn this incident into nationwide action, the latter orchestrating a student strike in

Tampico.[24] Yet while major educational unrest like that in Puebla or at the University of Guadalajara could have ripple effects throughout Mexico, each ripple inevitably diminished in size, especially when they reached the less Catholic, "shallow" regions of the country like the north.

LAZARO CARDENAS AND THE CATHOLIC RIGHT

The largest and best organized segment of the Mexican Right in the mid-1930s was the Catholic Church. Though the hierarchy shunned the political arena after the failed Cristero rebellion, the church at the parish level remained politicized. The Catholic Right was a force to be reckoned with because it rested on a base of mestizo and Indian peasants in the countryside. In 1934 half of Mexico's population resided on the central plateau, with the majority in rural areas. Although major urban areas added one million residents between 1930 and 1940 (up from 3.3 to 4.3 million) while the rural population stagnated (at 13.3 million), Mexico in 1940 was still 78 percent rural. Its Indians, devoutly Catholic, frequently lived in isolated villages of less than twenty-five hundred persons, subject to considerable influence from their priests. As Mexican historian Luis González explains, local clergy stayed "near the multitudes," and, despite intense government propaganda, they continued to enjoy the support of the rural peasantry.[25]

In 1934 Calles as Maximum Chief sought to install yet another puppet, his fourth in six years, into the presidential residence. It was a scheduled election year, and his nominee, to everyone's surprise, resisted him shortly after obtaining the office. Lázaro Cárdenas had been a faithful Callista, but his sudden disloyalty triggered a prolonged political struggle not resolved until the fall of 1935 when the Maximum Chief temporarily left the country and his political influence rapidly abated.

The anticlerical Plutarco Calles could not mobilize Mexico's religious peasants on his behalf in the showdown with Cárdenas, but from 1934 to 1936 he appears to have used a strategy of aggravating the Catholic Right as a means of upsetting his rival's new government. Consequently, the Mexican church underwent what one historian has termed "the worst ordeal of its history" in 1934 and 1935, when state and local political bosses loyal to Calles persecuted it with exceptional zeal.[26] These policies differed from the moderation of the Cárdenas administration, which sought to control the flames of passion over church-state issues fanned by its political rivals. The persecution did not, however, attract devout peasants into Cárdenas's camp. The president himself had a reputation as an enemy of the church, and his association with the Revolutionary establishment precluded the possibility of winning rural Catholics to his side by political means.

The possibility existed, however, that Cárdenas could woo the support of the *campesinos* by economic initiatives. If distribution of lands to the rural poor would win their favor, he certainly did not fail for lack of trying. His administration carried out the largest agrarian reform program in Latin American history, distributing 45 million acres to nearly one million recipients. Unlike the more modest distributions in the 1920s, these reforms featured the wholesale breakup of large estates, including those owned by Calles loyalists and many foreigners. And rather than distribute parcels as private property, Cárdenas turned to communal farming, the Indian *ejido*, as a model for restoration. He created the Banco Nacional de Crédito Ejidal to aid peasants in financing and modernization.

Although one can debate the extent to which land reform brought Cárdenas the support of the rural poor, there is no doubt that it weakened and alienated one already disorganized sector of the right, the *terratenientes*, or great land-owners. Mexico's landed elite had suffered considerable loss in the 1910–1920 Revolution, if not by lands seized, then at least in terms of political clout. Segments of the Porfirian elite vested heavily in land were more subject to loss than those with diversified holdings, although all the "old rich" tended to mingle with the new Revolutionary elite in the 1920s, frequently through alliances by marriage. During the Maximato the landed elite had begun to organize them-selves in the Cámara Nacional de Agricultura [CNA], protect themselves with paramilitary White Guards, and quietly endorse new anti-agrarian initiatives of the Calles-influenced government. The aggressive posture of Cárdenas, how-ever, dashed their short-lived optimism and doomed the CNA. Death squad activity abated after Cárdenas threatened to rearm peasant militias in 1935, though one Veracruz landowner, Manuel Parra, did arrange the sensational murder of the state's agrarian governor, Manlio Fabio Altamirano.

Because the great landowners were relegated to the role of villains in the Revolutionary political culture, the rest of the Mexican Right could illafford to come to their aid overtly. Luis Cabrera, the opposition politician who had declined to campaign in 1934, wrote a book criticizing land reform and the Banco Ejidal entitled *Un ensayo comunista en México*. In it he avoided allying himself with the landed elite, and dodged the issue of the Right's true convic-tions by ambivalently dismissing Cárdenas's land policy as "contrary to the principles of the Revolution."[27] On the ground, however, the alliance between the Catholic Right and landowners was persistent and real. Priests in small villages in Michoacán frequently beseeched their peasant parishioners to avoid the fires of hell by shunning government-distributed land, and fingered agrarian activists as "communists"—who not infrequently were murdered soon after-wards. Clinging to the notion of the sanctity of private property and obedience to authority, they threatened agrarians with excommunication and even allowed the privacy of the confessional to be violated, funneling names and information to the White Guards.[28]

While agrarian reform alienated landowners and annoyed the broader Mexi-can Right, it did not necessarily reap for Cárdenas the popular support he might have anticipated. Yet many sympathetic observers and historians have wrongly assumed that it did. This assumption rests on the belief that economics lies at the root of human motivation. Karl Marx and his orthodox followers have offered the theoretical construct for such a materialist world view, and it echos in the writings of some chroniclers of 1930s Mexico.[29] It has been challenged by what can be termed "cultural Marxism," pioneered by Italian socialist Antonio Gramsci. Gramsci undermined the material view by arguing that "cultural hegemony" holds modern societies together. According to Gramsci, genuine revolution can occur only by "overcoming the economic-corporative," which is to say that class consciousness must develop on both an economic and a cultural level. Students of Gramsci point to his fundamental critique of classical Marxism: that it "never gave sufficient weight to noneconomic factors like ideology and culture."[30] Fundamental to Gramsci's critique of orthodox Marxism has been his analysis of peasants. Peasants in quasi-capitalistic societies like Mexico cling to a simple understanding of their world and fail to see that economic and political institutions evolve and can be profoundly restructured.

Hence, the peasant still has the mentality of a plebe serf: he erupts in violent revolt against the "gentry" every now and then, but he is incapable of seeing himself as a member of a collectivity, nor can he wage a systematic and permanent campaign designed to alter the economic and political relations of society.[31]

For Gramsci, then, a reorienting of the peasantry is requisite to authentic revolution; socialist education, presumably, would be a logical avenue toward this goal, yet in Mexico even it was rejected by most peasants. Cultural values prevented the triumph of cardenismo in the "hearts and minds" of devout Catholic peasantry on the central plateau. At best, land reform divided them into agrarian and Cristero camps in some rural areas.

Agrarian mobilization at the grassroots level followed the initiatives of the Cárdenas government, rather than inspired them. The Cardenista project was ultimately undertaken from the top down. And any political support generated for the regime by land reform was largely offset by its simultaneous promotion of socialist education, which was roundly and spontaneously rejected by a vast majority of rural Mexicans. "We don't want land," peasants told Cárdenas in Guaracha, Michoacán, "we want religion."[32]

The pace of education reform quickened under Cárdenas and remained a continuity in policy with Maximato administrations. Though the new president had moderated the overt persecution of the church, he made no concessions in the area of education. In line with the October 1934 revision of Article 3 by the Chamber of Deputies, which called for increased secularization of the schools, he launched an ambitious program of school building. The number of rural primary schools rose by more than four thousand between 1935 and 1940, and the number of students rose by five hundred thousand.[33] A concomitant increase of teachers gave rise to unionization, with the powerful Sindicato de Trabajadores de la Enseñanza de la República Mexicana [STERM] integrating into the umbrella organization, the Confederación de Trabajadores de México [CTM].

Teachers became the target of the Right, which condemned the education policy as "the product of a conspiracy by fanatical communists and professional politicians." Between 1931 and 1940 at least 223 rural teachers were the victims of violence. Often the attackers had religious motives. This was especially true in the west central highlands where, for example, a band of alleged Cristeros killed María Salud Morales near Tacámbaro, Michoacán in 1937. The brutality of the assaults on teachers is shocking: some faced mutilation or died at the hands of lynch mobs.[34]

Professor David Raby has compiled impressive material on the persecution of teachers, linking the violence to economic motives. "There is ample evidence," he explains, "that popular hostility against the teachers was . . . often the result of deliberate manipulations on the part of privileged groups." Among those groups were the landowners opposing agrarian reform, though Raby concedes that "it is not possible to demonstrate this conclusively" in specific instances. Thus Raby analyzes findings from the materialist perspective that places economic motive at the root of human nature. Marx argued that the ruling classes used religion as a mechanism of working class control. As Raby reiterates, "more profound motives rested beyond this religious war."[35]

The research is thorough, but Raby's Marxist analysis is subject to critique. While it is certainly true that many teachers supported land reform and peasant unionization, which undoubtedly won them the ire of vested interests and elicited harassment, the conclusion that religious conviction was any less sincere and widespread does not necessarily follow. The concrete means by which the ruling class "manipulated" the poor through religion needs to be shown. What methods and tools of manipulation could the elite use? Many priests spread rumors against the schools and teachers, but evidence that they did so at the behest of landowners is exceedingly thin.[36] While one of the peasants Raby interviewed noted that Cristeros were "in reality serving the rich by impeding land reform," that does not mean that religion was not the primary motive of these counter-terrorists who resisted change even if it might better their own economic condition. Where does Raby get his analytical framework? It arises, perhaps inadvertently, from his primary sources. Beyond oral histories, the author relied heavily on two periodicals, but predominantly on *El Machete*.[37] *El Machete*, the official organ of the Communist party, was written by Marxists with a materialist world view that would want to see class warfare in the countryside. A great source for research material, it does not provide the basis of a sound analytical model.

In truth, the intense cultural penetration of deep religious values drove the vast majority of peasants to reject Cárdenas's education agenda and, for the most part, cardenismo itself. The hatred of socialist education was widespread and spontaneous. Raby himself chronicles cases where whole villages turned out to persecute a teacher, while lay Catholic organizations comprising ACM, which spent much of their energy fighting socialist education, mushroomed in size. ACM may have had upwards of three hundred thousand members by the mid-1930s, with its women's auxiliary boasting sixty thousand in 1936 alone.[38]

The success of the women's auxiliary reflects the importance of women in the education and anticlerical debates. Rural women found space for their own empowerment in the midst of church-state conflict, often assuming responsibilities in organizing villages in response to anticlerical excesses, such as occurred in the small village of Ario Santa Mónica, Michoacán, where local Cardenistas destroyed popular religious icons of the Virgin Mary. The role of women in the Catholic Right was so pronounced that some government officials viewed them as a kind of "clerical fifth column," and the regime was clearly uneasy about their national enfranchisement.

Indicative of the government's vulnerability to pressures from the Right is its incorporation of Mother's Day as a "patriotic festival" by the mid-1930s. As noted education historian Mary Kay Vaughan explains, "by honoring mothers, the state recognized the family's importance to national development and sought to counteract women's loyalties to the church."[39] Ideologically, Mother's Day was clearly not one of the regime's preferred reasons for festivals, but as it sponsored the celebrations through schools, it hoped to impute new social values about family and motherhood to the peasantry as well as co-opt, to at least some degree, the profound loyalty Mexicans feel toward mothers and popular values surrounding maternity. In this task, as Vaughan has demonstrated, the state project largely failed. Rather than follow strict guidelines, theatrical plays featured religious imagery and popular ideas concerning motherhood, including the "pathos of suffering" associated with both motherhood and the Virgin Mary. The government's attempts to promote national celebrations in place of religious fiestas in mid-decade enjoyed only nominal success, as local villages altered the nature of the celebrations as they saw fit. Indeed, in both festivals and schooling, "the central state could not impose its educational project" effectively, and in fact reflected the fundamental weakness of cardenismo, not its strength.[40]

In contrast, the religious Right experienced "massive growth" during Cárdenas's tenure, "which even exceeded in quantity that of the Cristero era of the proceeding decade." Many Catholics took to the streets in large protests, such as one in Veracruz in February 1937, and triggered street riots over socialists education, as in Ciudad González, Guanajuato in March 1935. In Aguascalientes police arrested ninety-nine men and fifty-seven women from a crowd of several hundred opposing education policy, though city officials interviewed each detainee and released the vast majority of them. In May 1935 a similar rally of five thousand persons in Hermosillo demanded the closing of schools and the opening of churches. When a smaller crowd, "in which women were conspicuous," marched on the governor's mansion in the evening, army troops forced them to disperse.[41] Beyond the relatively peaceful protests, some Catholics rearmed.

The Cristeros had always been a small fraction of the Right, though they receive disproportionate attention because of the extreme methods they used and the military threat they posed. They revived in 1935 because of socialist education. The odds of success in this "second" guerrilla war were even lower than those from 1926 to 1929. The church hierarchy withheld even tacit support, condemned the Cristeros, and forced lay organizations to ignore them completely. The army, equipped with new technologies such as radio and more airplanes, had greater effectiveness in the field. The Cristeros were weaker, with a maximum seventy-five hundred men under arms, many of them former fighters driven to despair by the weak economy and by the death squad executions of their comrades-in-arms during the Maximato.

The second *Cristiada* peaked in late 1935, with the largest rebel contingents and heaviest fighting in Durango, Jalisco, and Michoacán. Lauro Rocha led several hundred rebels in the highlands of Jalisco, supplied and funded by supporters in Guadalajara and armed with Thompson machine guns. The Cárdenas government sent in thousands of troops and aircraft to pacify the area, and heavy fighting ensued from late October through December. On October 23 at the village of Mesa Redonda, for example, a fifteen-hour battle left more than one hundred government casualties and twenty-six Cristeros dead. Though no match for the army, some of these detachments survived to the end of cardenismo. Rebels in Durango under Federico Vázquez remained in the field until 1941. Though the Bajío was the center of the insurrection, pockets of resistance flared up throughout the country. Northern Sonora heated up until the removal of Callista governor Ramos in December, while socialist education so enraged the Mayo Indians in southern Sonora and Sinaloa that the army marched four infantry battalions against them. The retreating Mayo were cornered and repeatedly bombed by planes, but their bitterness at the Revolutionary government continued into the late 1930s, when they joined the fascistic movement known as Sinarquismo in droves.[42]

The Cristeros engaged in terrorism and targeted agrarians and teachers. Rebels under Ramón Aguilar, the main guerrilla chieftain in Michoacán (and a former agrarian himself), ambushed and killed three *agraristas* near Cotija on December 5, prompting a survivor to ask Cárdenas for financial help for their widows. In August 1937 José Martínez told the president how Cristeros murdered his friend, an *ejidatario* named José García, in San Luis de la Paz, Guanajuato on August 7. Three days later the rebels returned and killed more civilians, while in Michoacán a flurry of attacks left several teachers dead.[43] While local acts of violence had deeply personal consequences, on a national scale they were politicized by the 1934 opposition. Leaders of electoral resistance to the regime tried to encourage the Cristeros. The CRPI's Aurelio Manrique shaved off his waist-length beard and smuggled himself back into Mexico in February 1935 to assess the situation. On his return, he told the San Antonio press that "religious persecution has increased discontent" and that rebellion against Cárdenas had spread throughout much of the country. Other

Texas exiles plotted from El Paso. Villarreal and Valenzuela, in touch with Vasconcelos, called for a revolution on November 20, 1934, to no avail, but took heart with the Cristeros. Leaflets appeared in spring 1935 calling for unity behind Vasconcelos. Entitled "Why Vasconcelos Is the Guide," these handbills concluded that Mexico's problem "is a moral rather than an economic one." Vasconcelos "represents the only way of returning to legality," explained the notices, "since legality disappeared in 1913" (with Madero) and gave way "to the general plunder of the day."[44]

Because of its military and organizational disadvantages, the second Cristero rebellion largely evaporated in 1936 and came to naught. The vast majority of the Right had concluded that armed resistance was useless after the earlier rebellion, and few peasants were willing, in the face of certain government persecution, to take up arms. The widespread rejection of the Revolutionary regime remained, however. There is little basis for arguing that land reform undermined the second Cristero uprising.[45] The Right, spearheaded by Catholics, had attempted popular mobilization through insurrection in the 1920s, the ballot box in 1929, and grassroots Catholic lay organizations since the early 1930s. Already formidable, after 1935 it would enjoy, with the demise of Maximum Chief Calles, a new alliance with the capitalist business elite deeply offended by Cardenista labor policies.

NOTES

1. Bailey, *Viva Cristo Rey*, pp. 249–51, 272, 280–81.

2. Jean Meyer, *La Cristiada: La guerra de los cristeros*, vol. 1 (Mexico City: Siglo Veintiuno Editores, 1973), pp. 330–35; Bailey, *Viva Cristo Rey*, p. 289.

3. Regarding the LNDLR, ACJM, and Cristeros, see Chapter 1. Bailey, *Viva Cristo Rey*, pp. 290–91; Hugh Campbell, "The Radical Right in Mexico, 1929–1949," (Ph.D. dissertation, University of California at Los Angeles, 1967), pp. 55–58.

4. Meyer, *La Cristiada*, vol. 1, pp. 345–46, 356; "Jalisco convertido en un matadero," *La Palabra* 2:70 (October 18, 1931): 1; Bailey, *Viva Cristo Rey*, p. 294.

5. Martaelena Negrete, *Relaciones entre la iglesia y el estado en México, 1930–1940* (Mexico City: El Colegio de México y Universidad Iberoamericana, 1988), pp. 67, 70; Charles Hackett, "Mexico's New War on the Church," *Current History* 35 (February 1932): 716.

6. Hackett, "New War," p. 17; "Información completa de la persecución en Querétaro," *La Palabra* 2:74 (November 29, 1931): 1; telegram, Cárdenas to Calles, May 14, 1932, APEC, Fondo Lázaro Cárdenas, 206/271.5.0. A complete listing of laws and modifications to laws restricting and registering priests may be found in Elena Sodi de Pallares, *Los Cristeros y José de León Toral* (Mexico City: Editorial Cultura, 1936), pp. 151–55.

7. Adrian Bantjes, "Politics, Class and Culture in Post-Revolutionary Mexico: Cardenismo and Sonora, 1929–1940" (Ph.D. dissertation, University of Texas, 1991), pp. 35–36; Campbell, "Radical Right," p. 83; Meyer, *Política del Maximato*, p. 181.

8. Hackett, "New War," p. 16; Sodi de Pallares, *Cristeros y Toral*, pp. 60–68, features a complete list of the closed churches.

9. Negrete, *Relaciones en México*, pp. 85–86. The faithful flooded the Secretaría de Gobernación with *juicios*, which the bureaucrats simply ignored.

10. "Text of Encyclical on Mexico's Church Laws," *New York Times*, October 1, 1932; Charles Hackett, "Mexico Reopens War on Church," *Current History* 37:2 (November 1932): 206.

11. J. Reuben Clark, ambassador, to SS, October 20, 1932, USDS, 812.00/29799; Richard Cummings, military attaché, to War Department, "Quarterly Stability of Government Report," January 17, 1933, USDS 812.00/29823.

12. A small number of Cristero incidents dot the pages of military attaché reports in 1930–1931, and even the increase in 1932 activity merits this caveat: the line between political action and banditry can be thin. See the Introduction to Paul Vanderwood, *Disorder and Progress: Bandits, Police, and Mexican Development* (Lincoln: University of Nebraska Press, 1981). Some Cristeros may have found the return to society especially difficult because of unemployment as the depression set in, yet still fancied themselves insurgents instead of bandits.

13. Acción Católica Mexicana, *Estatutos Generales de la Acción Católica Mexicana* (Mexico City: Gráficos Michoacán, 1930), p. 9. This small booklet is available in the Biblioteca Nacional. The ACJM technically dissolved in 1929, then reactivated as part of ACM in November 1930; see Bailey, *Viva Cristo Rey*, pp. 290–91; Negrete, *Relaciones en México*, p. 254.

14. ACM, *Estatutos Generales*, p. 7.

15. Negrete, *Relaciones en México*, pp. 243–44; Bailey, *Viva Cristo Rey*, p. 290; "Los Católicos se defienden," *La Palabra* 2:73 (November 29, 1931): 1.

16. "La colecta en favor de los sacerdotes Veracruzanos," *La Palabra* 2:69 (October 18, 1931): 1. Cummings, "Quarterly Stability of Government Report," April 7, 1933, USDS, 812.00/29845.

17. John A. Britton, *Educación y radicalismo en México: Los años de Bassols, 1931–1934* (Mexico City: Secretaría de Educación Pública, 1976), pp. 23, 27–33; "El culto al estado," *La Palabra* 2:73 (November 29, 1931): 5.

18. Britton, *Educación y radicalismo*, pp. 35–38; Frank Hanighen, "The Law in Monterrey," *The Commonweal* 17:15 (February 8, 1933): 399. Students graduating from unaffiliated schools could gain admission to state universities via a special exam.

19. Britton, *Educación en México*, pp. 40–42, 99–102.

20. Meyer, *Política del Maximato*, pp. 172–74. The University of Mexico had received limited autonomy in 1929.

21. "El problema estudiantil dio motivo a acalorada sesión de los diputados," *Excelsior*, November 23, 1933; "El gremio Estudiantil formula declaraciones," *Excelsior*, November 23, 1933. Donald Mabry, *The Mexican University and the State: Student Conflicts, 1910–1971* (College Station: Texas A & M University Press, 1982), pp. 104–6.

22. J. C. Miramontes to Calles, telegram, November 21, 1933, in *Plutaro Elías Calles: Correspondencia personal, 1919–1945* (Mexico City: Fondo de Cultura Económica, 1993), p. 322; "Manifiesto de la Confederación Nacional de Estudiantes," *Excelsior*, November 3, 1933. The CNE was formed in 1928 at the Culiacán Student Congress; see Azuela, *Aventura vasconcelista*, p. 72. Mabry, *Mexican University and State*, pp. 100, 119.

23. Britton, *Educación en México*, pp. 103, 112, 135–39; Peter Lester Reich, *Mexico's Hidden Revolution: The Catholic Church in Law and Politics since 1929* (South Bend: University of Notre Dame Press, 1995), p. 47; "Discurso del General Plutarco Calles,"

[excerpts], July 20, 1934, in Guadalupe Monroy Huitrón, *Política educativa de la revolución,1910–1940* (Mexico City: Secretaría de Educación Pública, 1975), pp. 92–93.

24. "Tumultos estudiantiles habidos en Puebla," *Excelsior*, October 5, 1934; "Se lanzaron a la huelga de los alumnos en Tampico," *Excelsior*, October 6, 1934; "Se forma el frente único para luchar en contra de la 'educación socialista,'" *Excelsior*, October 14, 1934.

25. Luis González, *Los artífices del cardenismo* (Mexico City: El Colegio de México, 1979), pp. 7, 19, 24, 65. Population statistics from John Gledhill, *Casi Nada: A Study of Agrarian Reform in the Homeland of Cardenismo* (Albany: State University of New York at Albany, Institute for Mesoamerican Studies, 1991), p. 8.

26. Bailey, *Viva Cristo Rey*, p. 296.

27. Heather Fowler Salamini, *Agrarian Radicalism in Veracruz, 1920–1938* (Lincoln: University of Nebraska Press, 1971), pp. 131–32; Mark Wasserman, "Strategies for Survival of the Porfirian Elite in Revolutionary Mexico: Chihuahua during the 1920s," *Hispanic American Historical Review* 67:1 (Winter 1987): 89–93. See also by same author *Persistent Oligarchs: Elite and Politics in Chihuahua, Mexico, 1910–1940* (Durham: Duke University Press, 1993). Luis González, *Los días del presidente Cárdenas* (Mexico City: El Colegio de México, 1981), pp. 153–54.

28. Marjorie Becker, "Torching La Purísima, Dancing at the Altar: The Constuction of Revolutionary Hegemony in Michoacán, 1934–1940," in Joseph and Nugent, eds., *Everyday Forms of State Formation*, pp. 251–53, 257; Gledhill, *Casi Nada*, pp. 80, 92.

29. See, for example, Weyl and Weyl, *Reconquest of Mexico*, which contends that the Cristero rebellion was merely "a symptom of profound economic disturbance," p. 7; materialism is the basis of Arnaldo Córdova's critique in *La política de masas del cardenismo* (Mexico City: Ediciones Era, 1974), pp. 93–122.

30. Walter Adamson, *Hegemony and Revolution: A Study of Antonio Gramsci's Political and Cultural Theory* (Berkeley: University of California Press, 1980), pp. 171–75. For added clarity on Gramsci's notions of "cultural hegemony" and "economic corporative," see David Forgacs, ed., *A Gramsci Reader: Selected Writings, 1916–1935* (London: Lawrence and Wishart, 1988), pp. 421–24.

31. Antonio Gramsci in Forgacs, ed., *A Gramsci Reader*, pp. 113–14.

32. Jean Meyer, *La Cristiada*, vol. 3, pp. 77, 81; Gledhill, *Casi Nada*, pp. 34–36.

33. Campbell, "Radical Right," pp. 206–9; Victoria Lerner, *La educación socialista* (Mexico City: El Colegio de México, 1979), p. 127.

34. David L. Raby, *Educación y revolución social en México, 1921–1940*, trans. Roberto Gómez Ciriza (Mexico City: Secretaría de Educación Pública, 1974), pp. 41, 147–51, 159.

35. Raby, *Educación en México*, pp. 158, 165, 172.

36. Raby, *Educación en México*, 163, 179–80. Raby's statements regarding linkage of persecution to vested economic interests are not followed by proof of the links; see pp. 165 ff and 179 ff.

37. *El Machete* changed its name to *La Voz de México*, but is the same source. Raby's citations of cases where he suspects ulterior motives are overwhelmingly from *El Machete*. See cites, pp. 147–98.

38. Raby, *Educación en México*, p. 159; González, *Los artífices del cardenismo*, p. 64; Negrete, *Relaciones en México*, p. 255.

39. Becker, "Torching La Purísima," pp. 248–250, 258; Mary Kay Vaughan, "Rural Women's Literacy and Education during the Mexican Revolution: Subverting a Patriarchal Event?" in Heather Fowler Salamini and Mary Kay Vaughan, eds., *Women of*

the Mexican Countryside, 1850–1990 (Tucson: University of Arizona Press, 1994), p. 120.

40. Mary Kay Vaughan, "The Construction of the Patriotic Festival in Tecamachalco, Puebla, 1900–1946," in William Beezley, Cheryl English Martin, and William French, eds., *Rituals of Rule, Rituals of Resistance: Public Celebrations and Popular Culture in Mexico* (Wilmington, Del.: Scholarly Resources, 1994), pp. 227–28, 235; see also Mary Kay Vaughan, "The Educational Project of the Mexican Revolution: The Response of Local Societies (1934–1940)," in John Britton, ed., *Molding the Hearts and Minds: Education, Communications, and Social Change in Latin America* (Wilmington, Del.: Scholarly Resources, 1994), p. 107.

41. Weyl and Weyl, *Reconquest of Mexico*, p. 168; Campbell, "Radical Right," pp. 198, 210; "Captura en masa de 150 personas de ambos sexos," *Excelsior*, October 14, 1934; A. F. Yepis, Vice Consul in Guaymas, to SS, July 5, 1935, USDS 812.00/30232.

42. Bailey, *Viva Cristo Rey*, p. 296; Jean Meyer, *La Cristiada*, vol. 1, pp. 367–69, 372–75; Daniels to SS, November 13, 1935, USDS 812.00/30293; Henry Norweb, Chargé d'Affaires, to SS, December 11, 1935, USDS 812.00/30309.

43. Jean Meyer, *La Cristiada*, p. 368; Ciro Basaldua Gallegos to Cárdenas, December 5, 1935, Archivo General de la Nación [AGN], Ramo Presidentes, Fondo Lázaro Cárdenas [FLC], 559.3/14.0; José Martínez to Cárdenas, August 20, 1937, AGN, FLC 559.3/2.3; Raby, *Educación en México*, pp. 149–50.

44. "Disguise Provides Revolt Insight," *San Antonio Express*, February 6, 1935; F. B. Mallon, Military Intelligence, Forth Sam Houston, Texas to War Department, July 6, 1935, in USDS 812.00/ 30254; Norweb to SS, May 10, 1935, USDS 812.00/30198. A copy of the handbill is attached; note the unwillingness of the Right to criticize Madero, though it dislikes the Revolutionary legacy.

45. Gledhill, *Casi Nada*, p. 35.

4

REVOLUTIONARY FAMILY TROUBLES: CAPITALISTS, CALLES, AND CÁRDENAS

The Catholic Right, though formidable in its continuing struggle to disrupt the Revolutionary government during the early 1930s, was undercut by the quiet alliance between the business sector and the Calles-dominated regime. Its Revolutionary rhetoric notwithstanding, the Maximato government pursued fundamentally conservative economic practices. As a North American observed in 1932, Mexico's "attitude toward clerical matters has swung toward the left," but "in an economic way, Mexico has been moving to the Right."[1] This paradox of the Maximato complicates the analysis of the Right, for business sectors in cities like Monterrey were quite content with the direction in which General Calles was taking the country. Only with the rise of Lázaro Cárdenas did the capitalist Right resolutely position itself in stark opposition to the regime. It began to do so in the midst of a difficult period of labor turmoil and political tension during the summer and fall of 1935, a crisis period that denotes the end of the Maximato. Before this, to the chagrin of the Catholic and political Right, industrialists were ambivalent toward the government and often even supportive.

In the decade of the 1930s, government policies on business and labor changed in an atmosphere of increasing turmoil wrought by worldwide economic depression. In the mid-1920s Calles had heartily supported the rise of the Confederación Regional Obrera Mexicana, which oversaw an enormous mobilization of labor directed by his political ally Luis Morones. CROM unionized workers, won mild concessions from capital, crushed more radical labor organizations, and provided Calles with a mass base for promoting the authority of the centralized state. At the outset of the Maximato, however, CROM's corrupt leadership fell into disfavor with much of the Revolutionary clique, including Provisional President Portes Gil, who promoted alternative unions. Independent unions multiplied, and schisms in CROM eroded its power. CROM membership decreased by half between 1928 and 1932.

CROM had never made particularly deep inroads in the Catholic regions of the country. Priests discouraged union membership, and the church "had a retarding effect on the development of the labor movement," especially in Guadalajara. The prerevolutionary Catholic congresses had produced Catholic Labor Circles, but these and subsequent church-sponsored unions in the 1920s resembled mutual aid societies more than anything else—sometimes they actually supplied employers with strikebreakers! In the context of the Cristero revolt, Catholic unions dissolved "without causing more than a faint ripple" in Mexican labor relations.[2]

The crisis in world capitalism after 1929 augured additional problems for labor as the government aligned itself with business in order to keep a lid on potential social unrest. Compared to most Latin American republics, Mexico weathered the depression quite well. Two reasons underlay this relative economic stability: first, an agrarian subsistence economy still dominated much of Mexico; and second, industries subject to export and worldwide price fluctuations were generally diversified. Some displaced workers fell back upon family members in the countryside, helping them till the land and survive the lean years. Export agriculture included production of henequen, cotton, coffee, and some tropical fruits—hardly the reliance on a single staple like sugar, which collapsed in the world marketplace and brought down the Cuban government of Gerardo Machado. Indeed, agriculture overwhelmingly fed the domestic market, and long-term statistical fluctuations in production do not even neatly reflect the depression. Much more serious, though, were problems in export-oriented oil, mineral, and industrial sectors, which comprised the backbone of organized labor. From 1930 to 1932, world prices in commodities such as lead and silver dropped dramatically, prompting production cuts and layoffs.[3] A deflationary spiral gripped Mexico until 1933, with real wages falling even more sharply than the cost of living. At the outset of deflation and a 78 percent drop in silver production in 1930, the Calles government took Mexico off the gold standard and began to mint silver coins; by 1932 a shakeup in the cabinet brought Alberto Pani back into the Treasury and he printed paper money in an effort to increase currency circulation. By 1934, due to Pani's efforts and other factors, the worst was over.

During the troublesome period from 1930 to 1933, organized labor faced a surge in unemployment and an unsympathetic government anxious to revive exports, even at its expense. Oil and mineral operations which had employed ninety thousand Mexicans in 1927 worked only half that number in 1932.[4] In September 1929 the government authorized layoffs without any labor recourse, and during the early 1930s salary cuts and dismissals became commonplace. When labor resisted, such as at the American Smelting and Refining Company's Monterrey plant in 1932, company officials used force and even the army joined in to break up labor demonstrations.

Government labor policy changed both on paper and in practice during the depression. Legal mechanisms dissatisfied both capital and labor, while practical measures appeased only the former. Efforts to expand Article 123, which constituted the labor section of the 1917 Constitution, and codify in detail capital-labor relations began in earnest with the so-called Portes Gil measures, a series of laws debated without resolution in September 1929 in the Mexican Chamber of Deputies. Secretaries Luis León and Aarón Sáenz in Ortiz Rubio's subsequent administration extensively modified the proposals, which garnered cabinet, congressional, and official party approval, while many "representatives of private interests . . . maintained a discreet silence."

The resulting Federal Labor Law of 1931 was, in fact, not overtly hostile to labor, though CROM condemned it and workers in Monterrey labeled it "fascist." In some aspects, such as legalizing the closed shop (where all workers in a factory are obligated to hold union membership), the law was actually several years ahead of legislation in industrial nations like the United States. Yet to the extent that the measure replaced state labor laws sanctioned by constitutional Article 123, it tended to be more conservative. Unions had to register with the government, report dues, expenses, and membership, and strikes required Federal approval.[5] Ultimately, the law determined management-worker relations by the nature of its enforcement. Since colonial times, when Spanish administrators liberally interpreted and even ignored legislation issued by their superiors in the distant motherland, Mexico has had a political tradition epitomized by the famous colonial saying "obedezco, pero no cumplo" ("I obey, but I do not comply"). There is frequently a wide gap between laws on the books and laws in practice. During the Maximato, officials selectively enforced provisions to the detriment of labor. Marjorie Clark, an astute contemporary observer, noted that the code was "arbitrarily interpreted and enforced," subject to "politics, personalism, favoritism, and bribery."[6] Not surprisingly, the business elite was in a better position to bribe and influence. Motives for the pro-management interpretation of the law also included fears of radical labor in an era of economic uncertainty. Often the two went hand in hand, as business groups repeatedly sounded the alarm with regard to "communistic" labor.

Fortunately for labor, business interests were neither well organized nor particularly effective lobbyists until the 1940s. As the Revolution wound down, myriad local and regional Chambers of Commerce had emerged throughout Mexico, responding to the apparent commitment of the Carranza government to enforce Article 123. An umbrella organization, La Confederación de Cámaras de Comercio [CCC], rose shortly thereafter, though its influence with the Alvaro Obregón and Calles governments (1920–1928) was limited. By 1930 the CCC inspired a new organization, La Confederación Patronal de la República Mexicana [known as El Grupo Patronal or COPARMEX], designed to lobby government and combat militant labor. In 1931 El Grupo Patronal undertook a study of the new Federal labor code, primarily in order to discover ways to evade it.[7] It recruited small businessmen to its banner by playing on their fears of the labor code. A pamphlet entitled "Why should you associate with El Grupo Patronal," for example, explained:

The crisis and economic panic are not permanent, but the new labor code is . . . and you will find a shackle in the form of the excessive demands of labor that will impede your march toward progress. Is it not more economical to pay a small [membership] fee now . . . than to knowingly permit the development of a pathological mind-set against the health of business, the spreading of the cancer of communism by apostles who say that "property is theft"?[8]

Appeals such as this had some effect, though El Grupo Patronal grew only modestly during the Maximato. Its most committed supporters were industrialists of Monterrey, who had voiced opposition to the labor reforms since 1929 and who began to assume "an eminent position in the relations between the private sector and the federal government."[9]

If business was not particularly well organized during the Maximato, neither was labor. The reasons were different, however. Business barely mobilized because it had little grievance with the government; labor frayed in the face of erosion and persecution. Unions independent of CROM had resented its domination of the movement in the 1920s, and vied for control in key industries as CROM slid into decline. Some of these unions, such as the Confederación de Transportes y Comunicaciones [CTC], struck during the wage cuts and dismissals of the 1930–1933 depression. Strikes during this period were primarily defensive in nature, seeking to preserve modest gains earned in the 1920s. Yet arbitration boards became "weapons of interunion warfare," as sometimes one union would vote against another union's cause.

Labor was also on the defensive rhetorically, often labeled as antirevolutionary or, worse yet, communist. Many politicians associated independent unions with anti-Callista factions. One wrote the Maximum Chief in 1931 that "without doubt the enemies of the Revolution are your enemies, those that have been spreading labor agitation throughout the Republic." A 1931 labor publication from the southeast felt the need to assure its readers, "We are nationalist labor, but not communist labor."[10] Communists bore the brunt of the persecution, which lasted for the duration of the Maximato. In 1929 the small Partido Comunista Mexicana [PCM], abiding by the Communist International's [Comintern] Third Period guidelines, refused to cooperate in any way with progressive elements of the Revolutionary government. The PCM sought to establish non-CROM unions, and even plotted overthrow of the new PNR, though such an enterprise was far beyond the abilities of the minuscule party. Hot rhetoric and minor intrigue instead triggered ruthless suppression: the Portes Gil government broke diplomatic relations with the Soviet Union, rounded up PCM members and their sympathizers, and sanctioned a massacre in the border town of Matamoros.[11] Intensified persecution revived in mid-1932 and continued under the last Maximato puppet president, Abelardo Rodríguez, a conservative who enjoyed the confidence of business. Authorities rounded up communists, holding them incommunicado and subject to torture, then shipped them to the penal colony at Islas Tres Marías off the Pacific coast. Many foreigners were among fifty communists arrested in July 1932 for distributing antigovernment leaflets to army troops. Arrests in Veracruz state and at the National Preparatory School followed, part of a vigorous anti-Left and anti-labor policy that, according to a North American consul, pleased the "reactionary element."[12]

The United States government was kept well informed of happenings in Mexico. It maintained a sizable office of the Federal Bureau of Investigation in Mexico City, and appears to have closely monitored sensitive events. The Mexican government also funneled information to its North American counter-parts. The persecution of the PCM prompted a July 1932 protest from the International Labor Defense [ILD], a New York–based, communist-led organi-zation which, among other activities, spent considerable energy in the mid-1930s winning political asylum in Mexico for leftists fleeing the European fascist states. The Mexican attorney general sent copies of the ILD's appeal to his U.S. equivalent.

Mexican officials persecuted the discredited PCM themselves, but increas-ingly relied on a surrogate force to harass labor as the Maximato drew to a close. The Acción Revolucionaria Mexicana [ARM] formed in March 1934 under a minor Revolutionary general, Nicolás Rodríguez, who had once served under Francisco "Pancho" Villa. Popularly known as the *Dorados*, or Gold Shirts, these fascistic thugs claimed to be the heirs of Villa's *Dorado* cavalry units, from which they took their name. Inspired by Benito Mussolini's Black Shirts and frequently wearing gold shirts and black pants, they operated under the motto of "Mexico for Mexicans," maligned Communists and Jews, and made the intimidation of strikers their primary activity. The government did little to stop them.[13]

Urban business interests, otherwise natural allies of the Right, were largely pleased with the Maximato regime. The agrarian elite, those with heavy invest-ments in agriculture and land in the countryside (though they often resided in the cities), also found hopeful signs under the governance of the Maximum Chief. Yet if businessmen were poorly organized, even more so were the rural elite. Porfirian landowners had been politically marginalized and economically crippled during the Revolution, and even as late as the Maximato many of them remained in self-imposed exile. And while businessmen could gain a modicum of public sympathy by slandering their labor opponents as "communists," popular opinion remained dead set against the landowners—after all, what did the Revolution of Emiliano Zapata mean, if not land?

Like businessmen, some landowners organized themselves at the outset of the Maximato in order to lobby the government. Similar to El Grupo Patronal was the Cámara Nacional de Agricultura [CNA], founded in 1930, which urged Mexico City to fix the time in which all land expropriations would be com-pleted. Calles and his loyal president, Ortiz Rubio, were sympathetic to this call, premised on the need of landholders to have assurance before they invested capital to increase production. Public sentiment, however, required that such termination dates be set quietly, at the state government level. Large landholders did not have much clout in Mexico City, but at the local level they found resources with which to defend their interests. Many formed and funded the paramilitary White Guards, which "physically eliminated the most dangerous agrarian leaders." Often, too, landholders were able to make use of municipal officers, as in the case of those in the vicinity of Guadalajara, who persuaded city officials to carry out reprisals against agrarians. Only a few betrayed their economic interests by helping the Revolutionary government and thereby winning its favor. Michoacán governor Lázaro Cárdenas, for example, appealed to Calles on behalf of María Pizarro, a widow who had assisted Federals in the neighborhood of her hacienda in suppressing Cristero rebels.[14]

During the Maximato, agrarian reform continued at an uneven pace, despite Calles's 1929 declaration that it was a "failure." Rarely were entire estates broken up, usually lands were allocated in small plots, and the entire process was subject to considerable local and regional variation. The most aggressive agrarian reform came in the state of Veracruz, where the Obregón governor Adalberto Tejeda rode the crest of a political current generated by leftist agitation in the 1920s. Peasants had been organized by Ursulo Galván, a hardworking communist who founded the Liga Nacional Campesina in 1926. Galván was fortunate to have steered his organization clear of dangerous alliances in 1929, shunning the PCM's call to revolt (which led to his expulsion from the party), and aiding in the suppression of Escobar and Aguirre. Tejeda opted to align himself with Galván's mobilized peasant leagues, which in turn made him "one of the more powerful political figures on the national scene" at the outset of the 1930s. He implemented land distributions from 1929 to 1932, despite opposition from ranchers, farmers, and Spanish commercial interests. Tensions led to bloodletting by both sides, as armed agrarians clashed with White Guards. By late 1932 the national government could take no more, sending in the army to disarm peasants and effectively dismantle the Tejeda political machine. The national press, and rightist papers annoyed by Tejeda's longstanding anticlericalism, welcomed the move.[15]

FROM MAXIMATO TO CARDENISMO: LABOR CRISIS

The capitalist Right, acquiescent if not actually in bed with the Revolutionary regime during the Maximato, was jarred from its slumber in 1935, when the newly elected president, Lázaro Cárdenas, sought to break free of the Maximum Chief's control. The rupture became public in June 1935 during a wave of labor unrest throughout the country. Unions, which had been weakened during the Maximato and had watched real wages decline since the outset of the depression, were ready to engage in strikes once given permission by the government. Frustration made them a ready ally for Cárdenas, who gambled his political life on worker support, letting loose the wave of strikes and alienating capital. Unfortunately for Calles, industrialists had failed to become a powerful political force during the Maximato, making him vulnerable in this, the political fight of his career. He had alienated the other sizable segment of the Right, the Catholic church, long ago, leaving him with little grassroots support as he lost control of a Revolutionary establishment weary of his domination and sympathetic to the independent aspirations of Cárdenas.

Born to a small-time merchant in Jiquilpán, Michoacán in 1895, Cárdenas began his climb to power, like most in the so-called Revolutionary Family, through the ranks of the Constitutionalist army. His military career, noteworthy though not spectacular, began with an appointment as a second captain of cavalry in 1913, and ended with the honor of the highest rank bestowed by the army, that of *divisionario*, in 1928. Subsequently he held several political posts, serving briefly in the cabinet of Ortiz Rubio, but working more importantly as governor of his native state. Early 1933 found him resuming cabinet duties as secretary of war, a post that afforded him the opportunity of solidifying army support. Cárdenas was an orthodox Callista all along the way: he fought against the Escobar revolt, assisted in ousting the briefly rebellious Ortiz Rubio from the presidency, abided by the dictums of the Maximum Chief, and duly curtailed church activities as governor of Michoacán.

Although decades later several Mexican scholars, disillusioned with their government, would charge that Cárdenas mobilized labor in order to create a powerful and lasting corporatist state, it is evident that he had a sincere desire to improve workers' lives. His administration also understood that the support of labor was "necessary for its own survival due to right-wing threats."[16] Hence the number of government-sanctioned strikes leapt from a paultry 13 in 1933 to 642 in 1935, unleashing new political tensions and economic disruptions throughout the country. Many of the strikes were directed at foreign-owned corporations, such as an early one targeting the Canadian-owned Mexican Tramways Company which managed Mexico City's streetcars. After workers received a successful settlement via government arbitration, other strikes followed. Oil workers living in awful poverty struck the Huasteca Petroleum Company owned by Standard Oil of New Jersey; employees of the European-financed San Rafael Paper Company struck and gained a potpourri of meaningful concessions. In nearly every case where the Cárdenas government intervened, labor made noteworthy gains.[17] The strikes were especially poignant to Plutarco Calles because at least one of them struck at his own pocketbook. Workers at the Mexican Telephone and Telegraph Company, a subsidiary of its North American counterpart, walked out in May 1935 in search of union recognition. The Maximum Chief, a well-vested stockholder, waited impatiently for Cárdenas to intervene on behalf of the company, but to no avail.

The telephone company strike prompted Calles to break with the president publicly.[18] Despite the relative political weakness of the business community, he appealed to it with his famous "patriotic declarations" in June. Quoted at length in Mexico City newspapers, Calles expressed strong displeasure at the restless atmosphere in Mexico, noting that "for six months the nation has been disrupted by constant strikes, many of them clearly unjustified." He argued that the unions, often "ungrateful," were damaging the government and troubling the country at a time when Mexicans needed political calm and economic stability. In truth, it was Calles who was misreading the political climate in Mexico. While his declarations generated a brief flurry of support from some Mexicans, including the only substantial business group, the Chambers of Commerce, they alienated much of the Revolutionary establishment. In the wake of the declarations and a public response by Cárdenas, official party operatives and members of congress fell into line behind the president.[19]

Within a week of his declarations, Calles left Mexico City for an extended retreat to Sinaloa and Los Angeles. Cárdenas pursued the advantage with vigor in the wake of his departure, purging the party and his cabinet of remaining Callistas, while he brushed aside the bitter condemnations of those who stood up for Calles. Some hate mail arrived at the National Palace: a group of "old revolutionaries" condemned the president as "the foremost traitor of Mexico," advising him that "in twenty-five years of betrayals . . . yours has been one of the worst, because you owed your whole political career to General Calles."[20] Quickly organizing labor and agrarian interests voiced warm support for the president, working to uproot vestiges of Callista power, and they celebrated the novelty of finally having an ally at the very top of Mexico's political structure.

In the critical period from June to December 1935, Cardenistas seized the initiative in the absence of Calles. Long before the public schism, Calles had attempted to aggravate the powerful Catholic Right in order to disrupt the consolidation of power by his newfound rival in the presidential palace. Mexican historian Lorenzo Meyer posits that "the objective of the Maximum Chief was to destabilize the new administration in order to prevent it from gaining the strength and confidence necessary to challenge his primacy." The irony, of course, is that the fiercely anticlerical Calles, viewed as the devil himself by millions of devout Catholics, should have tried to pester the Right into action for his own advantage. That he attempted to do so, however, is powerful testimony to the importance in 1930s Mexico of the Right.

The Calles strategy appears to have begun as early as 1934, during the election campaign, when he and his henchmen spouted volatile anticlerical rhetoric at a time when candidate Cárdenas refrained from such belligerence. The Callista who persisted most forcefully in the fire-fueling discourse was former Tabasco governor Tomás Garrido Canabal, a man so possessed with the anticlerical spirit that he named his eldest son Satan. As secretary of agriculture in Cárdenas's first cabinet, Garrido was perfectly positioned to stir troublesome waters in the capital itself. He brought his irreligious Bloque de Jóvenes Revolucionarios, or Red Shirts, to Mexico City, where they held "Red Saturday" assemblies in the Palace of Fine Arts, ridiculing priests and Christianity. In December 1934 Red Shirts visited the plush suburb of Coyoacán, assaulting worshipers at a church, killing five of them and triggering a small street riot. These incidents embarrassed the Cárdenas government and generated it considerable ill will.[21]

When the Calles-Cárdenas power struggle broke into the open in June 1935, the president ousted his troubling agriculture minister, replacing him with San Luis Potosí strongman Saturnino Cedillo, a known conservative on church-state issues. Catholic opponents of Garrido, understanding his vulnerability, financed an expedition of twenty-one young men (mostly students) under the leadership of thirty-five-year-old Tabascan Rodolfo Brito Foucher. The contingent flew into Villahermosa, the state capital, with the ostensible purpose of helping the political opposition in local elections, but also with the expectation that they would spark a showdown with the Red Shirts. The predicted clash took place on July 15, leaving three Catholics dead from gunfire.

The strategy of bringing down Garrido by confrontation and subsequent popular outrage, similar to the apparent Callista plans on a national level, worked perfectly. An outpouring of protest erupted from the Catholic Right throughout Mexico, sometimes cast in such a way as to take advantage of Garrido's position on the losing side of the political struggle in the Revolutionary Family. Manuel Gómez Morín, rector of the National University, led thousands of students on a march through Mexico City chanting "viva Cárdenas" and "Death to Calles and Garrido." Cárdenas, provided an opportunity by the Right to rid himself of a prominent Callista, forced Garrido out of power and into exile, subsequently rescinding most of Tabasco's severe anticlerical laws in August.

A second hotbed of anticlerical activity which generated difficulties for Cárdenas early in his tenure was Sonora, home of the Calles family and domain of a political machine run by Plutarco's son Rodolfo. In 1934 the state government stepped up its campaign against the church, imitating many of the techniques used by Garrido. Limits on clerics turned into complete expulsion in May 1934, while near-universal church closings followed. The authorities held dances inside some sanctuaries, desecrated others, and sponsored "cultural Sunday" services in Hermosillo that included parodies of Christian rituals and a play entitled "Death to Religion." The statue of San Francisco Xavier in the shrine at Magdalena, venerated by Papago Indians, was taken to the state capital and burned in the furnace of a beer brewery. Yet like the course of church-state tensions in Tabasco, religious persecution diminished with the removal of Callista governor Ramón Ramos in December 1935.[22] Late 1935 purges of local and regional Callistas brought relative peace in religious matters, allowing Cárdenas to temper the flames of passion that had been fanned by its political rivals for nearly two years.

If the Catholic Right slowly settled down into a prolonged period of sulking as Cárdenas gained the upper hand on Calles, other rightist sectors of Mexican society festered with heightened discontent. In many middle-class households, inconvenienced by the spate of labor strikes such as those by Mexico City transportation workers, sentiment was decidedly against the new government. The urban middle classes, never in Cárdenas's corner, were to drift farther and farther to the right during mid-decade. If not the president, the symbol of their wrath was Vicente Lombardo Toledano, who became a household name as he revived belligerent unionism through the Confederación de Trabajadores de Mexico [CTM]. Middle-class anger was also fueled in part by inflation: between 1934 and 1938 the prices of consumer goods rose by nearly 50 percent, and while blue collar workers stayed atop the increases through strikes and higher wages, middle sectors lost ground. The creation of an otherwise insignificant Confederación de la Clase Media [CCM], formed under Gustavo Sáenz de Sicilia in June 1936, testifies to the frustrations of the middle class. The CCM blamed labor unrest for many of Mexico's problems in a Manifesto, and called for "an end to using unions for political purposes" and "the protection of capital from unjustified attack."[23]

Of course, even more annoyed by the labor unrest was capital itself. Business leaders clamored for a return to the favorable policies of the Maximato, which they had expected to continue. Both foreign and domestic businessmen watched with anxiety as the Cárdenas-Calles fight broke open in mid-1935, with many North Americans expecting "the downfall of Calles and the inevitable swing of the government toward a still more radical policy." One executive of Goodrich Rubber Company, on the heels of Calles's "patriotic declarations," disagreed, expressing confidence that Calles would prevail and events would take "a decided turn for the better."[24] But as Calles left the country their hopes soured. General Motors, which had contemplated building a new assembly plant in Mexico City, backed out of the investment.

Mexican business interests, which had begun to organize during the Maximato, first appealed to, then actively opposed Cárdenas. In March 1936 the Chambers of Commerce sent him a letter expressing concern over his labor policies. "The alarming number of strikes that continue without interruption," the letter explained, "would bring management to bankruptcy if it were to yield to the unjust and exaggerated demands of labor." Businessmen expressed their conviction that, while communism did not exist in Mexico yet, the persistence of strikes threatened "to produce a social and economic state similar to that of communism." They ended with an invitation to dialogue, stating a desire "to collaborate with the government and improve the condition of the working classes."[25] Cárdenas, in a radio address, rebuked the private sector as he complained that they were not, in fact, cooperative enough. Monterrey businessmen, led by the Garza Sada clan, had founded the Chambers as well as El Grupo Patronal, and especially resented Cárdenas's policies as they grappled with a series of major strikes in their own city. When the president visited in February 1936, they shut down their factories in protest. El Grupo Patronal became the focal point of anti-Cardenista activity among employers throughout the country by 1936, counting five thousand members who affiliated in twenty-six branches.[26]

Mexican industrialists sought to turn public opinion against Cárdenas by employing rightist propaganda in the newspapers and on radio. The rhetorical ploys of both business and the government appealed to traditional values of work, home, and family. The conservative Regiomontano press attempted to discredit the CTM by convincing wives of "the dangers of the communist menace to their husbands." Elite women in the city, such as the wife of Luis Garza Sada, spoke out against the threat worker agitation posed to both church and family; concerned women visited working class women in their homes and distributed anticommunist literature. The Revolutionary regime countered with its own family value rhetoric. Cárdenas, as chief spokesman, explained in an interview with *Excelsior* that "the government is endeavoring to strengthen family ties by making the home an institution protected against poverty, unemployment, and the unsanitary living conditions that exist in the millions of homes of the poor."[27]

The Monterrey elite also formed Acción Cívica Nacional [ACN] in March 1936, an association of anti-Cárdenas activists that worked closely with ARM. ACN had among its objectives

1. to extol the concept of Motherland, foster allegiance to the flag, promote the love of our National Hymn, the veneration of our Heroes, and respect for the legally established authorities and the National Army as prime sustainer of the institutions of the Republic;

2. to dignify the concept of the home and preserve the family as the fundamental base of the Mexican social structure;

3. to combat the dark communist doctrines that we consider a threat to the home, country, and to liberty.[28]

These goals encompass nationalism and reflect the battle for the family. Interestingly, in both its objectives and its motto, "home, Motherland, liberty," ACN neglected the role of the church. In doing so it seemed to acknowledge the Revolutionary ideology that relegated the church to a modest place in Mexican society, opting instead to engage the familial discourse. Its reference to the army as "sustainer" of national institutions was, in light of the breadth of history, an imaginative description.

ACN had a small women's auxiliary known as Acción Cívica Femenina [ACF], headed by Esperanza F. G. de Santibañez and founded at the same time. ACF called on Mexican women to intervene in society and help restore social order. In its founding manifesto the organization vowed to develop each member's intelligence "in order to prepare her appropriately for civic duties, and in order that she may preserve her place in the home, thereby perfecting her femininity." In an April 1936 letter to Cárdenas, Santibañez expressed the desire of the ACF to work with the PNR on issues of agreement, such as women's suffrage and opportunities in civil service.[29] ACF then, was two-sided: though its ideological underpinnings were conservative, it could also serve as an avenue for women to social and political empowerment.

ACN and the business lobby failed to convince Cárdenas to change his course regarding labor (weighty evidence of his sincerity as a reformer), prompting the Right to back up its efforts in the media with intimidation on the streets. The doubling up of efforts to dislodge the government and change its policies coincided with the presence of Plutarco Calles, who had returned to Mexico in December 1935 and would remain until April. Business interests enlisted the help of the Gold Shirts, the organization of fascist thugs that reached its apogee in early 1936, attacking CTM organizers in Monterrey with the apparent financial support of leading industrialists.[30]

At this juncture in world history the Gold Shirts found much that inspired them in European fascism: anti-Semitism, anticommunism, and an obsessive need to protect national symbols from insult. Their hatred of Jews prompted them to advocate the seizure of all Jewish-owned businesses in Mexico (which, in truth, were not many), and some Gold Shirts even suggested a Mexican-Nordic racial link. Their founder, Nicolás Rodríguez, quoted a letter from a German sympathizer which contended that "serious studies by ethnologists . . . prove the racial equality of Mexicans and Nordics, and this can be shown today even by blood tests." Fiercely nationalistic, ARM stated in a March 1936 manifesto to the nation that it continued the work of Miguel Hidalgo, José María Morelos, and the "patriarchs" of the Reform and the Revolution. "We are not a party of assembled speakers," it proclaimed, "we are a party of action and fight."[31] There was recent proof that these words were true: Gold Shirts had ransacked the Mexico City headquarters of the Communist party on February 5.

While the same manifesto equated fascism with communism, ARM never called its opponents anything but "communists." After four Gold Shirts engaged in fisticuffs with some Mexico City university students in April 1935, Rodríguez retorted that they had been "provoked by communist elements." Leaflets distributed by members identified unionized workers as dupes of Soviet agents, contended that strikes were leading the nation to ruin, and called on Mexicans to resist imminent "communist enslavement."[32] When Hernán Laborde, leader of Mexico's small Communist party, promised "to fly the Red banner from Chapultepec Castle and stir the populace to acknowledge Soviet Russia as their fatherland," the Gold Shirts retaliated with a public assembly in April 1935 that featured a huge gold banner made of silk.[33]

The Gold Shirts had operated free of government interference when Calles was in control, but by spring 1936 Cárdenas, in the final stages of consolidating his power, began to repress them. Monterrey police cracked down, driving many Gold Shirts into the Laguna region west of Saltillo. Here local authorities monitored their activities, expressing concern about their weapons and the possibility that they would become hired guns for enraged landowners subject to expropriation under the agrarian reform. Agrarians protested the establishment of a new Gold Shirt headquarters in Torreón, while government officials suppressed a Gold Shirt publication printed with the help of Saltillo's newspaper publisher, Ortiz Garza.[34]

The president waited for an opportunity to crack down further on the fascistic movement, and such an occasion came in July, when labor and the militant Right clashed violently in Monterrey. A ten-minute gun battle involving Gold Shirts erupted outside ACN offices, leaving two workers dead and six injured. The CTM staged street demonstrations in protest and asked Cárdenas to dissolve both ACN and ARM. Cárdenas happily complied, moving against ARM in mid-August despite the pleas of Señora Leonor Guitérrez, leader of the Gold Shirt women's auxiliary.[35]

Police arrested Nicolás Rodríguez and put him on a plane to Ciudad Juárez, while military authorities expressed hope to the U.S. embassy that he would be granted asylum. Ambassador Josephus Daniels was receptive to their appeal, writing his superiors in Washington that exiling political opponents from Mexico was "a distinct improvement . . . over *ley fuga*," or their indiscrete assassination. On August 11 Rodríguez crossed the International Bridge into El Paso without incident. Holdover Gold Shirts in the Laguna issued a circular condemning the expulsion of their leader, charging that Cárdenas had "trampled upon the rights of citizenship constitutionally guaranteed to all men in Mexico." They sent a letter, addressed to the president, congratulating him for expelling their leader "in Callista dictatorial fashion."[36]

The departure of Rodríguez did not spell the organization's demise. Gold Shirts continued to pester Jews, communists, and labor throughout the duration of cardenismo. The Vanguardia Mexicana Nacional [VMN] served as a cover organization for the banned Gold Shirts, and some members filtered into the Unión Nacional de Veteranos de la Revolución [UNVR], a rightist group founded in 1935 but most active from 1937 to 1940. Rodríguez himself refused to accept exile quietly, becoming the target of both U.S. and Mexican surveillance as he contemplated counterrevolution from Texas. These modest efforts notwithstanding, "after the crackdown in August 1936 the ARM per se was no longer a significant political element in Mexico."[37]

ARM's demise came on the heels of the final exodus of Calles. The Maximum Chief, who had so brilliantly foiled countless political adversaries for more than a decade, had badly erred when he left his native land in summer 1935. Despite the flurry of rumors that greeted his return by airplane to Mexico City in December, he had ruined any chance of winning the battle against the now well-entrenched Cárdenas. On the evening of April 9, 1936, Cárdenas made his final move, placing Calles under arrest at his estate just east of Mexico City and whisking him to the airport and out of the country on the following day. At the airport terminal, as he awaited his flight into exile, Plutarco Calles, "Maximum Chief of the Mexican Revolution," continued reading Adolph Hitler's *Mein Kampf,* a book that had engrossed him for several days.

On arrival in the United States, Calles played his final card, employing rightist rhetoric in hopes of striking a chord with both Mexicans and North

Americans. "Communism is rapidly spreading in the country," he told an anxious Texas press corps at Brownsville. "If there is anything that can save Mexico now, it is for labor and the middle classes to organize and fight communism."[38] His warnings attracted considerable interest in the United States, triggering a debate over Mexican conditions in the media. Owen White, for example, authored an October 1936 *Colliers* article entitled "Next Door to Communism," which cited Calles and posited that Cardenista radicalism meant "danger ahead." Chronicling the wave of labor strikes, the author surmised that "already the disastrous effect that this new ideology is having upon the Mexican people is every apparent." Average Mexicans were happy until Cárdenas came along, but now these simple "Indians" are "so bewildered that under the whiplash of the agitators' oratory they become dangerous." The Mexican government is arming the "communistic laborers and agrarians" and insurgency could come "at any time," White warned, and "communism will be knocking on our back door."[39]

Such careless media bombast translated into individual alarm. A Texan warned the U.S. government's Office of Arms and Munitions Control that unrest in Mexico was a leftist plot. Once the United States is entangled in warfare with Mexicans, he cautioned, John Lewis and three million Congress of Industrial Organizations members "are to start a civil war and overthrow the American government." Not surprisingly, many conservative elements in the United States counted on the Mexican Right to resist the "communist" regime and avert disaster. When a group of Gold Shirts toured the United States in the fall of 1937 to raise money for their subversive activities, they received enthusiastic support.[40]

Not all North Americans reacted with such irrationality. Ambassador Josephus Daniels correctly attributed much of the hysteria to the work of Plutarco Calles and his cohorts in exile, noting that the "ex-Iron Man was following an American custom" by labeling his opponents "communists." Many lesser newspapers, especially those closer to Mexico with better access to reliable information, dismissed talk of chaos and communism. In Texas, *The Laredo Times* scoffed at thoughts of a new Mexican revolution, its editor arguing that Cárdenas, rather than advocating Marxism, was simply seeking to better the living conditions of poor Mexicans. Other Americans resented Calles's arrival in the first place. The Board of Aldermen in Chelsea, Massachusetts, a predominantly Roman Catholic community, condemned by resolution the Federal government's admission of the Sonoran, contending that "he personifies and has stood for all that is reactionary against the Catholic religion."[41]

The rantings of Callistas from across the border did little to trouble the Cárdenas government, which had gained firm control of Mexico's centralized political bureaucracy. Although historians tend to use six-year presidential terms, or *sexenios*, as natural time frames for periodization, cardenismo in truth only grasped the reins of power in late 1935. Even then, it faced a determined Right with great appeal to a healthy majority of Mexicans.

NOTES

1. Hanighen, "Law in Monterrey," p. 400.
2. Marjorie R. Clark, *Organized Labor in Mexico* (Chapel Hill: University of North Carolina Press, 1934), pp. 65, 87–94.
3. Lorenzo Meyer, *El conflicto social y los gobiernos del Maximato, 1928–1934* (Mexico City: El Colegio de México, 1978), pp. 15, 21, 29–37.
4. Lorenzo Meyer, *El conflicto social,* pp. 44, 71–73, 87–88.
5. Lorenzo Meyer, *El conflicto social,* pp. 112, 138–39, 149–52; Clark, *Organized Labor,* pp. 214–17.
6. Clark, *Organized Labor,* p. 259. In an extension of the statism of the 1920s, strikes triumphed or failed according to the attitude of the state; see Clark, p. 225. The distinctive co-optive nature of Latin American labor has been explored in the writings of Hobart Spalding.
7. Clark, *Organized Labor,* pp. 230–31, 241–42; Lorenzo Meyer, *El conflicto social,* p. 154.
8. Confederación Patronal de la República Mexicana, "Porque debe usted asociarse a la Confederación Patronal," pamphlet, Mexico City, 1934, APEC, Fondo Confederación Patronal, 48/10.0.0
9. Campbell, "Radical Right," pp. 155–58. Campbell briefly discusses the rise of El Grupo Patronal, identifying Monterrey's Unión Patronal as a precursor. Alex Sargoza, *The Monterrey Elite and the Mexican State, 1880–1940* (Austin: University of Texas Press, 1988), pp. 160–67.
10. Meyer, *El conflicto social,* pp. 131–34; Clark, *Organized Labor,* p. 252; Florinda Lazos León to Calles, June 20, 1931, APEC, Fondo Partidos Varios, 4334/1.1.0; slogan of pamphlet entitled *La Voz de Sureste* 1 (April 24, 1931): 1, APEC, 4334/9.1.0.
11. Barry Carr, *Marxism and Communism in Twentieth-Century Mexico* (Lincoln: University of Nebraska Press, 1992), pp. 92–93; Clark, *Organized Labor,* p. 134; Meyer, *El conflicto social,* pp. 127–28.
12. J. Reuben Clark to SS, "Political Report for July 1932," August 24, 1932, USDS 812.00/29754; Samuel Sokobin, consul in Saltillo, to SS, September 6, 1932, USDS 812.00/29788; Clark, *Organized Labor,* pp. 264–65.
13. Letter, ILD to National Palace, Mexico City, July 22, 1932, see attached August 11 memo and margin, USDS 812.00/29746; Campbell, "Radical Right," pp. 138–40. Under J. Edgar Hoover the FBI established branch offices in many Latin American capitals, but FBI archival material has proven difficult to access.
14. Lorenzo Meyer, *El conflicto social,* pp. 185, 211–15. Meyer posits that the influence of CNA petitions was probably negligible. Telegram, Emerenciano Alvarez to Calles, February 13, 1932, APEC, Fondo Partidos Varios, 4334/10.1.0; Cárdenas to Calles, June 21, 1930, APEC, Fondo Lázaro Cárdenas, 820/206.4.0.
15. Jean Meyer, "Revolution and Reconstruction," pp. 233–34; Fowler Salamini, *Agrarian Radicalism in Veracruz,* pp. 33–35, 54, 62–64, 90–92, 106; J. Ruben Clark, "Political Report," August 24, 1932, USDS; "Una revolución comunista," *La Palabra* 1:183 (January 8, 1933): 1.

16. This interpretation of cardenismo predominated in Mexican scholarship after 1968, in the wake of the massacre of hundreds of workers and students at Tlatelolco. See the historiographical explanation and citations in the Conclusion. Spencer, "Strategies of Institutionalization," p. 274.

17. Joe Ashby, *Organized Labor and the Mexican Revolution under Lázaro Cárdenas* (Chapel Hill: University of North Carolina Press, 1963), pp. 24–25. Figures on official strikes distort the reality of innumerable unofficial ones during the Maximato.

18. Ashby, *Organized Labor*, pp. 25–26.

19. "Sensacionales declaraciones del Gral. Plutarco Elías Calles," *El Universal*, June 12, 1935; Eduardo J. Correa, *El balance del cardenismo* (Mexico City: Talleres Linotipográficos, 1941), pp. 53–57.

20. "Un grupo de viejos revolucionarios," to Cardenas, telegram, June 29, 1935, APEC, Fondo Lázaro Cárdenas, 840/206.9.473.

21. Lorenzo Meyer, *Política del Maximato*, pp. 294–95; Luis González, *Días del presidente*, pp. 22–24.

22. Dulles, *Yesterday in Mexico*, pp. 650–58; Bantjes, "Politics, Class and Culture," pp. 36–38, 43.

23. Octavio Ianni, *El estado capitalista en la época de Cárdenas* (Mexico City: Ediciones Era, 1977), pp. 66–67; Weyl and Weyl, *Reconquest of Mexico*, pp. 232–33, 251–53, 361; "Manifiesto," *El Universal*, June 21, 1936.

24. Yepis to SS, June 21, 1935, USDS 812.00/30224; Report on Business Prospects, Norweb to SS, June 14, 1935, pp. 1, 8, USDS 812.00/30220.

25. "El comercio, la industria, y la banca se dirigen al ejecutivo," *El Universal*, March 12, 1936.

26. Daniels to SS, April 15, 1936, p. 7, USDS 812.00/30358; Sargoza, *Monterrey Elite*, p. 179; Campbell, "Radical Right," p. 155.

27. Sargoza, *Monterrey Elite*, p. 183; "Una entrevista con El Presidente," *Excelsior*, April 14, 1935.

28. Campbell, "Radical Right," p. 152; "Propositos de la Acción Cívica Nacionalista," *El Pueblo* (Hermosillo), March 29, 1936. This newspaper is filed in the Hemeroteca of the Sonoran state library. Headquartered in Monterrey, the ACN had its strength in the north.

29. Esperanza F. G. de Santibañez to Cárdenas, April 24, 1936, and "Manifiesto a la Mujer Mexicana," no date, both in AGN, FLC, 111/1568.0.

30. "Resume of Conditions," William Schott, secretary of embassy, to SS, March 11, 1936, p. 5, USDS 812.00/30341; Sargoza, *Monterrey Elite*, p. 183. Sargoza states confidently that business financed the *Dorados*, but his source is another USDS memorandum.

31. Campbell, "Radical Right," pp. 152, 167; Albert Michaels, "Fascism and Sinarquismo: Popular Nationalisms against the Mexican Revolution," *Journal of Church and State* 8 (Spring 1966): 235; "Los 'Dorados' han lanzado un manifiesto a la Nación," *El Universal*, March 4, 1936.

32. "Ha sido provocado el grupo de los 'camisas doradas' de la ciudad," *Excelsior*, April 14, 1935; ARM, "Abajo el comunismo escalvisante," leaflet, no date, a copy of which is attached to Clifton English, vice-counsel in Torreón, to SS, USDS 812.00/30399.

33. Nicolás Rodríguez to Cárdenas, April 8, 1935, AGN, FLC 606.3/20.0. Rodríguez invited the president to attend the ceremony; Cárdenas declined.

34. Unknown author, Memorandum originating from Saltillo, May 19, 1936; Francisco Castañeda and others, Sindicato Revolucionario "Ignacio Allende," to Cárdenas, April 19, 1936, both in AGN, FLC 541.1/41.0.

35. "Zafarrancho en Monterrey," *Excelsior*, July 30, 1936; "Una manifestación de obreros en Monterrey," *El Universal*, August 3, 1936; "Mensaje de las Mujeres 'Doradas' al Cárdenas," *El Universal*, August 4, 1936.

36. Daniels to SS, telegram, August 11, 1936, USDS 812.00/30392; Daniels to SS, August 25, 1936, USDS 812.00/30401; "Al pueblo de la Región Lagunera," handbill, in AGN, FLC, 541.1/41.0.

37. Weyl and Weyl, *Reconquest of Mexico*, pp. 359–60; Campbell, "Radical Right," p. 154. Regarding the VMN, UNVR and Rodríguez's activities, see Chapter 7.

38. Dulles, *Yesterday in Mexico*, pp. 659–65, 678; "Six Guard Calles on Flight to Texas," *New York Times*, April 11, 1936.

39. Owen White, "Next Door to Communism," *Colliers* (October 3, 1936), pp. 12, 53–54.

40. John Taylor to Office of Arms and Munitions Control, October 20, 1938, USDS 812.00/30637; Weyl and Weyl, *Reconquest of Mexico*, p. 168.

41. Daniels, *Shirt-Sleeve Diplomat*, pp. 62, 65; "About Mexico," *The Laredo Times*, May 7, 1936; Resolution, Board of Aldermen, Chelsea, Massachusetts, May 4, 1936, in USDS 812.00/30373.

PART II

CARDENISMO, 1935–1940

5

CARDENISMO AND
THE RISE OF THE RIGHT

The ascendancy of Lázaro Cárdenas to the presidency in 1934, and his consolidation of authentic political power by 1936, profoundly changed both the nature and the composition of the Mexican Right. Ideologically, the Right coalesced as never before, swept up in a sense of urgency as it pondered the "dangers" posed by cardenismo to the very foundation blocks of Mexican society: family, faith, and fatherland. The divisions over tactics, goals, and personal loyalties, which had plagued the Right since 1929, slowly gave way to a fresh ideological unity. This relative harmony matured during an era of public debate with the Revolutionary establishment over a series of emotionally charged issues from late 1936 through 1938. New organizations emerged to lead the Right, even as the stalwart institutions of the "old Right," the church and army, stepped away from the political arena. While military groups, including conservative veterans, mobilized against the regime, the army came under tight government control through the reorganized official party. The proliferation of nascent opposition groups should not be construed as factionalism: the Right prospered during the 1930s and extended itself in several directions, but its components shared common ground and often worked together.

These new organizations wrangled with the Cárdenas government and the Mexican Left through the print media. No study of the Right would be complete without attention to its periodicals and literature, which flourished during the mid-1930s. Through print the Right struggled to convince Mexicans of the wayward course of cardenismo. When possible, rightists also worked through the conservative mainstream press, often finding an arena in Mexico City's two largest daily newspapers, *El Excélsior* and *El Universal*, both edited by conservatives.[1] The latter was especially popular with rightists who published paid pronouncements and manifestos.

The most important press organ of the Right itself, during the 1936–1938 period, was *El Hombre Libre*, a Mexico City newspaper published three times a week with an average length of four pages. Its editor, Diego Arenas Guzmán, was not orthodox in his conservatism. Born in the capital in 1891, he had participated in the founding of the liberal Partido Nacional Democrático at the end of the Porfiriato, then helped organize the Casa del Obrero Mundial, a labor union infused with anarcho-syndicalism. As the Revolutionary bloodletting wound down, he turned his attention to journalism, publishing widely on the Revolution and political issues. An agnostic, he defended religious liberty to the point of serving jail time on several occasions.[2]

El Hombre Libre, begun in the Maximato, reached the apex of its influence in the mid-1930s before closing down in 1942 after the defeat of cardenismo. Little can be gleaned about its financial backing or its readership. Subscribers paid 8 pesos a year to receive it, and the recurrent advertising suggests that the readership may have been predominantly male. The Policia Privada, located on Tacuba Street in Mexico City, saw reason to advertise in *El Hombre Libre* often. "Before you accept an individual as the devoted boyfriend of your daughter, investigate his previous actions and conduct," it explained to concerned fathers. The Clínica Alemana tendered cures for "sexual weaknesses," including sterility, premature emissions, and diseases that loyal husbands probably should not have suffered.

Its colorful advertising and ideologically eclectic editor notwithstanding, *El Hombre Libre* was the major journalistic hotbed of criticism of the Cárdenas regime. Almost invariably it blamed all national problems on the leftist policies of the Revolutionary government, and in the process indoctrinated its readers with arguments against socialism. When Mexico, for the first time in its history, had to import grain to feed its burgeoning population in 1937, *El Hombre Libre* looked past the population statistics and unfortunate drought to the "real" culprits: land reform, collective farming, and the Banco Ejidal.[3] And while its attacks on the government were uneven in quality of argumentation, the paper did solicit guest editorials by prominent opposition thinkers such as Luis Cabrera, José Vasconcelos, and Justo Franco.

El Hombre Libre organized its own political party in 1937, the Partido Social Demócrata Mexicano [PSDM]. The platform, printed frequently in the newspaper, was a mixture of conservative and classical liberal proposals reflecting the beliefs of the party's intellectual father, Arenas Guzmán. Economically, the PSDM called for land reform, but only in individual tracts that preserved the concept of private property; the party allowed for state intervention in regulating production and ending monopolies, as well as in dividing up landed estates. Politically, it called for democracy in Mexico and affirmed that individual rights could be limited for the public good, although society should also "cultivate and invigorate the individual personality, elevating one's conscience and moral senses" to support the greater community.

In the social realm the PSDM program shackled high-sounding ideas with its conservative presumptions. While society may function under Enlightenment notions of the corporate good, it must accentuate "the familial structure, especially among the rural population, and consider the home as the true basis of society." Parents alone hold the right to shape a child's spiritual character. The PSDM endorsed the idea of equal rights for women, though "we do not advocate a feminism that causes our women to deny their role in shaping the mind-set of the child and in serving as the cornerstone of the Mexican home." Despite the clash of politically liberal and socially conservative ideas, the party made an honest effort to address women's issues and recruit their support.[4]

If there were any questions about the PSDM's attitude toward leftist ideologies, they were answered in the official program which appeared, among other publications, in *El Universal* on August 24. The document opened with a sharp attack on Marxist thought, though again it couched the critique in the context of classical liberalism's concern for the individual. Arguing that Marxism-Leninism is unnatural because it goes against the human attributes of reason, sentiment, and will, the program warned that "man in the Marxist system is nothing more than a grain of sand in the desert," since human dignity and individual will are lost. Next, in an argument that must have frightened middle-class readers to which the PSDM had an appeal, it contended that communism sanctions the destruction of the bourgeoisie, as the proletariat "exterminates the last man, woman, and child of the wretched middle class." Further,

The family can not coexist with a communist regime . . . . Communism must destroy the home, because as long as it and family affections endure, it is not able to completely take over the bodies and souls of men. And the Communist State needs absolute slaves!

The dismantling of the family leads in turn to the decline of religion, thereby assuring the damnation of human souls. This process, not surprisingly, came by way of socialist education, the perennial whipping boy of the Mexican Right.[5]

The PSDM's fascinating incorporation of Enlightenment notions of individual rights, undoubtedly the contribution of Arenas Guzmán, did not prevent it from uniting with other rightist organizations in a common fight against communism. This unity of the Right, in fact, was a stated purpose of the party, which attempted to link up with other groups and called "all democrats and nationalists" together for a June 26 convention of the "independent opposition." Among the organizations that responded were the original Partido Acción Nacional (begun in 1934), remnants of the Gold Shirts, and the nearly defunct Partido Anti-reeleccionista. The June meeting formally founded the PSDM, electing Jorge Prieto Laurens as its president and at least partially succeeded in uniting some of Cárdenas's opponents.[6] Another rightist group that cooperated with the PSDM was the Unión Nacional de Veteranos de la Revolución, a fiercely nationalistic organization comprised of military officers that began to play an active role in political agitation by 1937.[7] The basic maxim of the

UNVR appears in a letter it sent to President Cárdenas in May 1936, when he was still an honorary member: "The anticommunist campaign should be the principal activity of the UNVR," which orders members "to be on guard against every communist activity and to combat it in every legal way." Accordingly, the group spied on the PCM and collected data concerning its plans and alleged collections of weapons, which it turned over to authorities such as the secretary of war and the police.[8]

The UNVR attempted to influence public opinion by publishing an analysis of conditions in Mexico in *El Universal*. This paid advertisement outlined the primary concerns of the conservative veterans, who harked back to the Revolutionary tradition by comparing Cárdenas with Porfirio Díaz in his lack of appreciation of the populace's level of discontent. The UNVR identified four problems in July 1937: the "proven failure" of the *ejido* (communal land reform), internecine labor unrest which produced inflation, a burdensome public debt, and disregard for the Constitution and rules of law. Newly installed Guanajuato governor Luis Rodríguez, formerly the personal secretary of Cárdenas, served as the prime example of abusive government. This pronouncement constituted "the sharpest rebuke received by the government of President Cárdenas since his break with Calles two years ago," and raised deep concerns over the attitude of the Mexican army. The military attaché in the U.S. embassy advised his superiors that the critique represented "the point of view of the great majority" of active officers, who particularly resented Cárdenas arming peasant militias.[9] The UNVR's members put their politics into practice, agitating outside Mexico City and building ties with power brokers like Saturnino Cedillo, strong-arm governor of San Luis Potosí. Members battled land reform by defending wealthy landowners such as the Madero family in Coahuila which, despite its revolutionary heritage, hired them to protect their lands from local agrarians.[10]

Great landholders were not the only ones threatened by land reform, however, and while some turned to the UNVR for protection, many small and moderate landowners began to organize themselves, joining the Right in the loosely structured Unión de Pequeños Propietarios [UPP]. Mexico's lesser farmers were especially numerous in the north, where they raised cattle and horses. These ranchers, usually mestizo, were—like the peasant Indians and mestizos of central Mexico—deeply religious, scornful of the Revolutionary government's leftist rhetoric, and hostile to its socialist education. The UPP appeared in myriad farm towns in the north, primarily working to hinder government land distribution.[11]

In addition to the newcomers—the UPP, UNVR, and PSDM—several organizations founded earlier in the 1930s continued to agitate on the right, including El Grupo Patronal, Acción Cívica Nacional, Acción Cívica Femenina, Confederación de la Clase Media, and holdover elements of the Gold Shirts. In the 1936–1937 period the CCM was perhaps the most active of these, circulating pamphlets that attacked unions and warned *campesinos* that the state was their new "master." Organized on Mexico City university campuses, it raised money by selling "Anticommunist Campaign" stamps to its mostly urban business-class constituents. Though building a popular base, grassroots rightist groups faced harassment by local bureaucrats who owed their positions to the official party and government. The ACF in Durango, for example, complained that municipal officials were firing their members, even those with years of service, while the PSDM had difficulties organizing in Michoacán because of local government harassment.[12]

TAMING THE "OLD RIGHT" OF
CHURCH AND ARMY

At first glance, the Mexican Right appears on the wane in mid-decade because of the decline of its traditional institutional base. It is true that the two great bulkwarks of conservatism in Mexico, the army and the church, yielded to the authority of the Revolutionary state and continued to distance themselves from the political arena. The church hierarchy, which had acknowledged de facto defeat with the *Arreglos* ending the Cristero war, accepted its expulsion from political power; the army, less willing to exit gracefully, was ushered out, in part, through the reorganization of the official party by Cárdenas.

It will be recalled that the church hierarchy had begun to back away from a posture of confrontation with the Revolutionary regime at the end of the Cristero revolt. The retreat continued as Cárdenas came into power, made easier by the president's relative religious tolerance. Not only had the bishops reorganized Catholic grassroots organizations into Acción Católica Mexicana, but they completely shunned the revival of the Cristeros, sanctioning their second defeat. It was the church hierarchy that effectively clamped down on political activism by the laity, a policy that continued throughout Cárdenas's term.

This policy of accommodation did not prevent Catholic prelates from condemning Marxism, however. Mexico's bishops issued a pastoral letter in January 1936 which prohibited Catholics from embracing socialism or class warfare, and the pope joined the chorus with his worldwide encyclical "On Atheistic Communism" in March 1937. "Communism deprives man of his liberty, the spiritual source of his moral conduct," Pius XI proclaimed. *El Hombre Libre* found reason to quote the Pope repeatedly:

It rejects all hierarchy and authority established by God, including that of fathers . . . [Communism] denies the place of the woman with the family and in the home. In proclaiming the idea of women's emancipation it separates her from the domestic life and from caring for her children, dragging her into public life.

Yet the Vatican followed the encyclical with a pastoral letter to the Mexican church that avoided criticism of the government and struck an optimistic tone, predicting peace and growth. And lest any Catholics confuse his encyclical with a call to political resistance, Pius XI noted in the pastoral that practicing Christians must be "good citizens." Catholic lay groups followed the direction given them by the hierarchy. ACM had grown numerically in the mid-1930s as lay Catholics resisted socialist education, but by 1937 membership leveled off and ACM's agenda continued to drift toward the spiritual, that of "saving souls." National conferences, held biannually in 1936 and 1938, deemphasized the political for the spiritual. The subgroup for adult males, the UCM, increasingly focused on adult religious instruction, while the women's auxiliary, the UFCM, pursued charity work, home schooling, and church upkeep. The Catholic women's moral agenda included campaigns against divorce and illegitimate unions, and the promotion of modest dress—hardly themes that would provoke the government. The subgroups for youth, the ACJM and ACFM, sought to mitigate the effects of socialist education rather than confront it, so that all in all, by the late 1930s, lay organizations had become nearly apolitical.[13]

The church's shift in emphasis from the political to the spiritual may have had one additional practical motive beyond that of avoiding damaging confrontation with the government: in the 1930s it encountered a formidable spiritual challenge in North American Protestantism. Other denominations had long been active in Mexico, but their efforts had been slowed during the Revolutionary upheaval. By the outset of the 1930s stability had beckoned them back, while new transportation and communication links with the United States—such as cars and roads, telephones and radio stations—made their work easier (the increase in mission activities coincided with an increase in the number of U.S. citizens traveling to Mexico in general). The number of Mexican Protestants jumped from 130,000 in 1930 to 176,000 ten years later, a 35 percent rise. And even more alarming for the Catholic Church was the shift from Protestant reliance on foreign funds and missionaries to Mexican churches and preachers. Mexico had its first Methodist bishop take office in 1930, the Salvation Army arrived in 1937, and the Gideons, known for the Bible distributing, arrived a year later. Pentecostals made impressive inroads in particular, while Protestantism overall gained the most ground in northern Mexico.

Distracted by the spiritual challenges of Protestants and committed to peaceful coexistence with the Revolutionary establishment, the church withdrew from politics with much more grace than the military. The gradual process of cleansing the officer corps of its thirst for political power reached a turning point in 1938. Cárdenas, in one of his few victories over the Right, was able to tame the army. His success was rooted, in no small part, in the work of his predecessors who, since the early 1920s, had reorganized and reduced the huge Revolutionary army. In 1920, 680 generals commanded 118,000 troops; by 1937 both numbers were nearly cut in half. A second generation of high-ranking generals, or *divisionarios*, oversaw a more professional army less prone toward interfering in politics.

Still, the danger of such interference persisted. During the showdown with Calles, Cárdenas had replaced suspected Calles loyalists with generals from three other factions: those partisan to Juan Andreau Almazán, others tied to Saturnino Cedillo, and a smaller group in Veracruz comprised mainly of old Carrancistas. The three key positions in the War Department—secretary, subsecretary, and inspector general—were crucial to controlling the army. Cárdenas himself had been secretary just before winning the presidency, and opted to leave the post vacant. He had, as subsecretary, his own man, Manual Avila Camacho. As inspector general he appointed Heriberto Jara of the Veracruz clique. In the wake of the June 1935 cabinet shakeup, he was able to move Avila Camacho into the cabinet as Secretary and pass up Almazán loyalists altogether. Almazán would become the Right's 1940 presidential candidate, where he faced the official party nominee, Avila Camacho. Long before 1940, Cárdenas had both an enemy, and an ally to whom he was indebted, in the military.[14]

The threat of army discontent lasted well into the *sexenio* not only because of the recent power struggle, but also because the leftist policies of cardenismo "disturbed the army." After 1936 the president and his secretary faced three factions in the officers' ranks: loyalists of Almazán and Cedillo, and holdover Callistas like Manuel Pérez Treviño and Joaquín Amaro (the older Carranza faction was successfully ushered into retirement). Cedillo, a regional *caudillo* who had served in the cabinet as secretary of agriculture, was dangerous because of his ambition. Almazán, a conservative, enjoyed wide support and posed a grave ideological threat to the government.

Cárdenas and Avila Camacho countered the danger of military insurrection in three ways. First, they wooed and coddled junior officers and enlisted men, offered better housing, generous pensions, and free schooling, thereby potentially dividing the troops from the senior officers. Second, the government armed peasant militias that offset the position of the army. Last and most important, in 1938 the president reorganized the official party, the PNR, into the Partido de la Revolución Mexicana [PRM], incorporating the military into it as one of four divisions. "We did not put the army in politics," Cárdenas would later explain, "it was already there." But in the PRM it was outvoted. In addition, in the PRM the army was organized only on a national level, where Secretary Avila Camacho oversaw its selection of delegates. Junior officers were encouraged to join the peasant, labor, or popular sectors of the party, further diluting the army's influence. Powerful regional cliques of generals found themselves easily outmaneuvered, unable to influence national politics directly as before. Predictably, conservative generals, led by Almazán, opposed the incorporation into the PRM, which undercut the army's ability to pick official candidates.[15]

Within two months of the reorganization of the party, Saturnino Cedillo rebelled in San Luis Potosí. Viewed as the last of the old *caudillos*, Cedillo could never have been labeled an ideologue. He disappointed businessmen in his state by failing to court them, and had even implemented a modicum of land reform as a means of winning a rural power base. Yet after Calles was exiled, Cedillo had "set about maneuvering himself into a position where he could lead the reaction," turning San Luis Potosí into a refuge for half of Mexico's priests in 1935.[16] The Right increasingly looked to him as its champion; the Left pressured Cárdenas to oust him from the cabinet, from which he resigned in June 1937. Ironically, Cedillo had feuded with the political Right in his home state through much of his career. He succeeded in arranging the removal of Aurelio Manrique—the Obregón loyalist who had played an important role in the opposition during the 1934 elections—from the governorship in the late 1920s. Manrique sought revenge in the 1937 congressional campaigns by forming the anti-Cedillo Partido Renovador Potosino, a strategy that gained him nothing and caused him to lose his trademark beard, which was shaved off by Cedillo thugs during an assault.

Cedillo planned to run for president as an opposition candidate in 1940 and then revolt afterwards, but during 1937 he watched his position in San Luis Potosí deteriorate under pressure from Mexico City. In the fall the War Department closed an aviation school and stationed two regiments in the state, while in spring 1938 Cárdenas ordered him to military duty in Michoacán, a move tantamount to political exile. Cedillo opted to revolt instead. His May pronouncement evoked such a lame response that even he must have been surprised. Within days the rebel leader was on the run, retreating into the eastern mountains of his native state. Circulars issued by Cedillo from his hideout appealed to the Right:

Cárdenas knows that from 85 to 90 percent of the people are against him and his communist government . . . , for although he does not openly confess to be a communist, by his acts he has shown that he is a disciple of this false doctrine. He has planted the theories of Marx in the minds of the great majority of the innocent schoolchildren of this Republic.[17]

The futility of his efforts were obvious, however. Caught by Federal troops in January 1939, he died in a gun battle. With him died the last noteworthy military revolt in Mexico.

THE RIGHT, THE UNITED STATES, AND
THE OIL CONTROVERSY

Cedillo's failed revolt, a reflection of the decline of the "old Right" of church and army, came just weeks after the Cárdenas regime expropriated foreign oil interests—a bold and dangerous manuever even in the best of times. Cedillo himself probably expected to receive support from the United States (he certainly appealed for it), which because of its business interests was a natural ally of the Right. Yet the American attitude toward Mexico and its political Right, just like its policies in the mid-1930s, was not monolithic.[18] Conservative segments of the U.S. populace were decidedly supportive of their Mexican counterparts, sharing their apprehension of Cárdenas and the rise of Mexican "communism." Yet there were two surprising features of U.S.-Mexican perceptions of each other in the mid-1930s: first, the U.S. government did not, generally, share the concerns of the U.S. Right; and second, the Mexican Right so forcefully rejected the United States that, for the most part, it did not ally with its potential backers north of the border. Both features are vital to understanding the famous oil crisis and the Right's response to it.

The Franklin D. Roosevelt administration, though divided, held to its Good Neighbor policy for the duration of the decade, a position that favored hemispheric respect over a historical pattern of American intervention. Ambassador to Mexico Josephus Daniels was instrumental in persuading Roosevelt to take this course in U.S. dealings with Mexico, and he found a frequent ally in Treasury Secretary Henry Morgenthau, who had a healthy fear of fascism and continually advised the president to back the Cárdenas government. In fall 1937, Daniels and Morgenthau convinced Roosevelt not to curtail purchases of Mexican silver, a move promoted by Cordell Hull's State Department at the behest of Catholic and business lobbyists opposed to the Good Neighbor stance. Not even the dramatic 1936–1938 acceleration of land reform threatened to alter U.S. policy. Daniels quietly expressed concerns about the dispersement of U.S.-owned lands without sufficient compensation, while Hull demanded suspension of the seizures to no avail.[19]

The Mexican Right had no affinity for the United States and usually bypassed opportunities to ally with conservative American interests. Its staunch nationalism and disgust for Washington's frequent support of the Revolutionary regime lay at the root of this Yankeephobia. Cristeros resented the role of U.S. Ambassador Dwight Morrow in forcing their "surrender" through the *Arreglos*, while Vasconcelos had derided the well-known ambassador as "The Proconsul." The Escobar affair, Chamizal frontier controversy, and myriad other affronts to Mexican sovereignty—such as a proposal in the 1936 Arizona legislature to buy or lease part of Sonora—assured that the nationalist Right would remain hostile to Mexico's powerful northern neighbor. The Right was sometimes so anti-U.S. that it came to the defense of other foreign powers. In March 1937 *El Hombre Libre* complained that Cárdenas's oil policies were hurting British interests at the expense of the hated "Yankee Imperialists."[20]

The oil question had been the touchstone of U.S.-Mexican relations since the Revolution. Article 27 of the 1917 Constitution held that subsoil rights belonged to the Mexican people through their sovereign government, a position inspired by the perception that the Díaz regime had bartered away Mexico's mineral wealth to foreigners. During the 1920s the Sonorans walked softly on the idea of enforcement. Obregón granted U.S. oil companies a favorable interpretation of the provision with the 1929 Bucareli accords, while Calles reneged on Bucareli and required the multinationals to register for concessions, pushing the issue to the brink without engendering open confrontation with Washington.[21]

On March 18, 1938 the longstanding conflict between Mexico and foreign oil companies reached its apogee when Cárdenas went on national radio to announce the expropriation of all foreign oil holdings. The background to this decision is well known: oil workers, organized in the Sindicato de Trabajadores Petroleros de la República Mexicana [STPRM], struck in spring 1937 for higher wages, better benefits, and the forty-hour work week. The government arbitrated between STPRM and intransigent company management, granting a modest portion of labor's demands, a decision upheld by the Supreme Court. The continued refusal of the oil companies to honor Mexican authority pushed the Revolutionary regime to its dramatic decision.

The Mexican Right could not deny the correctness of the president's decision since it was rooted in nationalism and the precepts of the politically sacrosanct Revolution. The public euphoria over the expropriation was considerable, especially in Mexico City, and "briefly, the popular frontism of the CTM seemed to encompass the entire population." The Catholic hierarchy endorsed the action, and even many lay Catholics resentful of cardenismo assisted in raising money to pay for the expropriation. It was a great public relations coup for Cárdenas, one far superior to any other. Yet quietly, behind the scenes, rightist leaders muttered their disapproval. Always fearful of the growing power of the state, wealthy conservatives who had strong ties to the business community disagreed with the dangerous precedent of removing a major segment of the economy from the private sector. El Grupo Patronal opposed the move, Manuel Gómez Morín termed it "unpatriotic," Manuel Pérez Treviño remained strangely silent on the matter in a December 1938 manifesto slamming cardenismo, and Saturnino Cedillo looked for U.S. sympathy as he revolted.[22]

The dilemma for the Right, as it faced the brief popularity of the expropriation and tried to balance its fervent nationalism with its defense of capitalism, is exemplified in the response of the Mexico City newspaper *Omega*. Second to *El Hombre Libre* as a voice of the Right, *Omega* was founded and directed by Spanish-born Daniel Rodríguez de la Vega until his death just one month before the oil expropriation. The paper wavered in response to the crisis, but the underlying tone was one of criticism. On March 3, before the takeover, *Omega* saw fit to congratulate the Mexican Supreme Court for denying a writ of *amparo* to foreign oil companies on principles of national sovereignty. Nine days later, presaging the Right's warm regard for German and Italian fascism, it warned that Russia and the United States were conniving to deprive the anticommunist Axis powers Mexican oil.

Omega gave relatively little coverage to the expropriation in mid-March, but by the end of the month began to raise doubts about its wisdom. In an article warning that Mexico would suffer "terrible consequences" for its radicalism, the paper predicted economic doom via U.S. suspension of silver purchases (the United States in fact did suspend purchases for one week before Roosevelt accepted the counsel of Morgenthau and reversed himself). On April 7 it asked its readers if Mexico had the ability to administer the oil industry, warning that corrupt politicians of the Revolutionary regime would mismanage affairs. By April 30 *Omega* editorialized that "the original idea [of expropriation] is good," but the means and consequences would prove disastrous. Charging that the government was misleading the people as to the "grave situation" brought on by its action, *Omega* again expressed its conviction that government mismanagement of oil funds and profits would follow.[23]

If the Right's response to the expropriation was uneven, there was no doubt about the response of the oil industry. U.S. oil companies viewed the seizure of their properties with predictable anger. They waged a propaganda war in the United States in order to 'sway public opinion in their favor and force the Roosevelt administration to adopt a hard line against Mexico. Standard Oil of New Jersey led the attack, publishing twelve widely distributed pamphlets with titles such as "Whose Oil Is It?" These pamphlets used international law to condemn Mexico, portrayed the takeover as a communist plot, and argued that the "den of thieves" in charge of Mexico would ruin its economy and run the oil industry into the ground. Company executives reinforced these themes in press releases and interviews. Popular magazines like *Colliers* contended that Mexico, "harried by debt and mismanagement," could not afford to pay for the oil acquisition.[24]

The propaganda war extended beyond the border as oil companies promoted their cause in the Mexican press. Some of Standard Oil's literature appeared in the publications of the Mexican Right. *La Reacción*, for example, reproduced a pamphlet entitled "Confiscation or Expropriation" in 1940, written by Donald Richberg. It argued that the seizure of private property violated both Mexican and international law, and portrayed the Cárdenas government as criminal. The "expropriation" was, in truth, a confiscation, since the oil industry lost "properties worth hundreds of millions of dollars to a government that admits its inability to indemnify the owners." With no remedy possible in the courts, Richberg argued that upstanding U.S. businessmen would have to accept Mexico's paltry compensation payments and absorb an enormous loss.[25]

Despite the bombardment of oil company-instigated propaganda, Washington opted for a relatively gentle response toward Mexico. Ambassador Daniels and Henry Morgenthau were, again, the proponents of amity, while Cordell Hull's State Department balked at compromise and pressed for suspension of silver purchases and threats of military force. Cárdenas sent a twenty-member delegation to Washington to explain the expropriation, and published English-language tracts for distribution in the United States which may have modestly offset the powerful oil lobby.[26] The primary determinant of the U.S. response, however, was a profound fear of potential crisis in Mexico and the subsequent threats of fascism and the Mexican Right. As historian Lorenzo Meyer posits, international considerations were "in large measure" responsible for Roosevelt's unwillingness to fully back the oil companies. Morgenthau, in particular, argued for leniency, fearing that the Axis would step in if the United States allowed its relationship with Mexico to sour. The president's sympathy for Cárdenas, whom he viewed as a true democrat, and America's preoccupation with domestic problems also aided the cause of Mexico, Morgenthau, and Daniels.

Washington's fears that the Axis would step in where the Americans backed off were, at first glance, justified. Within days of the expropriation, Nazi Germany expressed interest in buying Mexican crude. The Cárdenas government obliged, later selling $17 million of oil in exchange for much-needed hard currency and manufactured goods, including aircraft. These developments, along with others, even prompted Hull and the State Department to support a softer line with regard to Mexico, and concern over Axis intrigue south of the border was a major reason for an end to the policy of isolation.[27]

Geopolitical concerns over Mexican and Latin American vulnerability to Axis designs resonated in the North American press. Even before the oil expropriation, some magazines such as *Current History* pondered whether or not the Americas were "safe." Carlton Beals, who had published widely on Latin America and Mexico in particular, repeatedly voiced his concerns about the fascist threat to the subcontinent in the late 1930s. In a 1938 *Current History* article entitled "Black Shirts in Latin America," he warned that Benito Mussolini's Italy was increasingly influential in the region, and that it was the probable major buyer of Mexican oil. A cartoon accompanying the article captioned "Hands Across the Sea" showed the shadow of a fascist salute over Latin America.[28] Beals reinforced his message with a 1938 book, *The Coming Struggle for Latin America*, demonstrating that the Left in the United States had its own conspiracy theories. In it he praised U.S. restraint in response to the expropriation, but warned that more had to be done. Spain was the linchpin, he contended, and a Franco victory in the Civil War would send fascism sweeping throughout Latin America. According to Beals, numerous pro-Franco German and Italian agents operated in places like Mexico, stirring up support for the Falange and fascism in general. In Mexico these agents were aided by Japanese spies, "trickling in" and setting up operations in strategic areas such as the Baja and Sonora.[29]

Beals's belief in secret Japanese operations in western Mexico in the late 1930s was a popular one because it played on U.S. fears of Japanese duplicity and the vulnerability of North America's Pacific coast. The author's paranoia over fascist conspiracies went to the point of contending that Mexicans had no prejudice against Orientals and that they would unite with Japan in war against America. In truth, such a declaration was ridiculous; Mexico, like the United States, had such deep-seated prejudice against Orientals that it even forbade their immigration. Nevertheless, U.S. Military Intelligence did everything possible to prevent the fulfillment of this prophecy, sending its own secret agents to monitor Japanese-Mexicans in the Baja, Sonora, Sinaloa, and Nayarit. Frequently Japanese manipulations were linked to the activities of the Mexican Right. The same military agents reported in 1940 that western Mexican states would rebel "upon Almazán's orders," while Sinarquista efforts to colonize the Baja triggered fears of an imminent Japanese attack through the peninsula.[30]

Concerns over Axis plots in Mexico grew in 1939 with the outbreak of the Second World War. New alarming articles and books appeared, including Frank Kluckhohn's *The Mexican Challenge*, which repeated the charge of Japanese spies in Mexico, contended that Germans influenced domestic policies, and predicted that Mexico would supply the Axis oil in the war. An article in the scholarly *Annals of the American Academy* reiterated the worrisome possibilities of Mexican oil exports to fascist states, while some U.S. government agencies even suggested military cooperation. The Federal Bureau of Investigation, nearly hysterical by fall 1939, told the White House that 250 Nazi pilots were in Mexico preparing to bomb the United States, that Nazi submarines operated from Veracruz, and that Mexico had signed a secret treaty to supply Germany oil in exchange for British Honduras.[31]

While U.S. accounts of foreign agents operating in Mexico were sensational, they did provide an opportunity for the government and press to discredit the Right. Fascism was, in the 1930s political culture, as unacceptable to Mexicans as communism. In May 1938 *La Prensa*, a pro-Cárdenas Mexico City daily, embraced allegations that fascists were at work, and told its readers exactly who they were: Saturnino Cedillo and Román Yocupicio. The former was plotting his revolt in San Luis Potosí, and the latter, the new strongman governor of Sonora, was an impeccable Cárdenas opponent.[32]

The vast majority of publications, authors, government agencies, and policy-makers in the United States demonstrated an astounding lack of knowledge of Mexico, and appreciation of Mexicans, in the late 1930s. They viewed their southern neighbor as simply another Latin American country, with all the stereotypes that such a label evoked. Even more remarkable, almost uniformly they failed to attribute any volition to Mexicans, believing them instead to be incredibly malleable people—easy prey to the suggestions and whims of white North Americans and Europeans. Because the whole region is so "backward," wrote an American scholar, it is susceptible to foreign influence. George Creel, noting in 1937 that "already Germany and Japan . . . have won fairly firm footholds south of the Rio Grande," argued that only U.S. tutelage could save Mexico. In the wake of the oil expropriation, rumors swept the U.S. government that Germans were working to overthrow Cárdenas. Never did it seem to occur to anyone that, in truth, many Mexicans actively opposed their government.[33] The United States exercised a logical response to the oil crisis, but it did so much more out of misperception than through intelligence. Fortunately for the Cárdenas government, the Mexican Right's own nationalism complicated its response to the expropriation and allowed the beleaguered president to have his brief moment in the sun.

NOTES

1. Regarding the press and major newspapers, see González, *Los artífices del cardenismo*, pp. 79–85. The largest pro-Cárdenas daily was Mexico City's *El Nacional*.

2. *Diccionario Porrúa: De historia, biografía, y geografía de México*, 5th ed., vol. 1 (Mexico City: Editorial Porrúa, 1986), p. 174. Arenas Guzmán moderated his views in old age, serving as director of *El Nacional* from 1956 to 1962.

3. Diego Arenas Guzmán, "Bendito el socialismo que nos está matando de hambre," *El Hombre Libre*, March 5, 1937. Regarding the common advertisements see, for example, the June 7, 1937 edition.

4. "Manifiesto constitutivo del PSDM, que será discutido en la próxima convención de los Independientes," *El Hombre Libre*, May 31, 1937; "La acción de la mujer mexicana dentro del PSDM," *El Hombre Libre*, April 19, 1937.

5. "Programa del Partido Social Demócrata Mexicano," *El Universal*, August 24, 1937. The program advised its readers to find proof of this chilling description by studying conditions in Russia and Spain. See the discussion below in Chapter 6.

6. "La convención independiente se reunirá el 26 de junio," *El Hombre Libre*, May 28, 1937; "Programa," *El Universal*, August 24, 1937.

7. "Se reorganiza el comité que convocó a la convención," *El Hombre Libre*, May 14, 1937. The UNVR was the first group to work with the PSDM, agreeing to help finance the June meeting. Manuel Fernández Boyolí and Eustaquio Marrón de Angelis, *Lo que no se sabe de la rebelión cedillista* (Mexico City: P.S.I., 1938), pp. 18–21. The authors of this book attempted to link rightist groups to the failed Cedillo revolt. The UNVR may have been funded in turn by COPARMEX; see Negrete, *Relaciones en México*, p. 203.

8. "Daniel Ríos Zortuche, vice president of the UNVR, to Cárdenas, May 16, 1936, AGN, FLC, 606.3/20.1.1. The letter also advised the president that the UNVR opposed schools with "communistic tendencies." Gabino Vizcarra, general secretary of the UNVR, to Cárdenas, telegram and memorandum, October 4, 1937, AGN, FLC 606.3/20.1.4.

9. "Habla la Unión Nacional de Veteranos de la Revolución sobre la situación actual de la República," *El Universal*, July 14, 1937; Pierre de L. Boal (chargé d'affaires) to SS, July 16, 1937, p. 2–3, USDS 812.00/30470.

10. Enrique Liekens to Lic. Ignacio García Téllez, secretary to Cárdenas, November 15, 1937, AGN, FLC, 551/14.2.25; Juan Guardiola, Agrarian Committee of San Carlos, Coahuila, to Cárdenas, November 30, 1938, AGN, FLC, 542.1/2415.1.17.

11. González, *Los artífices del cardenismo*, pp. 27–31; Agustín Lanuza to Secretaría de Gobernación, telegram, San Pedro del Gallo, Durango, September 11, 1937, AGN, FLC, 437.1/727.1.3.

12. Fernández Boyolí and Marrón de Angelis, *Lo que no se sabe*, pp. 36–43. Josefa Hernández, local president of ACF, to Cárdenas, September 7, 1936, AGN, FLC, 703.2/566.2; Arenas Guzmán to Luis Rodríguez, May 13, 1936, AGN, FLC, 542.1/1626.1.3.

13. "Carta encíclica del Papa," *El Hombre Libre*, May 11, 1937; Negrete, *Relaciones en México*, pp. 206–7, 248–60. Frustration with the depoliticalization of lay groups may have fueled the peasantry's embrace of Sinarquismo; see Chapter 8.

14. Negrete, *Relaciones en México*, pp. 279–81; Alicia Hernández Chávez, *La mecánica cardenista* (Mexico City: El Colegio de México, 1979), pp. 80–83, 91–97.

15. Lieuwen, *Mexican Militarism*, pp. 115, 122–26; Hernández Chávez, *La mecánica cardenista*, pp. 106–9.

16. Dudley Ankerson, *Agrarian Warlord: Saturnino Cedillo and the Mexican Revolution in San Luis Potosí* (DeKalb: Northern Illinois University Press, 1984), pp. 136–38, 152; Campbell, "Radical Right," pp. 175–76.

17. Ankerson, *Agrarian Warlord*, pp. 161–63, 178–80, 189; Hernández Chávez, *La mecánica cardenista*, p. 112; Pierre to SS, January 4, 1939, USDS 812.00/30670. A copy of a Cedillo circular is attached to the document; it appeals to the United States for help.

18. For details on U.S. and international relations with Mexico, both formal and informal, see Friedrich Schuler, "Cardenismo Revisited: International Dimensions of the Reform, 1937–1940" (Ph.D. dissertation, University of Chicago, 1990).

19. Nora Hamilton, *The Limits of State Autonomy: Post-Revolutionary Mexico* (Princeton: Princeton University Press, 1982), pp. 223–24; Bell, "Attitudes of Selected Groups," p. 184; Daniels, *Shirt-Sleeve Diplomat*, p. 69; "Mexico to Refuse Hull's Plea to Suspend Land Seizures," *Chicago Daily News*, September 1, 1938.

20. "Resumé," Daniels to SS, November 18, 1936, p. 23, USDS 812.00/30419; "Se ataca al imperialismo Inglés pero se protege al imperialismo Yanqui," *El Hombre Libre*, March 3, 1937.

21. For background on the oil question, the Bucareli accords, and Calles's policies, see Lorenzo Meyer, *México y los Estados Unidos en el conflicto petrolero, 1917–1942* (Mexico City: El Colegio de México, 1968), pp. 75–138. Labor problems leading up to the expropriation are thoroughly treated in Ashby, *Organized Labor*, pp. 179–272.

22. Knight, "Rise and Fall of Cardenismo," p. 282; Daniels, *Shirt-Sleeve Diplomat*, p. 246; Fernández Boyolí and Marrón de Angelis, *Lo que no se sabe*, p. 67. In 1940 Juan Almazán wisely refused oil company support for his campaign.

23. "Negación del amparo a los petroleros," March 3; José Perdomo, "Sabotaje petrolero contra los paises anticomunistas," March 12; "México sufre las terribles consecuencias de su politica de excesivos radicalismos," March 31; " Tenemos suficiente talento y honradez para administrar la riqueza petrolera?" April 7; and "No debe por ningun motivo ocultarse al pueblo la grave situación provocada por la expropriación," April 30, 1938, all in *Omega*.

24. Lorenzo Meyer, *El conflicto petrolero*, pp. 251–52; Bell, "Attitudes of Selected Groups," p. 176; George Creel, "Can We Prevent Chaos in Mexico?" *Colliers* (July 23, 1938): 12–13.

25. Lorenzo Meyer, *El conflicto petrolero*, p. 254; Donald Richberg, translated as "Lo que alegan los petroleros," *La Reacción* 3:73 (February 8, 1940): 10. A consensus exists among scholars that, in fact, Mexico paid a fair market price for the oil properties.

26. Lorenzo Meyer, *El conflicto petrolero*, pp. 231–34, 253. The United States did, briefly, suspend silver purchases in the first week of April.

27. Lorenzo Meyer, *El conflicto petrolero*, p. 238; Hamilton, *Limits of State Autonomy*, p. 218; David Haglund, *Latin America and the Transformation of U.S. Strategic Thought, 1936–1940* (Albuquerque: University of New Mexico Press, 1984), pp. 1–9, 74–75, 93–94.

28. Genaro Arbaiza, "Are the Americas Safe?" *Current History* 47:12 (December 1937): 29; Carlton Beals, "Black Shirts in Latin America," *Current History* 49:3 (November 1938): 32–34.

29. Carlton Beals, *The Coming Struggle for Latin America* (New York: Halcyon House, 1938), pp. 18–19, 159–62, 243–44, 421.

30. Beals, *Coming Struggle*, p. 39; National Archives, Washington, D.C., Military Intelligence Division, 2655-6-235/39, September 7, 1937, and 2657-6-768/197, May 31, 1940; Jean Meyer, *El sinarquismo*, p. 76.

31. Frank Kluckhohn, *The Mexican Challenge* (New York: Doubleday, Duran & Co., 1939), pp. 69, 78, 83, 91; Richard F. Beherendt, "Foreign Influence in Latin America,"

Annals of the American Academy of Political and Social Science 204 (July 1939): 3–4; Haglund, *Transformation of U.S. Thought*, p. 153.

32. "Se denuncian las ramificaciones de una conspiración fascista," *La Prensa*, May 16, 1938.

33. Beherendt, "Foreign Influence," p. 1; Creel, "Can We Prevent Chaos?" pp. 49–50; Haglund, *Transformation of U.S. Thought*, p. 75.

6

THE RIGHT'S LITERARY OFFENSIVE

From the outset of cardenismo, the Mexican Right began a vicious assault on the Revolutionary state through myriad publications. These writings, which range from simple booklets for popular consumption to sophisticated intellectual treatises, are invaluable for gaining an understanding of the political culture of 1930s Mexico. Where did the Right direct its appeal? What cultural values of political significance elicited the attention of the Right? Did the Right's critique elicit a meaningful response from the mass of the Mexican people? How did the Right's literary assault alter the political discourse of Cárdenas and his government? These and other questions have answers in the fabric of the political culture, and rightist literature is an avenue by which these answers can be found. There is no doubt that, from an institutional perspective, the Revolutionary state held the upper hand in Mexico with the growth in both the size and influence of an enormous centralized bureaucracy. By mid-decade the church and army were pushed aside. In the realm of popular values, however, it was the Right that held the edge. The Cárdenas agenda for Mexico was in danger from the start, vulnerable in a political culture that was fundamentally conservative and ultimately hostile.

Before examining specific political topics in the literature, one important theme appearing across the range of publications warrants special attention: anti-Semitism. Why was the Mexican Right, in a nation with so few Jews, fervently anti-Semitic? The answer is historical. Anti-Semitism has deep roots in Mexico, despite the presence of relatively few Jews. It was, of course, King Ferdinand and Queen Isabella of Spain who decreed in March 1492 that all Jews must convert to Christianity or depart in exile. The order of the Catholic monarchs, ruling in an era marked by an emphasis on religious orthodoxy, sparked both an exodus and an increase in the number of Jewish Christians, referred to by Spaniards as conversos. Many Jews sought to escape the hostile Iberian environs and carve out new lives for themselves in New Spain. Yet here, as in the homeland, they were subject to the Holy Office of the Inquisition if they did not fully renounce their faith. Hernando Alonso was the first Jewish martyr in Mexico, burned alive on October 17, 1528.[1]

The vast majority of Jews in colonial Mexico were able to avoid such severe penalties, and most at least outwardly evidenced some adherence to Catholicism in order to gain social and cultural acceptance. Mexican independence wrought little change for Mexican Jewry. Although the Inquisition ceased its work, in the nineteenth century a small Jewish community, centered in Mexico City, lived in a fervently Catholic society always suspicious of the "race" that rejected Jesus Christ (notwithstanding the fact that Jesus himself was a Jew). In the 1920s, immigration buttressed the size of the Jewish enclave, so that by the 1930s perhaps as many as thirty thousand resided in Mexico.

A particularly virulent anti-Semitism emerged in the Right as it thrived in the shadows of the rise of European fascism. The anti-Semitic pronouncements and policies of Nazi Germany fueled hatred around the globe. The literature of the Mexican right includes heavy doses of anti-Semitism, especially after mid-decade. Typical is the 1936 work of eccentric author and artist, Dr. Atl whose *Oro! Más Oro!* sought to explain to Mexicans the secret of world economics and the solution to economic depression. In a chapter entitled "From the Slopes of Mount Sinai to the U.S. Treasury," Dr. Atl charged that Jewish bankers created the U.S. Reserve bank system in order to horde the world's gold. The remedy to this Jew-generated depression, he held, was a dramatic rise in Mexican gold production, the worldwide shift back to the gold standard, and a general redistribution of the precious metal among the community of nations. Dr. Atl chided the Revolutionary regime for its failure to undertake such a program, outlining an ambitious exploration and mining scheme himself.[2]

The stereotype of greedy, rich Jewish bankers and moneylenders appeared frequently in the anti-Semitic newspaper *Omega*, which cast history as a series struggles against grand Jewish conspiracies. "The race of men that had assassi-nated Jesus Christ and his disciples," explained an *Omega* author in a 1938 editorial entitled simply "The Enemy," are above all else businessmen driven by a maddening "thirst for gold." Queen Isabella forced them to choose between the Bible and gold, and although Jews publicly embraced the Word of God, in private their cravings for money persisted. In a followup article, author Fran-cisco González Franco continued on the trail of world Jewry, contending that by the eighteenth century they had organized in secret Masonic societies. Through the Masons they came to dominate the nations, and in turn promoted liberalism, oppressed the poor, and shaped a world void of faith in God.[3]

Anti-Semitism was apparent in each of the three major topics that dominated rightist literature in the 1930s: the nature of communism, conditions in the Soviet Union, and the Spanish Civil War. Through much of the 1936–1938 period, Mexico's political culture hinged on the debate over the nature of communism and whether or not the Cárdenas government had put Mexico on the path to it. The position taken by the Right was obvious, stated effectively by Diego Arenas Guzmán in the pages of *El Hombre Libre*. Mexico, the editor wrote in March 1937, is slowly being turned into a "proletarian dictatorship," part of the Revolutionary government's plan to "sovietize" the country. He called on all sectors of society to organize against communism, especially through publications and pamphlets, and the formation of new groups and independent political parties.[4]

Among those answering the call was Acción Cívica Nacional, which published a series of seventeen tracts in 1937 concerning socialism and communism. Directed at a popular audience, these booklets usually ran about fifteen pages, explained concepts in simple terms, and sold for a maximum 10 centavos out of the ACN's offices in Mexico City. The first of the series was entitled simply "What Is Socialism and What Is Communism?", while subsequent works chronicled the dangers of these ideologies. In the third booklet, for example, the authors charged that socialism intends to destroy the family. It included an evocative subtitle of "Divorce and the Socialist School," positing that socialistic education undermines the authority of parents and priests, while sexual education corrupts the youth.[5]

Also responding to the call to combat communism with the pen was José Cantú Corro, a well-known religious orator in the 1930s. Born in Oaxaca in 1884, he was ordained a priest in 1907, and pursued writing with vigor after the Revolutionary upheaval of 1910–1920. Most of Cantú Corro's diverse works were nonpolitical material such as prayer books and devotionals, but the exigencies of the mid-1930s inspired him to publish pamphlets such as "El Comunismo," which sold for 15 centavos via a Mexico City address. "El Comunismo," which appeared under various titles, was a sixteen-page pamphlet that in fact attacked four ideologies which its author held hostile to Catholicism.[6] The first was liberalism, primarily an economic dogma that arose from the Enlightenment, preaching individual liberty and freedom from governmental tyranny. Cantú Corro advised his readers of its pitfalls: the exaggeration of the concept of liberty, the transformation of men into "hungry wolves" who fight each other for material gain, and the dangerous offshoots of Masonry, Protestantism, and "Jewish Capitalism." Next the cleric targeted socialism, charging that it turns people into units of production and consumption and undermines the family. "Society cannot exist without the family, which is its essential and organic component," he explained. Since marriage is central to the family, and since socialism is inimical to marriage because it promotes "free love" and communal loyalties, socialism is ultimately an enemy of society. Cantú Corro held that the idea of community based on something else besides the family was heresy. "What hell, worse than that of Dante, awaits the world if a society adopts these damning precepts!"[7]

The third ideology disparaged in the tract, though its author appears to have had some difficulty differentiating it from socialism, is communism. While communism replaces central government with administrative committees, like socialism it destroys family ties, "substitutes marriage with fleeting sexual unions, denies that fathers have rights over their children, and delivers these responsibilities into the hands of the State." Atheistic and "absurd," communism seeks to abolish borders and nations as well. It is similar to the final antireligious ideology, anarchism, also born of Marxism, which opposes all authority, family, laws, fatherland, private property, and the sacred faith.[8] José Cantú Corro, while a voracious critic of leftist theory, offered the readers of "El Comunismo" little insight on how to solve the world's inequities and social ills. He stated simply that Catholicism is the answer, since it is predicated in mutual help, caring, and generosity of spirit rather than the hate and vengeance that underlay class warfare. "Catholicism edifies," he explained, while "socialism destroys."

The best example of this destruction, according to the priest, was the Soviet Union, where Marxist dogma "has produced blood and tears, misery, hunger, and desolation." Because the state becomes master of the worker under Soviet-style socialism, it is the enemy of the worker. Even worse, Moscow has placed agents throughout the world, where they cause unrest in order to destroy civilization and allow for "a new society without God, home, or law." Jewish capitalists are aiding them in this quest. Similarly, ACN's series of tracts pointed to the nightmares of Soviet Russia. The "horrors" of Russian socialism received attention in one booklet, while another chronicled its failures, and a third focused on the cruel Soviet Cheka, or secret police.[9]

The attention Cantú Corro and ACN gave to the Soviet Union is not surprising. Central to the debate about communism was the nature of the Soviet state, which after the Bolshevik Revolution of 1917 had become a symbol of triumph for Marxists around the world. The Right attacked the Soviet model as a failed project, a brutal dictatorship that could not deliver meaningful improvements at home even while it continued to export revolution abroad. Its critics portrayed the Russian system as fundamentally opposed to democracy, church, and family; they frequently charged that Moscow was the inspiration behind the restlessness of Mexican labor and the leftist policies of Cárdenas. The extreme Right persecuted Soviet sympathizers. Gold Shirts, before their disbandment in August 1936, attempted to blow up a meeting of the PCM's Society of Friends of the Soviet Union with dynamite.[10]

Much of the Right's view of the Soviet system was expressed in the writings of former president Abelardo Rodríguez, who visited the country after leaving office and recorded his impressions in a short 1938 book entitled *Notas de mi viaje a Rusia*. Although he claimed the credibility of an "impartial" observer, and although many of his negative perceptions of the Stalinist regime were true, Rodríguez found reasons to defend capitalism and fear communism even before his trip. During the Maximato, by way of his association with Plutarco Calles, he had accumulated a small fortune in gambling enterprises, including race-tracks in Tijuana. He left the presidency a millionaire. Under Cárdenas many of Rodríguez's gambling houses were closed, alienating him from his successor.[11]

In Soviet Russia the ex-president uncovered a savage dictatorship under Joseph Stalin which rested on "oppression and slavery." The oppression was cloaked, he contended, by Stalin's brilliant demagoguery, and "insidious and constant propaganda" which convinced the Russian people that they lived "in an earthly paradise." Rodríguez saw little difference between Stalin, Mussolini, and Hitler, and in this conclusion he was, as history shows us, correct.

Notas de mi viaje a Rusia is far more fascinating, however, in its detail. The author evaluated the role of women in Soviet society, concluding them overworked as they performed upwards of 70 percent of the farm labor and comprised 40 percent of the industrial workforce. This exploitation of the weaker sex is called in

the Soviet tyranny, "the emancipation of the woman, the liberation of the woman from the fetters of the kitchen"! It is true that she must leave the home, the company of her family, her husband, her children; but only to be led to other cruel environments, to other even harder activities for which her sex and spiritual makeup are ill equipped.[12]

Russian women, he advised his readers, did not enjoy equal rights with men, but in fact faced harsher realities because they were denied the comforting presence of the home. The lack of nurturing mothers, in turn, had produced a sharp rise in the number of orphans and street children. Poor women, thirsting to be feminine again, fell to the temptations of sexy apparel and perfume, which yielded a "scandalous" increase in prostitution! In sum, Rodríguez posited, Soviet women were treated like beasts.[13]

The conclusions he drew outline by default the expectations many Mexicans had for women. First, they were to remain in the home, their natural habitat, where they can feel secure and fulfill their role as nurturers of children. Second, removing women from the safety of the home disrupts the very fabric of society: children degenerate to life on the streets without a mother's guiding hand, while husbands, presumably, suffer adverse effects. Women themselves long for the "comforts" of the home and turn to prostitution, a development for which, in Rodríguez's analysis, men bore no responsibility.

If the Soviet system ruined the family by taking women from the home, it crucified democracy by a culture of fraud and political oppression. With perhaps a mind toward Mexico's evolution under cardenismo, Abelardo Rodríguez charged that the Communist party was a political monopoly exercising supreme power through a huge state bureaucracy. Stalin, as absolute dictator, ignored his congress and the impotent president. Party vigilantes, local councils, and censors extended state authority into remote regions, while the Kremlin's candidates won fraudulent elections, the secret ballot and constitution notwithstanding.

A party of only 1.7 million members manipulated the entire country, in part, because of the skills of its seven hundred thousand Jews. According to Rodríguez, the Jews held key posts in finance and industry, "something not surprising, since their skills with money are known the world over." The consequence of all this was inflation (a timely observation given the inflationary cycle gripping Mexico during cardenismo): a kilo of coffee would cost Mexicans 55 pesos under similar conditions, leaving the readers of *Notas de mi viaje a Rusia* to conclude, as did its author, that all forms of communism and socialism have failed and that "democracy is the only hope for humanity."[14]

The anti-Semitism that marked Rodríguez's book appears in other rightist critiques of the Soviet Union. In addition to usurping democracy and displacing the family, Soviet communism assaulted the Christian faith and church. *El Hombre Libre* condemned Moscow's crusade against religion, carried out by Bolsheviks like "the Jew Yaroslavsky," who "clamors for a fight against the stupefacient religious populace," though their faith persists. Perhaps seeing a parallel to that of central Mexico's devout peasantry, the newspaper pointed gleefully to the failures of Soviet antireligion campaigns.[15]

The Soviet Union was a topic in the ideological debate made especially poignant by the Right's repeated charges that Moscow was orchestrating leftist activities in Mexico. The Partido Comunista Mexicana recovered in the late 1930s after suffering persecution during the Maximato, increasing its membership from around fifteen hundred to twenty thousand members between 1934 and 1938. Still, the party itself was paltry even at its zenith, able to influence Mexican society in only limited ways through its many front organizations.[16] Yet the Right implicated the Soviet government, by way of the PCM and its members, in labor activities in Mexico. Typical were the charges of *Ultimas Noticias*, which claimed in November 1938 that Moscow was behind infighting in the railroad unions. Railroad workers had a long tradition of belligerence and independent organizing, having paralyzed the nation in a 1929–1930 strike. They were divided, however, into different unions vying for power throughout the 1930s. According to *Ultimas Noticias*, which counted among its sources the secretary of Acción Femenina, the PCM was on the verge of gaining control of critical unions in order to make Moscow "master" of Mexico's railways. In truth, while communists comprised a healthy number of the members of the Sindicato de Trabajadores Ferrocarrileros de la República Mexicana, charges such as that of Mexico City's tabloid were fanciful at worst and exaggerated at best.[17]

Though some conservative mainstream papers like *Ultimas Noticias* cited rightist sources, which often compared and even attributed Mexico's problems and government policies to Moscow, much of the national press held to a more objective line. Hermosillo's *El Pueblo*, for example, rejected the Right's discourse on the dangers of socialism and communism, as well as its charges that national problems and policies were exogenous. On the contrary, *El Pueblo* found similarities between socialism and Christianity, and argued that cardenismo found its inspiration in Mexico's colonial past, in the utopian communities of Michoacán's Bishop Vasco de Quiroga. The Soviet Union was not "a communist island in a sea of capitalism," the paper charged, but rather "is a brutal Asiatic fascism."[18]

Another topic emphasized by the Right as well as the media in general was the Spanish Civil War, which became something of a national obsession as it unfolded in 1936 and raged through spring 1939. More than discussion of communism or Soviet Russia, events in Spain evoked deep emotions from Mexicans, in part because of the concomitant looming controversy over the immigration of Loyalist refugees. Spain had always held fascination for Mexicans, who viewed it as the "mother country" with a mixture of distrust and admiration.[19] In 1829 Mexico had expelled Spaniards from its soil in the wake of a bungled Spanish attempt to reconquer the former colony. And though economic and political ties between the two states were weak for the next century, the nature of events in 1930s Spain made it a natural subject on Mexico's own ideological battleground.

The background to the Spanish Civil War is essential in understanding its significance to Mexicans. In April 1931 Spaniards declared the Second Republic after King Alfonso XIII abdicated his throne. The Republican government, comprised of a coalition of liberals, socialists, labor leaders, and intellectuals, never rested on a tightly organized or ideologically unified foundation. Once in power, it undertook a series of reforms under Prime Minister Manuel Azaña. It attempted to weaken the church's role in both the state and society, distribute land to peasants, and promote secular education. These programs, undertaken in the lean years of worldwide depression, were accompanied by labor unrest in Spanish cities, as unions sought to make wage and benefits gains under a sympathetic government.

Much of the Spanish populace resisted the progressive Republican agenda and rallied around the stalwart opposition of the aristocracy, military, and church. The Fascist party, or Falange headed by General Francisco Franco, attracted devout Catholics and rightists aspiring to establish a corporate state like that of Mussolini's Italy. The Azaña government frequently played into Franco's hands by moving too fast in implementing policies that offended much of the populace in rural and conservative regions of Spain. When Article 3 of the 1931 Republican Constitution separated church and state, it and subsequent anticlerical measures such as removing crucifixes from schools "clashed with the sensibilities of the majority of Spaniards, for whom the church had continued to be equal to the state, with or without a monarchy."[20] The new government thus seemed unpatriotic. Azaña himself only aggravated tensions by proclaiming that Spain "has ceased to be Catholic." In 1936, amidst increasing ideological polarization, Spaniards elected a Popular Front government with a broader base of support. Efforts at compromise came too late, however. Army garrisons in Morocco revolted under Franco in July, triggering one of history's bloodiest civil wars.

For the Mexican Right, then, the parallels were frightening. Like Mexicans under cardenismo, Spaniards in the mid-1930s had endured waves of strikes, agrarian reform, socialistic education, and state attacks on the influence and status of the church. Only in the fact that Mexico had a long tradition of anticlericalism did the general historical contours differ. The result of these policies in Spain was civil war; could Mexico expect anything different? As the American consul general advised his superiors in Washington in 1936:

The very keenest interest is displayed in Mexico in the Spanish revolution. Many profess to believe that its results may profoundly affect Mexico, bringing about a similar conflict here; that it has already served to establish a clearer alignment of radical and conservative forces in the country; that it will help to encourage by suggestion the resort to violence . . . in part due to the definitely leftist policy of the government.[21]

The Right was drawn to a defense of the Spanish Falange for other reasons besides its natural ideological sympathies and the desire to avoid the perceived threat of civil war. The Mexican Revolution unleashed renewed anti-Hispanicism, in part via the government's support of artists who spearheaded *indigenismo*, the cultural glorification of Mexico's pre-Hispanic past. Muralists such as Diego Rivera and David Siqueiros portrayed Spaniards such as conquistador Hernán Cortés as cruel and greedy men with apelike features and physical deformities. In its opposition to the regime, then, coupled with a natural tendency to glorify Mexico's colonial past, the Right had added incentive to support Franco's counterrevolution.[22]

By 1936 Mexican sentiments regarding events in Spain were divided along ideological lines. Most intellectuals, as well as organized labor, supported the Republic; urban middle classes, elites, and devout Catholic peasants favored the Nationalists under Franco. Organizationally, the UNVR was decidedly pro-Franco, holding celebrations upon news of fascist victories. It worked in harmony with the Asociación Española Anti-Comunista y Anti-Judía [AEACAJ], a small group in Mexico City led by engineer and Spanish citizen Francisco Cayón y Cos. The AEACAJ drew nearly all of its membership from the Spanish community, which had reemerged in Mexico City gradually since the Porfiriato. Most of the fifty thousand Spaniards comprising the enclave were well-to-do, conservative, and at least sympathetic to Franco.[23] Yet despite having the strongest ties to Spain, the Spanish colony did not engage in as much political activism as might be expected. The AEACAJ did publish a small newsletter, *Vida Española*, from May 1937 to April 1938, but it suffered financial problems and limited interest. Cayón y Cos wrote Franco, claiming that 90 percent of the Spanish colony supported him, and explained the lack of more activities on interference by the Cárdenas government and the Spanish embassy.[24]

The Mexican Right uniformly held the Spanish Republic in disdain by the time the Falange incited rebellion in 1936. Like much of the world, it equated the Republican government with communism, even though the Spanish Communist Party had only limited political clout even during the civil war. And as evidenced in the name of the AEACAJ, rightists targeted Jews as part of the communist conspiracy at work in Madrid. *El Hombre Libre*, for example, explained to its readership in April 1937 that the real powers behind the Loyalist regime were Russian Jews, anarcho-syndicalists, and communists, "who control the 'nincompoop' Manuel Azaña." *Omega* also contended that Jews dominated Republicanism and that the cause faltered because the "only interests important to them are their own property and that of their race."[25]

Also leading the Right's assault on the Loyalist regime was José Vasconcelos, who had exiled himself in Spain after the 1929 election debacle and knew the country firsthand. In a featured article published in *El Hombre Libre*, Vasconcelos, who by 1936 was well on his way toward embracing the basic tenets of fascism, attempted to undermine worker enthusiasm for the Left. Communists, he argued, cloak their true intentions in united frontism, but once they triumph they devour their petit-bourgeois and labor allies. Real communism destroys unions and oppresses workers by keeping them subservient to the state, which is controlled by selfish Marxist intellectuals. Only in democracies are workers allowed to organize, strike, and collectively bargain with management, he explained, while Moscow continues to subvert such freedoms in France, Spain, and Mexico by using the "fascist illusion" to frighten workers into popular frontism.[26]

Resting largely on worker support, it is no surprise that the Cárdenas government backed the Republican regime with enthusiasm. Cárdenas himself attributed his policy to "ideological solidarity," believing that Spain was the key to stopping fascism and avoiding a second world war. He was amused and annoyed by the attacks in *El Hombre Libre*. When he read an article asking whether or not the government was sending arms to Republican Spain, he recorded in his diary "yes we are, *tonto*, we are selling them everything we have!" Events in Spain captivated the president, like the nation, and frequently became topics of conversation with his guests.[27]

The problem for Madrid was that Mexico had only a limited number of weapons to sell. The first arms shipment left Mexico in August 1936, and small caches continued into 1937. The Right, predictably, condemned the shipments when they became public knowledge in early 1937. It "impedes the ability of the Spanish people to resolve their own conflicts," *El Hombre Libre* roared, noting that other states and the League of Nations honored an arms embargo, even though they arguably had more to win or lose with the Spanish outcome than Mexico. The United States subsequently amended its neutrality law to prohibit arms shipments to Spain via third parties, and exerted pressure on Mexico to cooperate, undercutting the Cárdenas government's plans to ship more substantial aid including eighteen airplanes.[28]

Like his policies in general, Cárdenas's foreign policy won "only limited approval" from the Mexican populace. Most Mexicans rejected it. Government Loyalist sympathies particularly angered the devout Catholic peasantry in the Bajío. Vicente Lombardo Toledano advised the president in November 1937 that constitution anniversary celebrations in Querétaro were interrupted by rural "fascists" yelling "Viva Franco!" The laity were ahead of the church hierarchy, however, which remained largely silent on events in Spain as part of its continuing search for accommodation with the Revolutionary regime. Clerics squelched their strong convictions, for the most part, even after receiving a July 1937 letter from their Spanish counterparts which criticized the Republican government and attributed the war to "irreconcilable ideologies."[29]

As if the emotional divisions over aid and the war were not enough, the Cárdenas administration encountered a storm of protest with its refugee policy. Mexico became a haven for Loyalists seeking asylum; a trickle entered the country during the civil war, and a flood poured in afterwards. From the start, the Right decried the government's open door policy on ideological grounds and out of a sense of nationalism. The first refugees, however, made the rightist critique difficult: they were orphans. In June 1937 the Cárdenas government welcomed five hundred Spanish children to Mexico amidst considerable public attention. Declining offers to put the orphans (mostly of Loyalist parents) up for adoption, the president sent them to a school in Morelia, the capital of his native state. Teachers at the school were to educate the children in socialism and the principles for which their parents had fought and died.[30]

How could the Right, with its pronounced commitment to protecting the family from a "godless and communistic" Revolutionary establishment, condemn the feeding and clothing of orphans? The manner in which the president himself took an interest in the children further complicated matters. Cárdenas greeted the little ones and posed with them for photographs widely circulated in the press, making the very man the Right condemned as anti-God and anti-family appear compassionate and fatherly. Even in an age free of the excesses of political imaging and "spin," in all probability this was the intention of government—and it testifies to the importance of the political Right and the need of the Revolutionary establishment to defend itself on the same terms, that of saving the family.

The Right struggled to respond to this government public relations coup. Unable to condemn the succoring of orphans, it attacked the policy on tangential grounds. The Confederación de la Clase Media commended the government aid, but called for placing the children in homes and decried as shameful "that these orphans of the war are to be educated and prepared for communism" in Mexico. *El Hombre Libre* asked its readers if the new arrivals were, in truth, victims of the Azaña government. It denied that all of the children were even orphans, as the government claimed, and criticized their upkeep "when there are millions of Mexican children dying of hunger and abandonment." It joined the CCM in condemning leftist "indoctrination," noting that the Spanish colony had offered to care for the orphans to no avail. Thus the Right attempted to turn them into victims of Mexico's Revolutionary government! *El Hombre Libre* noted theatrically that the brainwashing began on arrival, when bands played "The International" to the little ones as authorities placed them on a government train.[31]

After the orphans arrived, other Spanish immigrants followed. In early 1938, with the help of Daniel Cosío Villegas, Mexico's ambassador to Portugal, the government arranged to rescue Spanish intellectuals from the civil war and establish them in the Casa de España, a scholarly commune that sponsored their work. These leftist scholars were integral in formulating Hispano-Americanism, a movement which reasserted the cultural unity of Spain and Latin America, and served as a counterpoint to Franco's Hispanism, or glorification of the Spanish heritage. Later, the Casa evolved into the Colegio de México.

In 1939 larger numbers of refugees began to arrive. In January, Franco's Nationalists launched a final offensive in the Loyalist stronghold of Catalonia, driving a half million refugees into France and dooming the government. Surrender came on April 1, as tens of thousands of additional refugees fled Spain in search of the safety of asylum. Cárdenas, sympathetic to their plight, appointed the controversial former education secretary, Narciso Bassols, to oversee the refugee selection process. The Right—alarmed by the role of their old nemesis, who had so vigorously promoted socialist education—joined much of the conservative mainstream press in rousing Mexicans to the dangers of "communist refugees" who would dabble in politics and steal jobs.[32]

With the arrival of the first shipload of sixteen hundred refugees in June, the fears of the opposition appeared justified. The immigrants exchanged greetings with government officials that included the raised clenched fist—the symbol of the Loyalists, but misinterpreted in the press as the sign of international communist solidarity. Yet tensions stilled as the Spaniards quietly assimilated into Mexico, a transition aided by a maturing *indigenismo* that had weakened anti-Hispanicism and support from the ideologically compatible sectors of the populace. And although, to the chagrin of the right, Cárdenas's successor would continue to admit Spanish refugees until 1945 (by which time they totaled twenty-five thousand), the massive influx that most Mexicans feared in 1939 never unfolded.[33]

Spain was, of course, not the only country generating refugees in the mid-1930s. Though much less numerous, some persons fleeing the growing horrors of Adolph Hitler's Nazi Germany also sought asylum in Mexico. *Ultimas Noticias* warned that the country could become the destination of enormous numbers of German and Austrian Jews, undoubtedly an ominous observation to the anti-Semitic Right. Though no large numbers of German refugees arrived, the Cárdenas government did frequently admit individuals from the United States who faced deportation back to Germany. Such was the case of Otto Richter, a communist who had left the Nazi state in 1936. Richter had been beaten by Brown Shirt thugs on the night of the Reichstag fire before fleeing to the United States, which, to his dismay, arranged to return him to the Nazis. A communist organization in New York City named the American Committee for the Protection of Foreign Born defended Richter, organizing protests and coordinating a massive letter writing campaign to President Franklin D. Roosevelt on his behalf. Richter, in the midst of a hunger strike that forced authorities to hospitalize him, received permission to migrate to Mexico. He was one of dozens of leftists whom New York communists routed to Mexico—spared from certain death in Germany.

Ironically, of all the refugees entering Mexico in the 1930s, the one that created the most stir came not from the dangers of fascist Europe, but from Soviet Russia. Leon Trotsky received asylum from the Cárdenas government in December 1936, and arrived one month later. One of the principal intellectual architects of the Bolshevik Revolution, Trotsky had lost a power struggle with his rival, the megalomaniac Stalin, who charged him with treason and plotted his murder. Though he abided by the conditions of his entry, Trotsky aroused the animosity of the Right, which called for his expulsion. He became a symbol to the Right of just how far left Mexico was moving; *El Hombre Libre* charged that he was engaging in political activities designed to ensnare the nation in communism. The Right could find solace, however, in the hostility that Trotsky encountered from segments of the Mexican Left. His presence spawned discord in progressive circles: labor leader Vicente Lombardo Toledano opposed Cárdenas's asylum decision, and the PCM, following the Stalinist line, viewed the move as a "provocation."[34]

The arrival of foreigners as refugees in Mexico highlighted the global dimensions of the issues that had polemicized the nation. Cardenismo coincided with an ideological crisis in the western world, driven by economic depression and the rise of fascism and communism, that challenged the supremacy of capitalist, democratic, and Christian civilization. The topics of rightist literature—the nature of communism, conditions in the Soviet Union, and the Spanish Civil War—implicitly spoke to the question of whether or not Mexico was crossing over from capitalism to communism and from Christianity to secularism. Usually, in its critique, the Right also explicitly raised the question and answered it in the affirmative. It was able to fuel a general sense of alarm among much of the populace, especially via debate with cardenismo over events in Spain, which captivated Mexicans and "helped define domestic alignments during the approach to the 1940 election."[35]

In combating the Right on this and other issues, Cárdenas was forced to incorporate rhetoric about saving the family into his political discourse, as when his government rescued orphans from the Spanish Civil War. The preservation of the family, in fact, was a primary theme in the Right's literary attack on communism and cardenismo. A wide range of publications, from popular books such as Abelardo Rodríguez's *Notas de mi viaje a Rusia* to party manifestos and *El Hombre Libre*, charged that the Left's agenda fundamentally undermined the home. Women, losing their femininity, would abandon their children; men, reduced to economic slaves of the state, were destined for lives of misery and a lapse of faith that led to eternity in hell. The Right reaped a rich harvest after sowing these seeds of fear among Mexicans. It was so effective that as early as September 1937 the Chamber of Deputies called for the disbanding of rightist groups because of their success at confusing and alarming the general public.[36]

NOTES

1. Seymour Liebman, *The Jews in New Spain: Faith, Flame, and the Inquisition* (Coral Gables: University of Miami Press, 1970), pp. 31–33, 113. Few Jews suffered death, and persecution by the Inquisition often involved sociopolitical motives, as explained in the scholarship of Richard Greenleaf.

2. Dr. Atl, *Oro! mas oro: El mundo lo necesita mejico puede darselo* (Mexico City: Ediciones Botas, 1936), pp. 49–53, 65–67, 167–73.

3. M. Siurot, "El Enemigo," *Omega*, March 5, 1938; Francisco González Franco, "El verdadero aspecto del problema," *Omega*, March 24, 1938.

4. Arenas Guzmán, "Medios eficaces para combatir comunismo," *El Hombre Libre*, March 1, 1937.

5. Acción Cívica Nacional, "Serie de folletos sobre el socialismo y el communismo ante el sentido común," 1937, Index of descriptions of booklets, available at Biblioteca Nacional, UNAM, Mexico City.

6. *Diccionario Porrúa*, vol. 1, p. 483. The most complete title of the pamphlet was "¿Qué es el Liberalismo? ¿Qué es el Socialismo? ¿Qué es el Comunismo? ¿Qué es el Anarquismo?" (Mexico City, 1937).

7. Cantú Corro, "El Comunismo," pp. 1–9.

8. Cantú Corro, "El Comunismo," pp. 12–14.

9. Cantú Corro, "El Comunismo," pp. 9–11, 13; ACN, "Serie de folletos," 1937.

10. Gonzalo Camacho, secretary general of the Sociedad de Amigos de la URSS, to Cárdenas, March 29, 1936, AGN, FLC, 606.3/20.2.

11. Abelardo Rodríguez, *Notas de mi viaje a Rusia* (Mexico City: Editorial Cultura, 1938), p. 9; Lieuwen, *Mexican Militarism*, p. 115.

12. Rodríguez, *Notas de mi viaje*, pp. 10–11, 22–23.

13. Rodríguez, *Notas de mi viaje*, pp. 23–27.

14. Rodríguez, *Notas de mi viaje*, pp. 83–86, 89, 93–94.

15. Dr. N. Salisniak, "Fallas de la acción ateísta en Rusia," *El Hombre Libre*, June 7, 1937.

16. Barry Carr, *Marxism and Communism in Twentieth-Century Mexico* (Lincoln: University of Nebraska Press, 1992), pp. 46, 53. Carr's work is the best source on the PCM and its activities in the 1930s.

17. "Moscú prepara la siembra de células en los ferrocarriles nacionales de México," *Ultimas Noticias*, November 2, 1938; "Está en manos de células de Stalin la Federación de empleados dícese," *Ultimas Noticias*, November 3, 1938; regarding railroad workers, see Meyer, *El conflicto social*, pp. 131–37; Carr, *Marxism and Communism*, p. 76.

18. "Cristianismo y socialismo," *El Pueblo*, March 20, 1936; "El gobierno obrero y campesino de la Rusia Soviética," *El Pueblo*, March 26, 1936.

19. González, *Días del presidente*, p. 129.

20. For background to the Spanish Civil War, see Hugh Thomas, *The Spanish Civil War* (New York: Harper & Row, 1961); Patricia Fagen, *Exiles and Citizens: Spanish Republicans in Mexico* (Austin: University of Texas Press, 1973), pp. 7, 11; Ascensión H. de León-Portilla, *España desde México: Vida y testimonio de transterrados* (Mexico City: Universidad Nacional Autónoma de México, 1978), pp. 31, 41–43.

21. "Monthly Report," Thomas Bowman, American consul general to SS, September 1, 1936, p. 7, USDS 812.00/30405. The fallacy in the argument that leftist policies led to the Spanish Civil War is, of course, that the Falange began the bloodletting.

22. T. G. Powell, *Mexico and the Spanish Civil War* (Albuquerque: University of New Mexico Press, 1981), pp. 28, 33–35. The Right did not uniformly reject the Spanish Republic at first: some of its voices, including José Vasconcelos and *El Hombre Libre*, praised the regime's democratic features in the 1931–1934 period at a time when they hoped for fair elections in Mexico. See same source, pp. 42–45.

23. González, *Días del presidente*, pp. 130–31; Fernández Boyolí and Marrón de Angelis, *Lo que no se sabe*, pp. 22–23; Powell, *Spanish Civil War*, pp. 26–27.

24. Cayón y Cos to Franco, May 3, 1937, and Cayón y Cos to Cardenal Segura, both in Fernández Boyolí and Marrón de Angelis, *Lo que no se sabe*, pp. 233–38.

25. León-Portilla, *España desde México*, pp. 52–53; "Homenaje al Generalisimo Francisco Franco," *El Hombre Libre*, April 19, 1937. The primary reasons many observers equated the Loyalist government with communism was Soviet support for the regime. "El régimen comunista de Barcelona exhibe su brutal tirania antipatriótica," *Omega*, February 17, 1938.

26. José Vasconcelos, "Las metamórfosis del comunismo y la revolución española," *El Hombre Libre*, November 2, 1936.

27. Cárdenas, *Apuntes*, vol. 1, pp. 366, 370–72. Cárdenas edited his diary before its publication long after his term in office, and may have tampered with these entries, given his forward-looking argument of stopping fascism to avoid world war.

28. León-Portilla, *España desde México*, p. 76; "La intervención de México en la guerra de España," *El Hombre Libre*, April 14, 1937.

29. Powell, *Spanish Civil War*, pp. 104, 110; Lombardo Toledano to Cárdenas, November 23, 1937, telegram, AGN, FLC, 551/14.2.41; Negrete, *Relaciones en México*, p. 216.

30. Fagen, *Exiles and Citizens*, p. 26. The best source on the school itself is Vera Foulkes, *Los "niños de Morelia" y la escuela España-México: Consideraciones analíticas sobra un experimento social* (Mexico City: Universidad Nacional Autónoma de México, 1953).

31. "La Confederación de la Clase Media y los huérfanos españoles," *El Hombre Libre*, March 15, 1937; "Son víctimas del gobierno de Azaña los pequeños llegados a México?" *El Hombre Libre*, June 11, 1937.

32. Fagen, *Exiles and Citizens*, pp. 27–28, 42–44, 149–50; "El comunismo y la guerra de España," *El Universal*, May 19, 1939. Bassols and muralist David Siqueiros led a protest against Mexico's antirefugee conservative press; see Powell, *Spanish Civil War*, p. 147.

33. Fagen, *Exiles and Citizens*, pp. 48–50; León-Portilla, *España desde México*, pp. 83, 93–94. While Fagen is the best source for information about the arrival of the refugees, see the sixteen interviews in *España desde México* for the long-term consequences.

34. "Los Nazis traen Judíos a México," *Ultimas Notícias*, November 4, 1938; Guadalupe Pacheco Méndez, Arturo Anguiano Orozco, and Rogelio Vizcaíno, *Cárdenas y la izquierda mexicana: Ensayo, testimonios, documentos*, 2nd ed. (Mexico City: Juan Pablos Editor, 1984), pp. 59–61; "La agitación comunista es repudiada en Zacatecas," *El Hombre Libre*, April 7, 1937.

35. Alan Knight, "The Rise and Fall of Cardenismo, c. 1930–c. 1946," in Bethell, ed., *Mexico since Independence*, p. 285.

36. Negrete, *Relaciones en México*, p. 215.

7

A BURGEONING OPPOSITION

"Nineteen-thirty-nine witnessed a surprising increase, without precedent, of opposition to the Mexican government."[1] Hostility toward the Cárdenas regime, evident since 1935, reached new heights at the end of the decade, in the wake of the Right's ideological offensive and in anticipation of the 1940 presidential campaign. Public euphoria over the oil expropriation, cardenismo's brief moment of popular triumph, quickly receded as the Right continued to define many of the parameters of debate in the broader political culture. The oil crisis, in fact, gave renewed impetus to opposition unity and its determination to halt the progressive agenda.

Discontent festered in multiple segments of Mexican society such as the central plateau's devout Catholic peasantry, but it soared among the middle classes. Comprising roughly 15 percent of the populace, these ill-defined sectors included two million small landowners, politicized in the midst of cardenismo by the perceived threat of continued agrarian reform. Urban components, which had demonstrated their dislike for the Revolutionary establishment by backing Vasconcelos in 1929, were even more hostile a decade later, roused by the Right's ideological attacks on the Cárdenas government as a communistic threat to family, free enterprise, and democracy. A U.S. newspaper contended in May 1939 that, "for the first time in history, the middle class in Mexico is organizing politically." Observers Nathaniel and Sylvia Weyl recorded in 1939 that the "middle class has moved from neutrality to definite hostility toward the Cárdenas program," posing a serious threat to the regime.[2]

Helping fuel the discontent among urban middle sectors in particular, as well as society in general, were economic problems. Inflation took hold in Mexico during the *sexenio*. The retail price index rose 38 percent, with food costs leading the way, spiraling by forty percent between 1936 and 1940. Rising prices discouraged investment and prompted some capital flight, and while, for the most part, unionized labor stayed ahead of the increases by wage gains, middle-class Mexicans suffered. Government supporters attributed the economic problems to capitalists seeking to discredit the regime. The Right, however, blamed Cárdenas's policies, such as agrarian reform and the oil expropriation, for the economic woes. The rightist news magazine *La Reacción* linked drops in food production (and subsequent inflation) to the inefficiency of the *ejidos* and the corruption of the Banco Ejidal.[3] Reflecting the popular discontent with the government was a disdain among many Mexicans for Lázaro Cárdenas himself. Some referred to him as *trompa chula*, a vulgar reference to his large and unseemly lips. Middle-class ranchers and businessmen in northern Sonora circulated a scathing poem about the president:

Siervo de los rusos, patrón de extranjeros,
que a los mexicanos has dejado en cueros
como una consecuencia de tu obstinación
que es madre y señora de tu entendimiento.
Por que es muy difícil que pueda un jumento
aceptar alguna rectificación.

Confórmate, hermano, con volver a Uruapán,
piensa que a los brutos de cierto los matan,
y si has de hacer algo en nuestro favor,
una cosa puedes de qué estar ufano,
córtale las uñas a tu ilustre hermano,
Lombardo Toledano.[4]

This poem, in the form of a short prayer, ended with the plea "have mercy on us, Lord." Its religious format is significant, reflecting the association of the regime with the anticlericalism that so many Mexicans of all classes rejected. It was also a chain letter, with closing instructions to its readers to "make ten copies and give them to your friends, knowing that if you break the chain you will be punished by the growth of your own lips and the turning of your head to stone."

The closing line attacking Vicente Lombardo Toledano is also noteworthy, for if anyone was more despised by millions of Mexicans than Cárdenas, it was the leader of the CTM. By the close of the *sexenio* Lombardo attracted so much of the ire of the Right that an uninformed observer would have thought him the most powerful man in Mexico. In truth, his efforts at developing worker consciousness fell far short of his own goals, and economic problems facing middle-class Mexicans could hardly be blamed on him. Yet the Right had made him its perennial whipping boy. *Omega* charged in 1938 that he was plotting to arm workers in order to establish a dictatorship, and blamed him for the government's support of Spanish Loyalists. The Right also began to promote the idea that Lombardo was an agent of Moscow. His "loyalty is to the sadistic Georgian" Joseph Stalin, *Omega* reported.[5] By 1939 he was the target of attacks not only from the Right, but in congress, military circles, and the mainstream press. Only CTM locals and agrarian committees came to his defense. One supporter complained in a telegram to Cárdenas that "the UNVR was attacking Lombardo all the time," while a union local in Veracruz urged the president to shut down *La Prensa*, *El Universal*, and *Novedades* in retaliation for their constant criticism of him. Senator Ezequiel Padilla, an old Calles loyalist, led a fight in congress to condemn the CTM, while a small group in Mexico City named the Federación Campesina y Obrera organized street protests against "the dictator, Lombardo Toledano."[6]

Much of the furor of the attacks on the labor leader, which transcended the narrower boundaries of the Right and engulfed a large segment of Mexican society, was fueled by suspicions—planted by the Right—that he was a closet communist. As such, he became a focal point of the ongoing ideological debate over communism in Mexico. Some Mexicans also thought him the real power behind the president. Fraudulent documents indicted Lombardo, such as a purported June 1938 "Report from Paris to the CTM Directors," apparently manufactured by critics. This two-page memorandum, ostensibly authored by him, called for war between the totalitarian states and the west, made frequent reference to "Jefe Stalin," and offered disturbing evidence of communist plots. "People may soon understand that the expropriation is a fraud," it explained, revealing that the true intent of the takeover was to ensnare Mexico in communist conspiracies. Despite this danger, conditions are favorable "because of the manageability of Cárdenas," an alliance with John L. Lewis's Congress of Industrial Organizations in the United States, and Franklin Roosevelt's continued cooperation with "our plans."

In the United States, as in Mexico, the great majority of the people are conservative and hate us because of unemployment and hunger. Lewis reported to Jefe Stalin that, besides, the CIO, he has under his control . . . more than three million unemployed, capable of paralyzing the country and transforming a world war into a civil war.[7]

Although the extent of this anti-Lombardo scam is unknown, another scurrilous report circulated among the highest officials of Mexico City's police department. In fall 1940 General José Manuel Núñez, the chief of police, spread rumors with other officers and government officials that eight secret Soviet agents had arrived in Mexico to carry out assassinations upon Lombardo's orders. The labor leader, interestingly, felt a need to rush a note to the president assuring him that the rumors were nonsense.[8]

There was no basis of fact for the popular belief that Lombardo was a communist operative. He drafted a new Six Year Plan in 1939 which reflected his Marxism and alarmed conservatives, but the document was subject to PRM approval, preserved private property, and was hardly the blueprint for communist dictatorship that critics like Manuel Pérez Treviño charged. Its author was not a Communist party member, nor did the PCM cooperate closely with the Cárdenas government. Persuading Mexicans of this was difficult, however, because Lombardo had visited Moscow and mingled with leading Comintern members.[9] Further, in 1939 the Revolutionary establishment blocked the Right's efforts in the Chamber of Deputies to outlaw the PCM. These measures, introduced in September, coincided with the Soviet Union's attack on Poland and the revelation of a Communist-Nazi alliance. Conservative deputies led by Ramón Iturbe and Miguel Flores Villar urged the disbanding of the PCM and the expulsion of its leader, Hernán Laborde, appealing to Mexican nationalism by charging the party was illegal as an organ of foreign control and "exotic doctrine."[10]

Not only did Cárdenas prevent the disbanding of the PCM, but he used the Chamber of Deputies in the fall of 1939 to pass legislation deeply antagonistic to the Right. The president and his secretary of education, Gonzalo Vázquez Vela, reopened still sensitive wounds over socialistic education by codifying it into Federal law, thus taking control of schools from the states. The centralization made a uniform socialist education system possible, a step viewed with suspicion by its opponents.

Despite Vázquez Vela's conciliatory gestures (in sharp contrast to the confrontational style of his predecessor, Narciso Bassols), the Right reacted to the law with hostility. Pedro Gringoire editorialized in *Excelsior*, for example, against the "seven sins" of socialistic education, including the oft-repeated charge that the state monopoly weakened the family by removing parents from the learning process. He contended that Revolutionary heroes rejected Marxism and would have rejected socialist education—making it anti-Mexican. *Jus*, a conservative news journal, attacked from a different angle, criticizing the program for neglecting the latest trends in education theory such as child liberty programs promoted by John Dewey and Maria Montessori. PAN, *Jus*, and the Unión Nacional de Padres de Familia, an organization revived by new controversy since its anti-Bassols days, feared state omnipotence, which the UNPF viewed "as part of a leftist effort to destroy the family and the morality of Mexican society."[11] A December 17 rally in the Zócalo featured PAN leader Manuel Gómez Morín, five hours of speeches, and chants of "down with communism" and "viva México."

The powerful assault on the federalization efforts had some effect, causing the administration to jettison the most radical features of the original draft, such as anticlerical passages and stiff penalties for unauthorized teaching. As John Britton, a leading authority on the topic, explains:

The preamble of the legislation reflected the moderate position of the Cárdenas government on education at the end of the 1930s. The first goal of education was "to consolidate national unity." The state did not exclude "private cooperation" under government supervision as a means of expanding education, an attitude very different from the aggressive anticlericalism of Bassols.[12]

If the Right was having some effect on the government by inspiring a softening of its education policy, a similar effect was taking hold in the ranks of the official party as it geared up for the 1940 elections. The reorganized PRM confronted the growing challenge of the Right as cardenismo polarized the Mexican body politic and drove an alienated majority into its ranks. The only solution to this dilemma, especially necessary if the PRM intended to conduct clean elections, was to move to the right itself.

The pre-candidates who aspired for the PRM's nomination understood the political ramifications of the surge of the Right. They undoubtedly took note of the quick demise of the early pre-candidacy of Luis Rodríguez, a leftist closely associated with Cárdenas who had served as presidential secretary and ambassador to the United States during the oil crisis. By early 1939 three men jockeyed for position within the PRM: Rafael Sánchez Tapia, Manuel Avila Camacho, and Francisco Múgica, representing the right, center, and left wings of the party respectively. Sánchez Tapia, former governor of Michoacán, had the least formidable political record and the added disadvantage of being too conservative to receive Cárdenas's blessing. His pre-candidacy soon faltered within the party structure, driving him into the ranks of the opposition. By spring 1939 the race for the nomination centered on the two remaining contenders.

If cardenismo had emerged victorious in the struggle for Mexican "hearts and minds" during the *sexenio*, there can be little doubt that the Revolution would have continued under Francisco Múgica. A committed reformer and close friend of Cárdenas, Múgica was a compassionate man whose background suggested that he was even farther to the left than the president. Born in poverty and obscurity, he rose within the Revolutionary ranks to lead the radical Jacobins at the 1917 constitutional convention, putting in place the legal mechanisms for far-reaching social reforms. On the outside of the Sonoran clique, he owed the rise in his political fortunes during the 1930s to Cárdenas, who arranged his appointment as superintendent of the Islas Tres Marías penal colony during the Maximato, then brought him into his cabinet as secretary of communications and transportation. Múgica worked tirelessly in his post, promoting the causes of labor unions, Loyalist Spain, and woman's suffrage. On the forefront of the debate over refugees, he persuaded Cárdenas to grant Trotsky asylum.[13]

It is a persuasive testimony to the strength of the Right that, in his early 1939 bid to become the PRM's nominee, Múgica cloaked his radicalism. In a February advertisement in *El Universal*, the pre-candidate struggled to allay the fears of his opponents. Promising to balance the needs of capital and labor, respect private property, and preserve freedom of religion and the press, he addressed charges that he was a communist in blunt terms:

Never have I been affiliated with the [Communist] Party. This is not to say that I am an enemy of the communists; the word does not scare me, like so many other revolutionaries, since Article 123 of our constitution is hardly a plan designed by Marx. This article was drafted by me and other revolutionaries before such ideas were ever known as "communism."[14]

These words reflect an attempt by Múgica to adopt to the dominant beliefs in the political culture: the interpretation of the Mexican Revolution as a positive experience and the disparagement of communism in the wake of the 1937–1938 ideological debates.

Múgica's efforts to move to the right and capture the nomination were undercut by the successes of the moderate, Secretary of War Avila Camacho. Popular with politicians and the army, he became the party favorite long before the November 1939 convention recognized him as its candidate. Cárdenas, whose personal power was waning, could probably not have imposed his choice on the PRM even if he had wanted to do so. This is not to say that Avila Camacho did not have to overcome some handicaps. In comparison to Múgica, his Revolutionary credentials left few Mexicans in awe. Dubbed "the unknown soldier" by his critics, he had risen to the rank of *divisionario* by 1929 without serious combat experience. As the military zone commander of Colima in the late 1920s, he exercised restraint in his campaigns against the Cristeros, rising to the cabinet post of subsecretary of war during the Maximato, then secretary under Cárdenas.

Within party ranks, some connections favored Avila Camacho. His influential brother, Maximino, had served as governor of Puebla and recruited support from among his counterparts. Manuel's popularity among the PRM's military contingent increased the odds against a *cuartelazo*, which many Mexicans feared and expected. Most surprising was the added endorsement of Lombardo and the CTM, motivated in part by the pro-Stalinist labor leader's resentment of Múgica's role in winning asylum for Trotsky. Cárdenas appreciated his potential as a candidate of national unity at a time of international crisis.[15]

Yet despite the momentum within the party for Avila Camacho, until late spring 1939 it was badly divided, with many leaders fearing open schism and massive defections to the opposition. Conservatives from inside and outside of the party vigorously attacked the PRM's left wing, led by Lombardo and party president Luis Rodríguez, which may have helped convince some moderates to back Avila Camacho. The two men had shared the podium at a November 1938 ceremony celebrating the anniversary of the Revolution, where they praised the PRM's progressive agenda and cooperation with the PCM. Veterans, in particular, were outraged. The next month, some rightist veterans were expelled from the party. Tensions persisted until Rodríguez resigned in May 1939, and unity revived under new party president Heriberto Jara.[16]

NEW OPPOSITION PARTIES AND
ATTACKS ON CARDENISMO

As the PRM settled on its presidential candidate in 1939, the Right mobilized through a series of new political groups, signaling the start of its own presidential campaign. These new parties, usually centered around an important opposition figure, employed the rhetoric of the previous ideological debates in order to attack the Cárdenas government and rally conservative forces to their cause. Most of these organizations were small, having little impact until they coalesced around the candidacy of Almazán in mid-1939. Comparisons of the lists of their founding members reveal many duplicate names, and quite a number of the agitators had held previous or concurrent membership in the UNVR.[17] Five organizations warrant attention, though only two of these—the Partido Acción Nacional [PAN] and the Partido Revolucionario Anti-Comunista [PRAC]—had lasting national significance.

The first new opposition party was the Frente Constitucional Democrático Mexicano [FCDM], founded by Ramón F. Iturbe, who served as its president. Born in Mazatlán of "obscure and humble origins," Iturbe attended a Catholic school before studying engineering in the United States. He fought in the Revolution under Carranza, served as governor of Sinaloa from 1917 to 1920, then temporarily made peace with Obregón until his participation in the Adolfo de la Huerta rebellion. Forced into exile for his disloyalty, Iturbe returned to Mexico in time to participate in the Escobar rebellion, coordinating a failed assault on his hometown. During the 1930s he prospered as an engineer for an oil company, returning to politics in 1937 with his election to the Chamber of Deputies, where he became an implacable enemy of Lombardo Toledano and Cárdenas. He also held, in 1937, one of the seven senior positions in the UNVR, that of visitador general.

Reflecting the convictions of its originator, the FCDM became a "bulwark of the reaction."[18] In a September 1938 manifesto, widely distributed in cities such as Ciudad Juárez, the party charged the Cárdenas government with usurping Madero's democracy by "hoisting the teachings of Russia in its place." In order to save Mexico it vowed to:

1. advance the democratic principles of the Mexican Revolution as outlined in the 1917 Constitution;
2. reveal to the Mexican people the truth of the fascistic and communistic elements at work; and
3. oppose these plots and the related propaganda.

The FCDM enjoyed early and substantial support among wealthy landowners and businessmen in Iturbe's home state of Sinaloa. It also attracted considerable support from conservatives in the army. Six *divisionarios* signed its manifesto, including Francisco Coss, Pablo González, Marcelo Caraveo, and Jacinto Treviño; a multitude of junior officers also offered their allegiance, among them Colonel Bolívar Sierra, who became the front's secretary. The presence of such a prominent military contingent may have been one reason why the creation of the FCDM aroused widespread interest; it became a topic of hot debate in the Chamber of Deputies.[19]

Although headquartered on Independence Avenue in Mexico City, the FCDM enjoyed its broadest support in the northern states, where a number of its leaders agitated against the government. Iturbe, Coss, and two colonels visited District Judge John Valls in Laredo, Texas in November 1938, warning him that Mexico would have a communist government within two years unless the army intervened. Across the border, many of Nuevo Laredo's wealthiest citizens endorsed the FCDM, which staged a rally in Plaza Hidalgo.[20]

The second significant opposition party to form after the FCDM was the Comité Revolucionario de Reconstrucción Nacional [CRRN], launched with a January 31, 1939 manifesto to the nation. The CRRN was led by Gilberto Valenzuela, the old Obregón loyalist who had drafted the Escobar rebellion's Plan de Hermosillo and participated in the 1934 electoral opposition as a PNA presidential candidate. Valenzuela held the post of president, but the CRRN's founding membership list reads like a who's who of the Mexican Right. Generals Iturbe, Caraveo, Treviño, and González signed on as vice presidents, making the leadership highly duplicative of that of the FCDM; other participants included leaders of the rightist press—Arenas Guzmán of *El Hombre Libre*, and Aquiles Elorduy, founder of *La Reacción* in 1938.

A fascist artist named Gerardo Murillo served the CRRN as its propaganda secretary. Murillo, better known as Dr. Atl, was by 1939 an open admirer of Adolf Hitler. Confident of impending Nazi victory over the western democracies, he published several small booklets that called on Mexicans to renounce all ties to the United States and join the winners. The struggle was, he argued, between German militarism and Jewish commercialism. Using Nietzsche as his inspiration, he concluded that war was the highest form of human expression. After considering the bloodletting of the Revolution, the artist concluded, Mexicans had a past of which to be proud.

Dr. Atl's strange rhetoric notwithstanding, the CRRN remained quite moderate in its official pronouncements and platform. Beyond a call to revoke the amended Article 3 of the Constitution of 1917, its agenda was vague. The January 31, 1939 manifesto urged "the impartial application" of the constitution, "without sectarian, demagogic interpretation." The party resolved to work for the "economic, social, and moral redemption" of Mexico, as well as national harmony, and balance the rights of labor and capital under the law. Perhaps reflecting the influence of the UNVR, it resolved to increase army salaries and generously reward Revolutionary veterans, "whose accomplishments demand recognition."[21]

The reason for the CRRN's ambiguity was its intention to become an umbrella group for the broader and diversified Right. Technically the organization referred to itself as a "coordinating body" rather than a political party, laboring in the spring to unite opposition groups under its banner. The effort met with limited success because of competition from other organizations and the lack of a consensus on a presidential candidate (and few would have seriously considered the ambitious Valenzuela, a political lightweight). The CRRN did dialogue with other groups, however, including the FCDM and PAN.[22]

A third minor group, emerging in March 1939, was the Partido Nacional de Salvación Pública [PNSP, often Nacional was omitted from its name], led by General Francisco Coss and its press and propaganda secretary, Adolfo León Osorio. Coss was xenophobic and anti-Semitic, having been involved in organizing anti-Spanish refugee demonstrations in early 1939 that forced Cárdenas to reverse his asylum decision for International Brigade members. The PNSP's manifesto, which appeared in *El Universal* on March 13, reflected Coss's convictions, implying that the real problem in Mexico was business monopolies run by foreign (and presumably Jewish) interests. The PNSP drew only a few hundred members, most of them residing in Mexico City, and failed to evolve into a significant organ of the opposition.[23] General Coss received a private meeting with Cárdenas at Los Pinos, the presidential estate, on April 24. As president of the PNSP, Coss raised a number of political concerns with the chief executive, including the nature of agrarian reform and his opposition to Spanish refugees. He argued on behalf of small ranchers and landholders, who still feared the seizure of their lands. He also expressed a desire "to see the *ejidatario* given title to his own parcel of land" in place of the communal control of a *ejidal* commission, contending that such was the type of land reform envisioned during the Revolution.[24] Though Coss's interview received press coverage, the PSNP remained obscure.

In addition to the FCDM, the CRRN, and the PNSP, in the closing years of cardenismo the Right produced an astounding number of fringe political groups, most of which were so small that they had no effect on the body politic. The Partido Revolucionario Antifascista, despite its name, spent its limited energy denouncing communism; lesser groups like the Frente Universitario de México, a student organization in Mexico City, seemed to appear and disappear overnight.[25] Since they endured for at least a few months and generated some national interest, the FCDM, CRRN, and PNSP constitute a higher level of political mobilization. Above them were two parties of even greater import: PAN and PRAC.

PAN, the Partido Acción Nacional, was distinctive from the start. Unlike every other rightist political party in the 1938–1940 period, it rested on sophisticated political philosophies rather than the charisma of some national figure. Wealthy Catholic intellectuals created the party, conceiving it in 1938, publishing doctrinal principles in July 1939, and formally founding it in September. These thinkers included Manuel Gómez Morín, Efraín González Luna, José González Torres—men of letters rather than activism. As such, the U.S. embassy dismissed them in a confidential memorandum to Washington: "Gómez Morín is incapable of directing a political party . . . surrounded by intellectuals like himself who, also like himself, are absolutely unprepared for this type of work."[26] Of all the rightist groups formed at the close of cardenismo, only PAN endured and flourished.

The most important founder was, without doubt, Manuel Gómez Morín, PAN's first president. Born of Spanish immigrants in Chihuahua in 1897,

Gómez Morín attended a Protestant school before moving to the conservative Bajío city of León by 1910. A teacher in early adult life, he gravitated toward Vasconcelos's thinking in wake of the Revolution, serving as treasurer in the 1929 campaign after a stint as chairman of the Bank of Mexico. He served as rector of the national university during the tumultuous years of Narcisso Bassols's anticlerical education reforms in the Maximato, then, in the mid-1930s, working in business, moved even farther to the right. Gómez Morín's political reasoning is not neatly boxed ideologically, however. He believed that Mexico needed to cultivate the "fundamentals of democracy," including labor and agrarian organizations free of government paternalism, a constructive economic program (not based on panaceas such as industrialization or agriculture), and protection from the dangers of an all-powerful state. In calling for democracy and political institutions free of excessive personalism, Gómez Morín and his cohorts harkened back to Maderismo; in their view of society they echoed the precepts of Catholic social action and the earlier Partido Católico Nacional.[27]

These philosophical underpinnings included the concept of society as comprised of intermediate corporate entities such as families, unions, *ejidos*, towns and cities, schools, and professional organizations. These entities, and individual liberty itself, had to be protected from state interference. Every human being, comprised of body and soul, must participate in the many tiers of community out of personal faith. Only then could Mexico, or any society, be simultaneously "saved" in an economic, social, political, and spiritual sense. "I am not able to conceive of a prosperous and wealthy Mexico," Gómez Morín later confided, "without the force of a nucleus of basic moral values which serve as the foundation to collective life."[28]

PAN's doctrinal principles of July 1939 were abstract, reflecting the philosophical ideas, rather than specific convictions, driving its founders. Above the corporate entities resided the nation-state, which won PAN's ultimate allegiance. "The national interest is preeminent," it declared, and "whatever conspires to break national unity must be brought down and opposed by all." In concrete terms, the party initially called for indirect democracy, with delegates elected from the various corporate entities; Gómez Morín condemned Article 3 and the government's persecution of the church, rejected the oil expropriation as "unpatriotic," and sought a decentralized state that would regulate, but not manage, industry.[29]

PAN, over the long term, was destined to become the major opposition party of the Right. Without doubt, the most noteworthy new organization in the short term was PRAC, the Partido Revolucionario Anti-Comunista, born of a December 1938 pronouncement by its founder, Manuel Pérez Treviño. An old Calles loyalist who had been Cárdenas's primary rival for the PNR nomination in 1934, Pérez Treviño had personal as well as ideological motives for his staunch opposition to the administration, which had ushered him from political power in the wake of Calles's exile. His "Call to the Mexican Citizenry," printed in

Excelsior, constituted a blistering attack on cardenismo and generated considerable public debate.

In his pronouncement Pérez Treviño, claiming that "a wave of discomfort and unrest is sweeping Mexico," laid several charges before the Revolutionary establishment which held great appeal to the Right. He contended that the PRM was modeled on the Soviet Union's Communist party, designed with the intention of subverting authentic democracy and the goals of the Revolution. Specifically, the party was using communal land distribution as a means of state control, stifling "the initiative of men and groups, which is the most elementary human liberty." Its attacks on landholders was an effort "to put an end to private rural holdings" and reduce the *campesino* to a slave of the state.

Similarly, the dictatorial regime promoted "class hatred" in industry, antagonizing capital and slowly sapping the work ethic from employees. Workers failed to understand that "a certain political goal is screened behind what appears to be a genuine labor movement," namely, the imposition of the communist state.

Mexico needs, therefore, a government that will return to its proper function as a regulator between conflicting economic and social interests. A government that becomes an agitator breaks the balance between opposing interests and leaves one of the parties without resources for defense, and attracts demagogic rabblerousers who are motivated by greed.[30]

In the realm of education, Pérez Treviño charged that the teaching mission had been distorted under Cárdenas, replaced with the goal of "instilling communism in the minds of Mexican children." He closed his manifesto with an appeal for Mexicans to join PRAC, which in turn would select a candidate for president in 1940.

The Cárdenas government responded to the attacks of Pérez Treviño in an *Excelsior* editorial published three days later by the PRM's Executive Committee. Placing its author in the ranks of "the reaction," the PRM leadership decried his personal and ideological hypocrisy.

What moral authority does a man like Pérez Treviño have to speak of democracy? He, who presided over a government of lies [as PNR chairman under Calles], who sold offices and delivered governorships and congressional seats at the orders of his chief, against the expressed will of the Mexican people!

Fascism, by its very nature, subverts democracy in the name of fighting communism. The PRM offered the Axis powers as the best evidence of this, noting that Berlin, Rome, and Tokyo united to resist Marxism, while in practice they only "unleashed violent aggressions on western democracies."[31]

Cárdenas himself also answered his Callista rival, engaging the debate over democracy in Mexico by defending his government as the facilitator of political pluralism. Democracy "rests on a better distribution of wealth, the elevation of basic living standards, and equal opportunity" in work and access to power—the very conditions envisioned by cardenismo. Previously, the president charged, oligarchs and landowners manipulated the masses for the purpose of feigning democratic procedures; education was integral to undoing this tradition of political manipulation.[32]

Interestingly, while both sides contested the notion of whether or not cardenismo was democratic, neither challenged the desirability of true democracy in Mexico. The Right's condemnation of the Revolutionary establishment as anti-democratic, a criticism recurrent in vasconcelismo, the 1934 election, the literary debates, and the campaign of 1940, appealed to the electorate's suspicions of balloting fraud since the end of the military phase of the Revolution. Mexicans held Francisco Madero's democratic aspirations for their country in high regard (one obscure opposition group christened itself the Madero Party in 1939); if either side had denied the need for popular elections, it would have been labeled anti-Revolutionary.

PRAC aspired to become an umbrella group of the right, incorporating four lesser organizations into its ranks in early 1939. Two of these, the PSDM and the Vanguardia Mexicana Nacional [VMN], were substantial. The PSDM, organized and promoted by *El Hombre Libre* editor Arenas Guzmán from 1935 to 1938, had passed into the control of Jorge Prieto Laurens, an opportunist whose poor management had caused the party to decline to about one thousand members at the time of its PRAC merger. The VMN was even smaller, but more active than the PSDM.[33] Led by one Rubén Moreno Padrés and descended from the disbanded Gold Shirts, its members handed out leaflets in major cities.

The salient feature of the handbills, not surprising given the VMN's predecessor organization, was a virulent anti-Semitism, which by 1939 had been made even more sharp by the worldwide shadow of Nazi Germany. At the gates of the Consolidada Steel Company in Monterrey in February, for example, workers received leaflets entitled "Cárdenas Is Responsible," which blamed the president for "supporting Jewish immigration and loathsome communism." In Mexico City during the January antirefugee demonstrations, VMN members handed out circulars declaring that "Jewish blood, Jewish blood, and still more Jewish blood must flow if Our Beloved Fatherland is to be saved." The organization offered to employ "direct action" to eliminate thirty thousand Jews living in Mexico.[34]

After absorbing lesser groups like the VMN, PRAC became the most significant opposition front. It thus attracted the support of the next national figure and presidential aspirant to condemn publicly the Cárdenas administration, Joaquín Amaro. Amaro, a native of Zacatecas state, had served in various army posts through the 1920s before becoming secretary of war under Calles and Ortiz Rubio from 1925 to 1929. As secretary, and as director of the Military College during the Maximato, he worked to reorganize the army and assure its loyalty to the Maximum Chief, making his name forever synonymous with Callista politics. Even more of a political heavyweight than PRAC's founder, Pérez Treviño, Amaro vied with Juan Andreu Almazán for leadership of the opposition from January to March 1939.

Amaro issued a proclamation on March 7 in which he condemned cardenismo and portrayed himself as savior of the nation. Warning that "the very postulates of the Revolution are at stake," he assured the Mexican people of his devotion to both the Revolutionary heritage and the army, that institution "which is forever faithful to the democratic principles" of Francisco Madero. Claiming political detachment and a judgment "unaffected by passion or self-interest," he outlined the errors of Cárdenas and the appropriate remedies to the "national crisis" facing Mexico:

First, we must completely eradicate the communistic and fascist tendencies and activities which . . . characterize the present regime. . . . I condemn the communistic tendency with regard to the granting of communal land holdings, which has brought about a new form of slavery to an omnipotent overlord.

Amaro further repudiated the threat that land reform posed to small landholders, and rejected Cárdenas's labor policies, which fueled a "lack of discipline which benefits no one and will only lead to anarchy." Calling strikes against the utilities "disastrous," he signaled his commitment to capital over labor. The closing paragraphs of the manifesto repeated some of the Right's common criticisms of the Cárdenas government, charging it with nepotism and favoritism, and noting the inflation ravaging Mexico with a call to fiscal conservatism.[35]

Amaro's pronouncement "provoked much excitement and debate." Predictably, the Revolutionary establishment condemned him as the "voice of the reaction," with its various contingents lining up in a chorus of condemnation. The majority of the Chamber of Deputies rebuffed the attack on the government, and some members charged that Amaro was guilty of serious insubordination, even though he had received a license from the army to leave it temporarily in order to participate in politics. The CTM pointed out that Amaro's declaration, with its reference to "squandering of money from a poor nation," implied his opposition to the oil expropriation. Yet segments of the Right, not surprisingly, welcomed the assault on cardenismo. The small Partido Nacionalista commended Amaro for his "brave declarations."[36]

Many of the counterattacks on Amaro focused on him more than on his message. It was perhaps unfortunate for Amaro, in retrospect, that he spent so much time in the opening of his manifesto talking about himself; such bold statements concerning his impartiality and sound judgment rightfully invited critique. Both Francisco Múgica and Manuel Avila Camacho pointed to his lifelong loyalty to Plutarco Calles. The Confederación Nacional Campesina [CNC], in a paid response appearing in El Universal, emphasized the hypocrisy of a man such as Amaro, who blindly served Calles, charging the present government with favoritism and nepotism. What right did he have to claim "devotion to the Revolution," it asked, when he often opposed land reform as a large landholder himself? Even the conservative newspaper Excelsior editorialized against Amaro, cleverly noting that *amaro* in Italian meant "bitter." The paper pointed out that the candid attack on cardenismo, while largely valid and in line with popular sentiment, was made unbelievable when espoused by Amaro.[37]

Indeed, Amaro's message was overshadowed by the man himself. Historian Luis Medina has argued that the hostile response to the manifesto irreparably damaged his bid for opposition leadership, since the Revolutionary establishment bore down on him as the first spokesperson to breach the subject of cardenismo's flaws. In truth, Pérez Treviño had preceded Amaro as Cárdenas's first prominent campaign-era critic, and he weathered the consequences quite well. Amaro, however, had too much baggage to carry from the past. Even the Right was lukewarm in rising to his defense, not surprising given Amaro's role in the Calles machine that crushed Vasconcelismo and the Escobar revolt. Medina is much more on target when he notes that "the truth contained in the accusations of Amaro's despotism made his candidacy less than viable."[38] The Mexican Right had yet to find its candidate, but it did not have to search much longer.

NOTES

1. Albert Michaels, "Las elecciones de 1940," *Historia Mexicana* 21:1 (July–September 1971): 100.

2. González, *Los artífices del cardenismo*, pp. 13–14; "A Return to Common Sense," *El Paso Times*, March 21, 1939; "Mexico's Middle Class Awakes," *El Paso Times*, May 8, 1939; Weyl and Weyl, *Reconquest of Mexico*, pp. 232, 251.

3. Knight, "Rise and Fall of Cardenismo," pp. 290–91; Hamilton, *Limits of State Autonomy*, p. 225; Ignacio Vázquez Gómez, "El maíz, los números y los campesinos," *La Reacción* 3:70 (January 18, 1940): 6.

4. Loosely translated: "Serf of the Russians, patron saint of foreigners, you have left Mexicans only their hides because of your obstinacy—which is the mother of your understanding; for it is very difficult to get a fool to accept correction. Be content to return to Uruapán [Cárdenas's hometown], since fools are certainly killed. And if you care to do something in our favor, something you can be proud of, then stop the work of your illustrious brother, Lombardo Toledano." A copy of the poem, which appears to have been well circulated in spring 1939, is attached to the memo from Lewis Boyle, counsel in Agua Prieta, to SS, April 22, 1939, USDS 812.00/30727.

5. "Un general pisotea la ordenanza militar y se erige en amenazador dictador rojo," *Omega*, August 25, 1938; "Lombardo Toledano aliado del imperialismo," *Omega*, September 22, 1938; "Régimen comunista," *Omega*, February 17, 1938.

6. Juan Guardiola, Agrarian Committee, San Carlos, Coahuila, November 30, 1938; Jesús Escobar, Sindicato de Trabajadores de la Industria Azucarera in Villa José Cardel, Veracruz, August 2, 1940; Vicente Castillo, Sindicato de Trabajadores de Industria Eléctrica, Saltillo, August 17, 1937; and Efrén Saucedo Palacios, April 12, 1939, all addressed to Cárdenas and all in AGN, FLC, 542.1/2415.2.

7. Source unknown, supposed Lombardo Toledano "Report from Paris" to CTM Directors, June 4, 1938, AGN, FLC, 542.1/2415.3.

8. Lombardo to Cárdenas, November 13, 1940, and Cárdenas to Lombardo, November 26, 1940, both in AGN, FLC 542.1/2415.2. The president expressed complete confidence in his associate. The inspiration for such rumors may have been the sensational August 20, 1940 murder of Soviet refugee Leon Trotsky by Stalinists. Lombardo Toledano had opposed granting Trotsky asylum.

9. Daniel Cosío Villegas, *La sucesión presidencial* (Mexico City: Cuadernos de Joaquín Mortiz, 1975), pp. 52–53; Lombardo in Wilkie, *Visto en siglo XX*, pp. 320–21.

10. "Piden la expulsión de los Stalinazis," *Ultimas Noticias*, September 30, 1939; "Varios diputados elaboran una ley a fin de eliminar cualquier doctrina exótica," *Excelsior*, September 30, 1939. Some PRM deputies counterproposed the suppression of rightist groups.

11. John Britton, *Educación y radicalismo en México: Los años de Cárdenas, 1934–1940* (Mexico City: Secretaría de Educación Pública, 1976), pp. 105–9.

12. Britton, *Los años de Cárdenas*, pp. 111, 113–15.

13. Luis Medina, *Del cardenismo al avilacamachismo* (Mexico City: El Colegio de México, 1978), p. 98; Michaels, "Las elecciones de 1940," pp. 83–90.

14. "El general Múgica y su programa de gobierno," *El Universal*, February 3, 1939.

15. Knight, "Rise and Fall of Cardenismo," p. 296; Michaels, "Las elecciones de 1940," pp. 90–100.

16. Medina, *Del cardenismo al availacamachismo*, pp. 77, 84; "Abajo Toledano y Rodríguez," *Omega*, November 24, 1938; "A los veteranos de la revolución," *Omega*, November 20, 1938; Ariel José Contreras, *México 1940: Industrialización y crisis política* (Mexico City: Siglo Veintiuno Editores, 1977), pp. 30–31.

17. This and subsequent comments on UNVR membership are primarily based on letterhead lists found in AGN, FLC, 606.3/20.

18. Carlos Tresguerras, "Quién es quién en la revolución?" and Ramón F. Iturbe, "El Petrolero," *La Prensa*, May 16, 1939, pp. 12–13, 22.

19. William Blocker, Consul General in Ciudad Juárez, to SS, October 25, 1938, USDS 812.00/30641. A copy of the manifesto is attached. Ramón Sánchez Martínez, representing agrarians in Gatal de Ocoroni, Sinaloa, to Cárdenas, November 29, 1938, AGN, FLC, 544.61/133.2.4.

20. Romeyn Wormuth, consul in Laredo, to SS, November 25 and 28, 1938, USDS 812.00/30650 and 30651.

21. "Comité Revolucionario de Reconstrucción Nacional," *Ultimas Noticias*, February 2, 1939; Medina, *Del cardenismo al avilacamachismo*, p. 101; Michaels, "Fascism and Sinarquismo," pp. 237–38.

22. "Sobre bases sólidas estase logrando la unificación de los partidos independientes," *Excelsior*, April 25, 1939.

23. Medina, *Del cardenismo al avilacamachismo*, p. 102; Daniels to SS, March 17, 1939, USDS 812.00/30706; see also document 30697 for antirefugee demonstration; "Manifiesto del Partido Nacional de Salvación Pública," *El Universal*, March 13, 1939. Ironically, León Osario was, reputedly, a foreigner. See confidential memorandum entitled "Political Parties in Mexico," no author, September 7, 1939, p. 2, USDS 812.00/37093.

24. "Conferencia entre el General Coss y el presidente," *Excelsior*, April 24, 1939. Note that Coss, like the Right in general, could criticize the government but not the Revolution.

25. Identifying the myriad organizations is made even more difficult by the Right's penchant for using different names. The PSNP, for example, was also known as the

Centro Unificador de la Revolución. See Medina, *Del cardenismo al avilacamachismo*, pp. 102 for a list of groups.

26. "Political Parties" memo, p. 3, USDS 812.00/30793.

27. Gómez Morín in Wilkie, ed., *México visto en siglo XX*, pp. 143–46, 192–95; Franz von Sauer, *The Alienated "Loyal" Opposition: Mexico's Partido Acción Nacional* (Albuquerque: University of New Mexico Press, 1974), pp. 14–21, 42–43. Von Sauer attempts to link PAN to these precursors, but his effort suffers from a poor grasp of Revolutionary history.

28. Gómez Morín in Wilkie, ed., *México visto en siglo XX*, pp. 221–23; Negrete, *Relaciones en México*, p. 231.

29. Quotes from Interview with Gómez Morín, and Doctrinal Points of PAN, both attached to Daniels to SS, July 22, 1939, USDS 812.00/30782.

30. Manuel Pérez Treviño, "Llamamiento a la masa ciudadana de México," *Excelsior*, December 8, 1938.

31. "Llamiento a la masa," *Excelsior*, December 8, 1938; "Luis I. Rodríguez, et al., "Declara el PRM que Pérez Treviño está ya con la reacción," *Excelsior*, December 11, 1938.

32. Lázaro Cárdenas, "Contesta las agresiones el Sr. Presidente," *Excelsior*, December 10, 1938.

33. Medina, *Del cardenismo al avilacamachismo*, p. 103; "Political Parties" memo, p. 2, USDS 812.00/30793.

34. Daniels to SS, February 2, 1939, USDS 812.00/30686, copy of handbill is attached; Negrete, *Relaciones en México*, p. 291; Weyl and Weyl, *Reconquest of Mexico*, pp. 359–360. The actual number of Jews in Mexico was closer to twenty thousand, most of whom were well assimilated into Mexican society and culture. See Krause, *Judíos en México*, p. 261.

35. Medina, *Del cardenismo al avilacamachismo*, pp. 100–104; González, *Días del presidente*, p. 222; Joaquín Amaro, "Manifiesto a la nación," *El Universal*, March 7, 1939.

36. "Causan sensación las declaraciones de Joaquín Amaro," *Ultimas Noticias*, March 8, 1939; "Ha causado indignación el manifiesto de Amaro," *El Universal*, March 9, 1939; "No ha terminado todavia la tormenta de protestas por el manifiesto de J. Amaro," *Excelsior*, March 11, 1939.

37. "Ha causado indignación," *El Universal*; CNC, "Falta a la verdad Joaquín Amaro," *El Universal*, March 9, 1939; "Amaro quiere decir amargo," *Excelsior*, March 9, 1939.

38. Medina, *Del cardenismo al avilacamachismo*, pp. 103–6.

8

THE 1940
PRESIDENTIAL ELECTION
AND ITS AFTERMATH

As the 1940 presidential campaign began, Mexico's ruling party and government, in a pattern that would become commonplace, once again faced a cynical and largely hostile electorate. What was different about 1940 was that the government was in the hands of an idealist, a true reformer who promised, and might actually deliver, clean elections. But the Right was not prepared to reengage in electoral politics based on the promises of its enemy. Its opposition was spawned from widespread popular disgust with cardenismo. Millions of Mexicans believed that the president was ruining the country: out-of-control strikes, inflation, rural chaos, and uncertainty about the future drove Mexicans to the polls. The Right had convinced millions that Cárdenas and Lombardo Toledano had placed their nation on the road to "communism" through land reform and socialistic education. Sentiment was decidedly against the government on the issue of Spanish Loyalist refugees, as well.

The anticlericalism of the Calles years had alienated many Mexicans, though the business elite could remember the Maximum Chief with considerable goodwill. The problem with Joaquín Amaro, who sought to lead the opposition with his March 1939 declaration, was that he was tainted by his association with the Revolutionary regime. And the regime was so unpopular by 1939 that what the Right needed was an independent champion, someone who could harken back to the hagiographic Revolutionary tradition while at the same time have little connection to the largely unpopular Revolutionary government. The Right found such a crusader in Juan Andreu Almazán, leader of a faction in the army bypassed by the Cárdenistas and hungry for power. An Almazán candidacy also avoided the mesh of personal loyalties to Calles and Obregón that had plagued the opposition in 1934.

General Almazán positioned himself for leadership of the Right in early 1939, even though he personally remained silent about his intentions until midsummer. Behind the scenes, Almazán operatives worked feverishly to generate support and unite the various opposition parties in the wake of Amaro's early April decline. Most important in these efforts was Eduardo Neri who, working through a new headquarters in Monterrey, established a network of pro-Almazán committees throughout the country that numbered some twenty-five thousand members by late summer. Also on the forefront of early efforts for Almazán was Gilberto Valenzuela. Though his early-1939 CRRN had been largely unsuccessful in its bid to become an umbrella group for the Right (and perhaps launch his own candidacy), it became a focal point of early Almazán efforts by drafting a general platform that the diverse opposition groups could endorse. This document, which called for electoral reform and repudiated "communist agitation," offered few concrete proposals or specific attacks—it even refrained from criticizing Article 3, the constitutional provision behind socialist education. While this can be interpreted as an effort to position the Right more in the center, it also bespoke a strategy of contesting with the PRM for the middle of the political electorate.[1]

Almazán himself had uneven Revolutionary credentials and the image of a moderate—not unlike his predecessor, José Vasconcelos, when he led the Right in 1929. Born in Guerrero in 1891 and raised after age five in the city of Puebla, Juan Almazán made propitious choices at the outset of the Revolution. He knew Aquiles Serdán, the Puebla resident who, after his stockpiled weapons had been discovered by Porfirio Díaz's agents, became the Revolution's first martyr; Almazán reputedly had attempted to liberate his followers from prison. An early adherent to the Madero revolt, Almazán served it as the youngest brigadier general in Mexico. Briefly reenrolled in medical school in 1911, he returned to military service shortly thereafter, making decisions that proved embarrassing in the 1939–1940 campaign: he participated in efforts to disarm the Zapatistas and allied with Victoriano Huerta in the wake of the coup during the Tragic Ten Days. A *divisionario* by 1914, he supported the counterrevolutionary efforts of Félix Díaz before leaving Mexico for self-imposed exile in Guatemala and the United States. Almazán cleared his name of the stigma of a reactionary only in 1920 when, back in Mexico fighting Carranza, he declared his support for Alvaro Obregón's Plan de Agua Prieta.[2]

After 1920 Almazán spent most of his life in Nuevo León, managing his Anáhuac road construction company and building a considerable private fortune. Aligning himself with Calles in the late 1920s, he played a key role in suppressing the Escobar revolt and gained considerable popularity in the army. He augmented this popularity by treating his own troops unusually well. When tensions with Pérez Treviño and Amaro in 1931 resulted in the loss of road-building contracts for the Anáhuac firm, Almazán used it to build a model military camp instead. In the late 1930s Almazán continued to cultivate army and regional popularity and practice conservative politics. He visited Europe, returning in July 1937 to a week of banquets and picnics sponsored by local civic and military authorities. His troops participated in some of these events, diving into a new, one-hundred yard swimming pool constructed by Almazán for their enjoyment. A U.S. diplomat who visited with the general during one of the July celebrations noted his sympathy for the Spanish forces under Franco. Another diplomat, Ambassador Josephus Daniels, once visited Almazán in his mountain home, Chapingua, overlooking Monterrey. He had "all the dash of a soldier," Daniels recorded in his diary, and had won the enduring affection of his soldiers by placing family living quarters beside their model barracks.[3]

By the summer of 1939, after Neri and Valenzuela's CRRN had laid the groundwork, Almazán openly declared his desire to become Mexico's next president. On June 30 he resigned his commission as the highest-ranking officer in the army, miffed by the PRM's clear intent to overlook him as the party nominee. One month later, on July 29, he issued a manifesto printed in Mexico's major newspapers. These "declarations," identified by Almazán not as a program but simply his own ideas, signaled the beginning of the opposition's campaign.

The declarations were typical of what the Right had been espousing for several years. Condemning "the enemies of the Revolution," Almazán claimed the status as a patriot and authentic Revolutionary; he rejected the labels placed upon him by his critics such as "fascist" and "reactionary." The bulk of the manifesto addressed major issues with considerable elusiveness. Opening with the unusual question of race, the candidate decried the isolation of Indians and called for their integration and the advancement of "all of Mexico." Agrarian reform should be rooted in the concept of private property, with titles given to peasants, small landholders guaranteed their property, and entrepreneurial incentives for investors to cultivate fallow tropical lowlands. While labor unions and strikes are legitimate, political syndicalism must end. The state "should protect workers," but also "respect the autonomy of worker organizations." Almazán addressed other concerns, including the need for honest government, expanded women's rights (harking back to vasconcelismo), clean elections, and warm foreign relations with the United States. In keeping with his moderation, he made only an ambiguous reference to Article 3 on education. A promise to improve conditions in the army likely came as a surprise to no one.[4]

One month after the declarations appeared, Almazán began the campaign proper, launching it with a mammoth rally in the capital. He arrived at the Buenavista train station on August 27 at 11:30 in the morning, greeted by more than eight thousand supporters. "The presence of women, beautiful maidens, was especially evident," noted one newspaper account of the arrival. "They carried bouquets of flowers in their hands, mostly red carnations," and cheered the candidate wildly. Neri and Valenzuela were also on hand, as were contingents from the PNSP, the army, and the VN, which flew its tricolor.

By noon Almazán reached the rally site, the Monument to the Revolution, where an estimated two hundred thousand Mexicans greeted him. The meeting lasted ninety minutes and featured several important speakers in addition to the candidate. The first to take the podium was Blanca Trejo, a thirty-three-year-old woman recently returned from Spain, where she had served as a low-level diplomat in the consulate in Barcelona. A critic of the Madrid government, Trejo published a book in 1940 entitled *Lo que vi en España* that portrayed the Loyalists as immoral communists and decried in particular Republican policies regarding women, including the use of women in militias. At the rally, however, she kept her remarks on Almazán, calling women to back him for the good of the country. Next, a labor leader named Rivera addressed the crowd, representing the Federación Revolucionaria de Obreros y Campesinos [FROC], an independent union of textile workers that endorsed Almazán. Rivera blasted Vicente Lombardo Toledano to the chants of the crowd. He called the Revolutionary regime's old charge, that the Right constituted the "reaction," a lie, declaring "our cause represents only the triumph of the Revolution."

Juan Almazán then rose to speak, reading a text that emphasized the need for democracy and challenging Cárdenas to honor his promise to deliver clean elections. In exchange he vowed a peaceful campaign. He urged his supporters to action: "I am not concerned with the dirty maneuvers of the enemies of the popular cause; that which really causes me to lose sleep is the fear that we will not succeed in organizing the people—an indispensable requirement to an indisputable electoral triumph." Several orators addressed the rally after Almazán, including Salvador Azuela, a lawyer who had helped steer the Vasconcelos effort, León Ossorio, the rabid PNSP anti-Semite who opted to spend his energy lambasting the PRM, and Antonio Soto y Gama, a participant in the 1934 opposition. Two students from the National University, representing the small rightist student groups Juventud Universitaria and Juventudes Nacionalistas, also greeted the crowd.[5]

The candidate's concerns about mobilizing the electorate were well founded, for despite the impressive beginning, the Right had organizational divisions. At about the same time as the rally the Almazán camp tried to corral various rightists into a new umbrella group, the Confederación Nacional de Partidos Independientes [CNPI]. An August 4 CNPI meeting did not go well, however, as FCDM participants attempted to shift support to the candidacy of General Rafael Sánchez Tapia. Although Almazán backers foiled this plan, the FCDM split, with a majority of its membership backing the rival candidate under the new party presidency of Marcelo Caraveo. A remnant of the FCDM, along with PRAC, UNVR, and the PSD, worked on behalf of Almazán during the fall, coordinating their efforts with only limited success. PRAC continued to toy with the possible candidacy of Amaro late into the year, then eventually declined amidst rumors that the opportunistic Amaro was secretly bartering with the PRM for political clout with Avila Camacho.

The FCDM stayed with Sánchez Tapia through the election. The candidate, commander of the military zone centered in Mexico City, ultimately only had the effect of siphoning off tens of thousands of potential votes from Almazán (the official vote count was fifteen thousand). Sánchez Tapia was a disappointed pre-candidate from within the official party, so upset with the ascent of Avila Camacho via a CNC convention in February 1939 that he opted to leave the PRM and undertake an independent campaign. His efforts, however, suffered from "ideological ambiguity." From the outset, hoping to capture both the affections of rightists and cardenista factions in labor and agriculture (the CTM and CNC, respectively), he was ambivalent about his program, stating simply that the next president "should consolidate the gains of the Revolution." Even after his break with the PRM, his ambiguity continued, as evidenced in a November 1939 platform that had limited appeal to diehard rightists.[6]

In January 1940 Almazán partisans disbanded the CNPI in favor of a new coalition party, the Partido Revolucionario de Unificación Nacional [PRUN] which, despite its name, still had only partial success in uniting the factious opposition. PRUN evolved primarily out of the CRRN, which folded, and attracted similar urban middle-class support. Headed by Emilio Madero, its program echoed that of Almazán, supplementing conservative planks with a populism that called for higher worker wages, increased university budgets, and women's suffrage. The party appealed for donations based on whatever one could afford, and asked each of its members to solicit contributions from five friends. Despite this, PRUN finances came overwhelmingly out of Almazán's own pocket. The campaign through election day on July 7, and subsequent efforts to continue the opposition, cost a total of 4 million pesos, of which 3 million came from the wealthy candidate.[7]

Tied so closely to Almazán, PRUN, not surprisingly, fell apart after the 1940 campaign. The more institutionalized and ultimately long-lasting PAN, in contrast, did not give Almazán its full support. A PAN convention voted in September 1939 to endorse the candidate conditionally, with a reluctant Manuel Gómez Morín pointing out the futility of election efforts in the face of PRM fraud. PAN's Catholic leaders sought to steer their party clear of the personalism dominating opposition politics, and also likely had misgivings about Almazán's overtures to the center in order to garner the greatest possible electoral advantage. During the campaign, PAN locals spent much of their effort outside the Almazán camp, criticizing the government and the "anti-Mexican pronouncements and practices" of Lombardo Toledano in particular. PAN's approach to the elections was largely a reflection of Gómez Morín, the party's founder who expressed some of his eclectic views in a July 1939 interview with *Christian Science Monitor* reporter Betty Kirk. He suggested that Cárdenas had actually advised Almazán to head to the opposition, and predicted that after engineering an Almazán-Avila Camacho stalemate, the president would appoint a "dark horse" candidate and extend his dictatorship.[8]

With PAN on the fringe and other groups divided, Almazán had difficulty orchestrating unified organizational support. He also encountered open hostility from leading figures within the right. In addition to Sánchez Tapia, both the flag bearers of the 1929 and 1934 opposition campaigns broke with his 1940 efforts.

José Vasconcelos, encouraged to return to Mexico from self-imposed exile with the government's conciliatory passing of a 1939 amnesty law, granted an interview to *El Universal* in which he argued that 1929 proved that opposition electoral plans were in vain and that in 1934 they only legitimized the regime. Expressing a personal dislike for Almazán, whom he blamed in part for the persecution and exile of his own followers, he decried his campaign as "a way for the opposition to commit suicide and to provoke the union of all Revolutionaries against it." By early 1940 Vasconcelos rested his hopes for Mexico on the European fascists, editing a small news magazine named *Timón* which dealt with international affairs and praised Mussolini and Hitler.[9]

In November 1939 Antonio I. Villarreal, leader of the Right in 1934, condemned Almazán personally, attacking him as a fraud who helped impose Revolutionary dictatorships on Mexico by his close cooperation with Huerta, Calles, and the Maximato administrations. His attack elicited responses from Almazán apologists like Antonio Díaz Soto y Gama, the aged Zapatista who had vied with Villarreal for the leadership of the CRPI in 1934 but now charged that he had been bought off by the government. University students from the Juventudes Demócratas Mexicanas also countered Villarreal, identifying him as a traitor to the opposition.[10]

Perhaps even more damaging to Almazán than the attacks of Villarreal and Vasconcelos, or the lack of organizational unity, was the depoliticalization of tens of thousands of peasants caught up in a burgeoning movement called Sinarquismo in the Bajío region of west central Mexico. The ultra-Catholic Unión Nacional Sinarquista [UNS] had arisen from the ashes of the second Cristero insurrection during the mid-1930s, born out of a secret society in May 1937 known as La Base, and headed by the young and charismatic Salvador Abascal. Born in Morelia, Michoacán in 1910 as the fourth of eleven children, Abascal attended a Catholic preparatory school in the 1920s and completed law school in 1930. The anticlericalism of the Revolutionary government alienated him, while the success of European fascists entranced him. Abascal led a movement that grew with rapidity as cardenismo faltered, enjoying success especially among women and Indians who found appeal in a fervently nationalistic and anticommunist message.

Abascal and Sinarquista leaders steered their adherents away from electoral participation and completely rejected the Revolution and its "anti-Mexican" heritage. They "did not admire Madero, nor Carranza or Zapata, but found their inspiration in the Catholic and autocratic centuries of colonial Mexico." They perceived both Avila Camacho and Almazán as products of the "godless" Revolution, and "took very little interest in the elections."[11] This notwithstanding, there is evidence that many Sinarquistas still supported and perhaps voted for Almazán. In Guanajuato, UNS officials reported to Abascal that PRUN was working to discredit them and noted with concern that it was having an effect on popular opinion among the uneducated peasants. "No doubt the same procedure is taking place throughout the Republic," they warned, urging UNS leaders to counter the attacks and keep the faithful in line.

Other opposition groups also criticized the anti-electoral position of the Sinarquistas and wooed their rank and file into the campaign. In Michoacán, for example, PAN officials paid visits to Sinarquista activists such as Gregorio Marroquín of Ario de Rosales, who complained that they "nearly scolded" him for the UNS voting ban. In Chihuahua, the small Partido Demócrata Republicano distributed leaflets on the eve of the election, calling on all devout Catholics to vote, particularly Sinarquistas. Abstaining from the ballot box is morally wrong, it warned, placing it among other infamies (such as voting for the wrong candidate) "for which one must someday give an answer before the tribunal of God."[12]

Thus Almazán and the Right faced three complications in the 1940 election effort: some disunity among the various parties, the lack of support from previous candidates, and the refusal of at least some of the disillusioned Catholic peasantry to participate. In 1929 Vasconcelos had been unable to unite urban opposition to the regime with the rural discontent of the Cristeros, and eleven years later the advent of Sinarquismo threatened to do the same. Yet despite the Right's disunity, Almazán enjoyed "a large popular following" as he toured Mexico in the months prior to the July 7, 1940 election. Enthusiasm for his campaign was greatest in the north, and was so strong among Mexicans living in the southwestern United States that sympathetic newspapers advocated giving immigrants the vote, while PRUN solicited their donations.[13] A second strength area rested with the urban middle class, including professionals, five thousand of whom signed a manifesto as members of the Frente Nacional de Profesionistas e Intelectuales [FNPI]. Although Almazán held lesser appeal for the devout Catholic peasantry in the interior of Mexico, he pitched his message with great success to women throughout the country, and spouted a populism that even aroused the interest of labor. The army, and especially its senior officers, though barred from politics, clearly sided with the challenger.

In campaign speeches the candidate shared his vision of a U.S.-like Mexico, prosperous and filled with ranchers and other small property owners. Vowing to protect private property, he repeatedly evoked the name of Emiliano Zapata, even as he condemned state-controlled farming collectives. Promising to give land titles directly to individual peasants, he charged that the Banco Ejidal and other government agencies were rife with corruption. Regarding the United States, Almazán proposed a limited alliance against the European fascists, argued that foreign capital was critical to Mexico's development, and hinted that he disagreed with the popular oil expropriation. He blamed labor leaders for tensions between workers and capital.

With great success the opposition candidate attacked cardenismo on matters relating to the family. He lambasted socialist education as "atrocious" and promised to end the unpopular implementation of Article 3. Playing to popular fears of communism, he defended the home, family, and morality as fundamental to social stability—order was the overarching theme of his campaign. He warned that Mexico could yet become a vassal state of the Soviet Union, and suggested that the Six Year Plans were a Russian invention. Labeling his opponents *imposicionistas*, because they imposed on Mexico an unpopular government, Almazán targeted Lombardo for special criticism as the leading "charlatan." Díaz Soto y Gama, who campaigned on his behalf, bluntly told his audiences that the election was a choice between Mexico or Russia and Lombardo and Almazán.[14]

The candidate, broadening his support by appealing to the political center, at times sounded like a populist. He called for hospitals, social security, and better living conditions for workers, and repeatedly addressed the need for women's suffrage, contending that only then could they "defend two things: the family and peace." The key to peace, just and moral government, required the feminine touch; in contrast, he explained, the unjust tyranny of "our official communism has not liberated women, because materialistic communism liberates no one."[15]

Evidence suggests that Almazán's strategy of reaching out to the center worked. He cut into the segment of the Mexican populace that should have been most loyal to cardenismo: industrial labor. A number of independent unions joined the opposition campaign, including the Partido Central Ferrocarrilero Pro-Almazán, headed by Eladio Medina and organized in April 1939 among disenchanted workers. Other Pro-Almazán groups formed among miners, electrical, and streetcar workers, as well as textile employees organized in FROC. CROM backed Almazán, and the candidate who enjoyed the warm support of much of Monterrey's business elite even captured the hearts of many oil workers within the CTM! A striking number of industrial workers, perhaps even a majority, sympathized with Almazán—not so much because of his populist rhetoric, but rather out of a longing for independent unionism, democracy, frustration with rising costs of living, and the success of the Right in the ideological debates over the family and communism. Signs of labor's defections even marred Mexico City's May Day parade, where participants yelled out antigovernment slogans. Even the Trotsky group, the Partido Revolucionario Obrero Campesino [PROC], led by muralist Diego Rivera, opted to back Almazán.[16]

In the face of the Almazán onslaught, Manuel Avila Camacho's campaign seemingly sputtered. A November 1939 PRM convention in Mexico City's Palace of Fine Arts formally delivered the nomination to the secretary of defense, with 81 percent of the 1,478 delegates voting in his favor. Getting the convention's nod was the only easy step for the official candidate, however. Even before the convention adjourned, he must have realized the essential need to move to the right. Avilacamachistas assigned to a committee revising Lombardo's second Six Year Plan pressed for changes; the revised document, dubbed the Plan of Government in an apparent effort to avoid the Sovietlike title, shunned Marxist terminology and radicalism. Avila Camacho and Heriberto Jara, the PRM chairman, both avoided reference to the plan in their closing convention speeches.

On the campaign trail the PRM candidate frequently employed conservative rhetoric. At times he sounded like Almazán. In an attempt to allay the fears of northern ranchers, he promised to respect private property, while he echoed his rival's call for foreign investment and friendship with the United States. The Right ridiculed him for his undistinguished military record, referring to him as the "unknown soldier" and "virgin sword" (the latter clearly an assault on his masculinity). The candidate answered his critics by arguing that his moderation in war reflected his "respect for human life and preoccupation with the home and the family"—once again an appeal to Mexicans on the terms of the Right. Using the theme of unity throughout the campaign, in his final speech Avila Camacho extended the rhetoric on family, calling on voters to unite, "not as winners and losers, but as Mexicans, all of the same family." Shortly before the election, in an apparent attempt to help his man, Cárdenas announced a halt to Spanish refugee immigration.[17]

Conservative Mexicans might have been more predisposed to heed Avila Camacho's words if the campaign had not been racked by violence and marred by intimidation. The one sector of society firmly controlled by the Revolutionary establishment was, of course, the government. State and local authorities, along with PRM and CTM militants, harassed and persecuted the opposition against the express wishes of the president. Even the federal government was apparently not above reproach: in early 1940 the Right charged that the regime was spreading rumors about Almazán, manufacturing stories that he intended to lead a rebellion in order to set himself up in a manner similar to that of Saturnino Cedillo.

Frequently it was through local police forces that the opposition encountered harassment, however. Mexico City police shut down the PNSP's offices in June 1939, prompting a small riot in which protesters jeered Cárdenas and Spanish refugees, shouted their support for Almazán, and fought with Avila Camacho supporters until two dozen were left wounded. Police from Pachuca assaulted a trainload of Almazán partisans outside their city in August 1939, killing two and giving the opposition a cause célèbre.[18] In Querétaro, police arrested PAN members and Sinarquistas who were distributing leaflets. Often the police seemed to sanction the violence of CTM militants. In Mexico City, CTM members broke up one FCDM rally and attempted to disrupt another two weeks later. Police kept the counterdemonstrators away from the six hundred participants until the end of the meeting, when fights broke out and authorities seized FCDM literature and detained nine persons. CTM members sacked the Puebla headquarters of FROC in September 1939, one month after its spokesman had so forcefully criticized Lombardo at the Almazán rally in Mexico City.[19]

Harassment of the opposition for two years prior to the balloting produced "a climate of anarchy and violence that culminated on election day." The same local officials that had so often discriminated against the Right during the campaign largely managed the registration lists and voting procedures, assuring Avila Camacho of a victory by fraud. Almazán, in a final manifesto to the Mexican people on the eve of the election, rallied his forces, but indicated that he understood the inevitability of the outcome. Mexicans are "tired of the farce," he proclaimed, and demand that the Revolutionary regime honor the popular will. He closed his appeal for an enormous voter turnout by honoring the Mexican woman, "unjustly deprived of her political rights" by a regime that spouted rhetoric about social justice.[20]

Election rules fueled the widespread violence of July 7. The Electoral Law of 1918 stipulated that polling booths were to be monitored by the first citizens to arrive (an invitation to then try and manipulate the vote via control of lists and ballots). The 214 polling stations in Mexico City were especially problematic, because the CTM had assigned groups of fifty to one hundred men to reach them first. Almazán was strong in Mexico City (there is little doubt that he would have won the capital hands down in a fair election), and there PRUN also fielded vigilance committees. Confrontation between partisans was inevitable. In the morning, some stations under the watch of Almazanistas were seized by force by unionists and local bureaucrats. Foreign correspondents found extensive evidence of fraud throughout the capital, and Cárdenas himself was turned away from one station that had been closed to prevent hundreds from voting for Almazán. The disturbed president decided to tour other booths, only to encounter crowds of would-be voters shouting "we want Almazán," decrying the fraud, and telling him they wearied of the rule of "communists and thieves." By the afternoon, under cloudy skies, the situation in the capital deteriorated. Gun battles erupted at several polling booths and downtown on major thoroughfares. An angry crowd of thousands of Almazán supporters assembled outside PRUN headquarters and marched to the Zócalo, where they faced army troops and police who soon opened fire, leaving at least six protesters dead.[21]

Despite PRUN efforts to monitor election day balloting, the PRM won a victory with official results that are best classified as ridiculous. The earliest tabulations credited 2,265,199 votes to Avila Camacho, 128,574 votes to Almazán, and 14,056 votes to Sánchez Tapia. Tensions over the election fueled unrest far beyond Mexico City, where election day violence claimed thirty lives alone: sporadic gunfights and repression left hundreds injured throughout the country. Sánchez Tapia returned to army duty within days of the election, thus acknowledging his defeat, but Almazán opted to flee the country, sailing to Cuba on July 17 in search of U.S. support. In an August 12 radio address from Havana, he vowed to declare himself president of Mexico on December 1 (inauguration day) and decried Mexico's antidemocratic regime. He closed his speech with an appeal to Mexican women, asking them to "to compel the men of Mexico to defend their votes and save her dignity."[22]

The fate of Almazán's efforts to reverse the election outcome, of course, was beyond the control of Mexican women. Attempts to gain U.S. approval for resistance to the regime unraveled after a promising early meeting with Eliott

Roosevelt, the president's son. The Cárdenas government countered Almazán's overtures by sending Miguel Alemán, Avila Camacho's campaign manager, to Washington, and by playing on U.S. fears of the Mexican Right's sympathy for the Axis powers. Heeding the advice of Ambassador Josephus Daniels, both the White House and State Department adopted the line of "no intervention in Mexican internal affairs," signaling recognition of the official results by sending Vice President Henry Wallace to the inauguration. Shortly before the ceremony, Almazán himself returned to Mexico and made peace with the regime, realizing the futility of revolt and unwilling to endanger his vast personal fortune.[23]

THE AFTERMATH OF 1940: SHIFT TO THE RIGHT

The Right failed to unseat the Revolutionary regime yet again in 1940, despite the outpouring of popular support for Almazán. Three reasons stood behind the general's electoral appeal, which had even surpassed that of Vasconcelos in 1929. First, his campaign came on the heels of the Right's effective ideological offensive which had convinced a majority of Mexicans to reject cardenismo. Almazán harped on the popular themes of family and social order. Second, Cárdenas repeatedly promised fair elections, as in an interview with *Hoy* magazine in November 1939, which prompted droves of Mexicans to flock to the polls in order to vote the regime out. Third, Almazán appealed to the center, knowing the Right was secure, in order to capture as many votes as possible and overwhelm the PRM by an undeniable margin of victory.

The failure of the Right to justly win the 1940 elections led to further disillusionment and anger among millions of Mexicans. The response of the most determined rightists was to embrace new forms of resistance and even place their hopes in the rising tide of world fascism. Sinarquismo boomed in the postelection years, reaching an apogee of more than a half million members by early 1943. UNS members practiced rigid military formations, sang nationalist songs, and listened to the diatribes of their leaders (though Abascal had lost control of the organization in December 1941). Several hundred Sinarquistas, with the consent of the Avila Camacho government, relocated to the Baja peninsula to establish a colony in 1942, raising fears that they were preparing to aid a Japanese invasion of North America.

Sinarquistas and the far Right had decided sympathy for Nazi Germany, especially during the 1939–1942 period when Hitler's armies enjoyed stunning military success. *La Reacción* expressed views typical of the Right when it employed anti-Semitism to explain the war and the role of Great Britain:

The most important reason why the Jews are enthusiastic partisans of British imperialism and politics is that they can continue their business activities in the British Empire, with their mines, cotton plantations, and the like, filling their bags with gold. Jews venerate the British regime, with its pseudodemocracy . . . [and its] press is completely dominated by Jews.

La Reacción and the far Right resented the increasingly anti-Axis official press in Mexico, claiming that it distorted the origins and nature of the war. In February 1940 *La Reacción* published fake documents showing that the British wanted the war. In April 1941 it mocked the charges of the mainstream press which explained Nazi successes as those of "brute force," pointing out that in the Balkans the Germans were outnumbered, and arguing that their mechanized units represented intelligence, science, and technology rather than brutality.[24]

The Right's position on World War II notwithstanding, most Mexicans were ambivalent about the distant fighting and were slowly making peace with their government. The hysteria over communism in Mexico declined as the direction of the regime under Avila Camacho shifted away from reform. The Right had convinced many Mexicans that the Cárdenas government was leading their nation down a road toward communism, atheism, and the destruction of the family. Yet while emotional arguments can sway a populace, they are poor substitutes for a villain. By 1939, Cárdenas's friend and labor leader, Vicente Lombardo Toledano, had became the most hated man in Mexico, perceived by millions as a shadowy figure obedient to Moscow and the true power behind a gullible president. With the 1940 elections, the villains—Lombardo and Cárdenas—were gone.

Defeated in the vote counting, the Right had in fact accomplished a great deal leading up to, and through, the historic elections. Its strength had been so great as to disrupt cardenismo from the start and block any ideas of its continuance. The PRM's Left, led by Francisco Múgica and resting in the CTM, had to feint moderation in a bid to capture the official nomination, but to no avail. Cárdenas had little choice but to turn to Manuel Avila Camacho, the pre-candidate representing the party's center, even though he was still farther to the left than the general populace. On the campaign trail he moved to the right, distancing himself from Lombardo and engaging in a similar discourse on the family as that of Almazán. Local party officials and police forces, their interests vested in the PRM, repressed the opposition and employed ballot fraud to assure Avila Camacho's victory, probably against the will of Lázaro Cárdenas.

In short order the Avila Camacho government shunned radicalism and gradually returned to the pre-Cárdenas policies favorable to Mexico's economic elite. Instead of an avenue to worker belligerence, the CTM slowly began to evolve into a means of worker control, with increasingly compliant union leaders answering to Fidel Veláquez, a conservative who replaced Lombardo as its head. The Confederación Nacional de Organizaciones Populares [CNOP], which represented the urban middle class, took precedent over the CTM within official party politics. Soon after his inauguration, Avila Camacho signaled an end to the regime's anticlericalism, confessing in a famous phrase, "I am a believer." The undertaking that had so alienated millions of Mexicans was, of course, socialist education, and within the first month of his presidency Avila Camacho conceded ground to a feisty Right that mobilized masses of Mexicans against it. A new organic law addressed education, and in November and December the

Right staged huge rallies to dictate its aims: PAN organized ten thousand protesters in San Luis Potosí, the all-but-defunct LNDL revived and drew between twenty and forty thousand in Mexico City, while fifty thousand congested downtown Puebla at the behest of the CNPI, which remained active for months after the election. The Right was successful in intimidating the newly installed president into action. The government redefined "socialist" and effectively ended the experiment in leftist schooling, which had been uneven in its implementation from the start. Religion and the role of the family received recognition as valid rationales in the education process, though the government persisted in some socialistic rhetoric in order to "pretend that it was not yielding to the pressures from the Right."[25] Pretend or not, the fact was that the Right largely had its way on education.

In other areas the moderation of the Avila Camacho government bridged the gap between the radicalism of cardenismo and the conservatism that was to follow. Landholders found a favorable climate under the new president, while bureaucratic support for the *ejidos* dissipated (though the CNC remained an avenue for political mobilization for decades to come). World War II brought Mexico into a much closer relationship, both culturally and economically, with the United States—with a concomitant dependency that would largely define Mexican life by the end of the century. In the midst of the war, Avila Camacho returned Cárdenas to public service as his minister of war, a post from which the former president revived the ire of the Right as he managed conscription efforts. "Death to Cárdenas and to conscription" was a common cry, and the program fueled the continued growth of Sinarquismo until the issue evaporated with the turn of war against the Axis by 1944.

In all things, then, the trend in Mexico "was inexorably right" under Avila Camacho. His successors proved even more conservative. After the elections, as historian Alan Knight notes, "much of the dissident right of 1940 was incorporated into official politics," and both PAN and the UNS "conformed to the rules of the game."[26] The Right lost the election battle but won the war. Its role became that of what observers have dubbed a "loyal opposition" because, in fact, the Mexican government itself has ruled primarily from the Right since 1940. An era of meaningful reform, that might eventually have led to wealth redistribution and a more just society in Mexico, was past.

NOTES

1. Medina, *Del cardenismo al avilacamachismo*, pp. 106–8; "Political Parties" memo, p. 1, USDS 812.00/37093. Medina makes the argument that Almazán softened his rightist rhetoric after observing the fall of Amaro. The implication of this argument, that the body politic was more to the left of Amaro and the Right, does not follow. The CRRN platform reflected the need to unquestionably unite the entire opposition and attract the most overwhelming support possible—including the political center.

2. Michaels, "Las elecciones de 1940," 106–9. In the campaign, Almazán faced criticism of his political career, especially his allegiance to Huerta, but pointed to his stellar military rank and record.

3. González, *Días del presidente*, p. 221; Medina, *Del cardenismo al avilacamachismo*, p. 100; William Blocker, consul at Monterrey, to SS, July 19, 1937, USDS 812.00/30472; Daniels, *Shirt-Sleeve Diplomat*, p. 80.

4. Lieuwen, *Mexican Militarism*, p. 133; "Declaraciones del Gral. Juan Andreu Almazán," *Excelsior*, July 29, 1939.

5. "Almazán mantendrá su resolución de llegar pacíficamente a las elecciones, sin apelar a la violencia," *La Prensa*, August 28, 1939; "El candidato aclamado al arribar ayer," *Excelsior*, August 28, 1939; Blanca Lydia Trejo, *Lo que vi en España: Episodios de la guerra* (Mexico City: Editorial Polis, 1940), pp. 42–43. On FROC see Contreras, *Industrialización y crisis política*, p. 83.

6. Contreras, *Industrialización y crisis política*, pp. 110–13; Medina, *Del cardenismo al avilacamachismo*, pp. 58–59, 71–75, 102; "Almazán Rally Sunday to Open His Campaign," *San Antonio Express*, August 25, 1939. Iturbe served briefly as president of the CNPI before being ousted.

7. Contreras, *Industrialización y crisis política*, pp. 182, 185; "Un importante circular del PRUN," *La Reacción*, 3:75 (February 22, 1940): 8. Juan Andreu Almazán, *Memorias: Informe y documentos sobre la campaña política de 1940* (Mexico City: E. Quintanar Impresor, 1941), pp. 17–18. Most of the remaining one million pesos came in the form of a few large donations.

8. Contreras, *Industrialización y crisis política*, pp. 165–67; Gómez Morín in Wilkie, *Visto en siglo XX*, p. 177; Betty Kirk, notes of interview with Gómez Morín, attached to Josephus Daniels to SS, July 22, 1939, USDS 812.00/30782.

9. "El licenciado Vasconcelos señala un rumbo," *El Universal*, April 9, 1940; Contreras, *Industrialización y crisis política*, pp. 117–19, 122. Unlike Vasconcelos, Rodolfo Brito Foucher, the young Catholic student who helped bring down Garrido Canabal, also returned from exile and endorsed Almazán. See memo, no author, June 24, 1939, p. 7, USDS 812.00/30768.

10. Villarreal, "De como y por que el Gral. Almazán siempre ha sido imposicionista," in Bernardino Mena Brito, *El P.R.U.N., Almazán, y el desastre final* (Mexico City: Ediciones Botas, 1941), pp. 188–90; Contreras, *Industrialización y crisis política*, p. 185; "Condenan la actitud del Gral. Villarreal," 3:73 (February 8, 1940): 11.

11. Campbell, "Radical Right," pp. 220–21; Vicente Vila, "Abascal: Cabeza sinarquista," *Así* 33 (June 28, 1941): 22–23, and vol. 35 (July 12, 1941): 39; Michaels, "Elecciones de 1940," pp. 101–3. Though written late in life, Abascal's steadfast convictions are best expressed in his *La revolución antimexicana* (Mexico City: Editorial Tradición, 1978).

12. Dagoberto Moncada, Comonfort, Guanajuato, to J. Francisco López C., June 12, 1940; Gregorio Marroquín, Ario de Rosales, Michoacán, to Manuel Zermeño Pérez, no date; and Partido Demócrata Republicano pamphlet attached to Jesús Barrera, Chihuahua, to Zermeño Pérez, July 5, 1940, Unión Nacional Sinarquista Papers, Subdirección de Documentación, Museo de Antropología e Historia, Mexico City.

13. Lieuwen, *Mexican Militarism*, p. 134; Boyle to SS, June 20, 1939, pp. 3–4, USDS, 812.00/30754. This call for immigrant enfranchisement has continued to the present.

14. Cosío Villegas, *Sucesión presidencial*, pp. 78–80; Contreras, *Industrialización y crisis política*, pp. 151, 188; Michaels, "Las elecciones de 1940," pp. 124–30.

15. Contreras, *Industrialización y crisis política*, p. 188; Paulino Machorro Narvaez, "El programa de Almazán," *La Reacción* 3:74 (February 15, 1940): 11.

16. Contreras, *Industrialización y crisis política*, pp. 80–84; Michaels, "Las elecciones de 1940," pp. 109, 123; Knight, "Rise and Fall of Cardenismo," pp. 291, 299.

17. Cosío Villegas, *Sucesión presidencial*, p. 66; Michaels, "Las elecciones de 1940," pp. 116–21; Albert Michaels, "The Crisis of Cardenismo," *Journal of Latin American Studies* 2 (1970): 76.

18. Medina, *Del cardenismo al avilacamachismo*, p. 117; Rubén Salazar Mallen, "La 'cedillización de Almazán,'" *La Reacción* 3:69 (January 11, 1940): 8; Daniels to SS, June 30, 1939, USDS 812.00/30759.

19. J. Aceves to Cárdenas, telegram, November 29, 1939, and Ildefonso Tapia Niño to Cárdenas, telegram, September 1937, both in AGN, FLC, 542.2/748.1; Federico Montes, chief of police, to Cárdenas, telegram, April 30, 1939, AGN, FLC, 542.1/2415.13; Contreras, *Industrialización y crisis política*, p. 83.

20. Medina, *Del cardenismo al avilacamachismo*, pp. 118–19; "El Gral. Almazán dirige un manifiesto al pueblo en vísperas de las elecciones," July 2, 1940, in Almazán, *Memorias*, pp. 120–23.

21. Medina, *Del cardenismo al avilacamachismo*, pp. 118–20; Betty Kirk, *Covering the Mexican Front* (Norman: University of Oklahoma Press, 1942), pp. 240–44.

22. Medina, *Del cardenismo al avilacamachismo*, pp. 119–21, 125; "El Gral. Almazán dirige por radio, desde la Habana, un Mensaje al Pueblo Mexicano," in Almazán, *Memorias*, pp. 125–26. The final ballot count, entered into the records on August 15, cut Almazán's votes to 15,101, or .6 percent of the total.

23. Medina, *Del cardenismo al avilacamachismo*, pp. 127–30; Lieuwen, *Mexican Militarism*, p. 138. For more on Almazán's post-election activities in the United States, including the establishment of a rump congress in Texas, see *Memorias*, pp. 34–92.

24. Meyer, *Sinarquismo*, pp. 47, 71–74, 81. The membership figures drawn from UNS documents by Meyer may be too high. "Guerra de los Judios," *La Reacción* 3:75 (February 22, 1940): 2; "La Gran Bretaña quería la guerra," *La Reacción* 3:72 (February 1, 1940): 2; Pedro Zuloaga, "En defensa de la barbarie," *La Reacción* 3:15 (April 28, 1941): 5.

25. Medina, *Del cardenismo al avilacamachismo*, pp. 360–61.

26. Knight, "Rise and Fall of Cardenismo," pp. 302–4, 308.

Conclusion

It has long been accepted that 1940 was a turning point in Mexico's political history. Something profound took hold of the institutionalized Revolution. Some contend that it shifted gears, others argue that the Revolutionary process, begun in 1910, died.[1] At the very least, after 1940 the nation's body politic began to lurch to the right, a slow process during the moderation of the Avila Camacho years, but one embracing a developmentalist agenda that repudiated cardenismo and set Mexico on the course along which it continues today. Concomitant with this observation has been the popular belief that, under cardenismo, the Revolutionary process reached its apogee. With agrarian reform, labor organization and agitation, socialistic education, and the oil expropriation, the Revolution went as far to the left under Cárdenas as it ever would.

Largely within the confines of these two overarching theses, historical interpretations of Lázaro Cárdenas and his project for Mexico diverge. An earlier school of historians and observers praised Cárdenas as a sincere man who accomplished much for his generally appreciative fellow citizens. In the wake of government repression in 1968, however, primarily Mexican social scientists traced many of the roots of modern authoritarianism to cardenismo, when a populist president restructured the official party, brought the military into its ranks, and created a corporate political entity which has stubbornly refused to yield power ever since.[2] Among these critics, cardenismo was not very revolutionary. It was capitalistic and had the counterrevolutionary goal of mobilizing the working classes in order to manipulate them into supporting an economic model based on industry and capital accumulation.[3]

This study answers two major problems that trouble the respective interpretations of cardenismo by filling an important gap in our understanding of Mexican political history. The gap, of course, is the history of the Mexican Right in the

1930s. Except for limited studies of the radical Right such as that by Hugh Campbell, historians have neglected the Right from the relative demise of its religious components (primarily the Cristeros) in 1929 to the advent of Juan Andreu Almazán's campaign in 1940.[4] This omission has allowed contradictions to mar the broader interpretations of cardenismo.

For the earlier interpretation that praised Cárdenas and emphasized his triumphs, the 1940 election debacle fundamentally contradicts the image of his popularity. How can we reconcile the apparent successes of cardenismo with its undisputable failure to endure? The answer lies largely in the impressive strength of the Right. Present throughout the 1930s, it attacked cardenismo on multiple levels and kept it off balance. It undermined the regime with a barrage of emotionally charged issues in the middle of the *sexenio* which redefined the political culture in favor of the opposition. The nature of these attacks, carried out in the press, literature, and political discourse, may have partially cloaked them from the eyes of some earlier, institution-oriented historians, since the institutional Right of army and church was, in fact, brought to heel and in political decline. But the Right adopted new grassroots and literary initiatives, and discredited Cárdenas by appealing to Mexicans in defense of family, God, and country. Cardenismo failed, from almost any angle within the political culture, to win the "hearts and minds" of a healthy majority of Mexicans.

Even some traditional institutional historians have detected the limitations of cardenismo toward the end of the *sexenio*. As one has explained:

Cárdenas's reforms had provoked hatred and anxiety among small landowners and the growing urban middle classes. . . . The average middle-class Mexican, terrified by the growth of organizations like the CTM and CNC, and dismayed by the economic dislocation caused by the oil expropriation, yearned for order and stability.[5]

Middle class discontent festered at a time when socialist education continued to alienate large segments of the countryside, especially in the Bajío. The rising industrial elite, obviously, had little affinity for the regime as well, annoyed by its labor policies. The landed elite were impotent but angry in the wake of extensive agrarian reform.

As recent scholars have delved into the cultural history of Revolutionary Mexico, they have found that the state's attempts to remake Mexicans through education and other state-sponsored sports and holiday programs largely failed. Culturally "the revolutionary 'new man' did not materialize." The litany of failure includes sex education, anticlericalism, and socialist education, as the state's attempts to redefine social values proved transient.[6] Political opposition to the government from 1938 to 1940 reflects deep-seated hostility, so the limited results of its cultural project should come as no surprise. The earlier historiographical school's apparent contradiction between Cárdenas's popularity and the 1940 election opposition is resolved: he was not particularly popular.

The second interpretation that criticizes cardenismo as constructing a corporate political machine also suffers a contradiction. Social scientists who contend that Lázaro Cárdenas willingly compromised Revolutionary principles and created a leviathan that continues to rule Mexico have largely failed to answer the earlier historiography emphasizing his idealism and sincerity. In fact, he desired to restructure Mexican society in ways that favored the economically disadvantaged (although a full embrace of this interpretation awaits an authoritative biography). Hence cardenismo, in the words of historian Alan Knight, was "a genuinely radical movement" that "faced severe resistance," not just visible but "also of a more surreptitious, covert, and successful kind."[7] Cárdenas's hand was forced in a different direction by 1940, however, not only by the forces within the Revolutionary party and government which wanted to preserve their political control of the country, but also by the relentless and growing opposition of the Right. It was the fundamental conservatism of the majority of the populace that brought about the demise of Cárdenas's progressive agenda, not the imposition of a corporate state apparatus by a Revolutionary regime willing to discard its principles in order to promote elite capitalist well-being.

In order to support the contention that Cárdenas set up a political system that controlled the masses and imposed on Mexicans an authoritarian political structure, many of the revisionists emphasize his reorganization of the official party in 1938. It is true that the PRM, with its four sectors representing labor, peasants, "popular" groups, and the military, evolved into the Partido Revolucionario Institucional [PRI] in 1946 and has governed Mexico ever since. One problem with the significance of the restructuring is, however, that of numbers. At its inception the PRM claimed just under four million members. Even if one were to accept these inflated figures at face value, that still leaves 80 percent of the populace outside the party. With a population of 19.4 million in 1940, the core of the process of sustaining a regime in Mexico rested in the continued use of election fraud. Cardenismo simply did not "mobilize" the great majority of the "masses."[8]

Even if, as Marxist historian Dana Markiewicz contends, the reorganized party placed peasants "firmly in the grasp of the regime," why did they stay there? Markiewicz has argued that agrarian reform under Cárdenas allowed the government to gain "control" of the peasants and "lay the conditions for . . . the end of reform." Such an argument is a non sequitur. Even if the Mexican government implemented reform in order to terminate reform, what mechanisms of control existed after 1940 that were not in place beforehand? It is true that the PRI incorporated the peasantry (on paper at least) after 1938, but what, exactly, prevented them from leaving its "grasp" after the reforms had ended? What methods of coercion existed? Certainly the PRI has won most of the meaningfully contested elections since 1940 by fraud, but that tactic predated cardenismo.

Markiewicz, like others in the Marxist school before her, tries to identify continuities between cardenismo and the Maximato in her 1993 book, *The Mexican Revolution and the Limits of Agrarian Reform*. Much of what she says about the cynicism and limitations of the supposedly "revolutionary" regime between 1917 and 1934 is true. There is much evidence, for example, to support her contention that, "despite its often radical-sounding agrarian reform rhetoric, the post-Porfirian regime never intended to fulfill peasant aspirations" and instead sought to preserve the inequitable status quo. To the degree that Markiewicz and other Marxists question the traditional historiography about the "institutionalized Revolution" before 1934, their position has merit. But in their zeal to discredit the corruption of Mexico's contemporary regime, they incorrectly swallow up cardenismo. The continuities they seek between the Maximato and Cárdenas's administration, for the most part, do not exist. Markiewicz, for example, explains:

Ideological gradients and even sharp conflicts did, of course, exist [between the two periods]; Cárdenas, for example, was tolerant of the Communist Party . . . and figures like Abelardo L. Rodríguez were quite flagrantly anticommunist. These were differences of style and strategy only; all agreed on the paramount importance of regime consolidation and stability.[9]

On the contrary, those "differences of style and strategy" were substantial. In the case of communists, it meant the difference between arrest, torture, and imprisonment on Islas Tres Marias and being able to live in safety and organize freely. It is true that both governments sought to consolidate their position and enjoy stability, but what government does not seek to endure? In their misdirected critique of cardenismo, a younger generation of Marxist historians have accepted, and even strengthened, the older historiographical notion that cardenismo was in the current of two decades of "institutionalized Revolution." Both views are wrong.

Also pivotal to most of the revisionist interpretations that view cardenismo as capitalistic populism has been the role of the industrial elite, centered in Monterrey. Ariel José Contreras, for example, offers a Marxist interpretation that contends that the industrial bourgeoisie quietly made a pact with the Revolutionary government, in the midst of the 1940 campaign, to rule on its behalf.[10] Even if one was to accept the assumption that Cárdenas and the PRM were willing to reach such an agreement, it would be necessary to emphasize that widespread popular discontent with the regime, at the very least, allowed the business elite to have their way.

The problem that this poses for the orthodox Marxist view of history, however, is obvious: while the ruling class operates in harmony with its own economic interests, lower classes often do not.[11] Such was the case in Mexico, where millions of peasants and poor workers flocked to the polls in 1940 in hopes of voting out of power a regime that largely had their own interests in mind. Gramsci's notion of cultural hegemony helps explain this phenomenon. Perceptions of the Revolutionary government (and particularly its education program) as anticlerical, inimical to the family, and communistic alienated the vast majority of Mexicans across class lines. The Right actively promoted these perceptions, along with its popular appeal for democracy in Mexico, in its publications and political rhetoric, with great effect, as demonstrated by the groundswell of political opposition in 1939–1940.

Counted among the revisionism is Nora Hamilton's *The Limits of State Autonomy*, which breaks ground theoretically and offers an interpretation of cardenismo with a vital new twist. Hamilton, a Marxist, modifies the orthodox Marxist notion of the state as an instrument under the control of the wealthy. She finds that, under certain conditions, the state can obtain a limited degree of independence, or autonomy, and be used "for ends other than those of the dominant class." Such was the case of Mexico under Cárdenas, who explored quasi-socialist policies and envisioned "a much more radical restructuring of society than his predecessors or populist regimes in other Latin American countries."[12] Thus Hamilton restores Cárdenas to his proper place as a visionary. She still concerns herself overwhelmingly with the role of the ruling class in reasserting its control over the state, rather than examining the grassroots, transclass Right in its rejection of the regime. This is a critical shortcoming because, like most political systems employing elections (however wrought by fraud) and subject to coverage in mass media, the Mexican government sought a degree of popular legitimacy beyond simply the approval of the ruling elite.

That the strength of the Right prevented it from doing so under Cárdenas is significant, and helps answer some of the more difficult questions of twentieth-century Mexican political history. The Right did not disappear after 1929 and then suddenly revive in 1940; it took on new forms and means of expression. Thus the bizarre swing in the body politic from right (Maximato) to left (cardenismo) to right (post-1940) can be partially explained by acknowledging the continuity of the political climate—it was Cárdenas and his progressive agenda that were fleeting. Rather than view his administration as the apogee of the institutionalized Revolution, we would do well to see it as the exception. It was at odds with the conservative political culture in Mexico nearly from its outset. It had little continuity with what came before, as well as what followed after. The continuity that cardenismo did share with the prior government of the Maximum Chief, Plutarco Calles, is in the nature of its opposition: a healthy number of Mexicans rejected it as corrupt, anti-God and family, imposed on them through electoral fraud. There was, in fact, very little "revolutionary" about Calles or his administration of Mexico, his anticlericalism (used as a tool against Cárdenas) notwithstanding.

Another troublesome aspect of Mexico's political history is the reluctance of the regime to enfranchise women. Indeed, Mexican women first voted for president in 1958, long after most of their counterparts elsewhere in Latin America. Cárdenas sent a constitutional amendment through congress in 1938, but the states failed to ratify it. He and the PRM were well aware that a majority of women supported the opposition. Women were integral in the work of the Right and targets of its rhetoric on preserving the home and family. In 1940 they would have disproportionately voted for Almazán.[13] Hence, despite its vaunted commitment to social justice, the regime denied women the vote until long after the crisis years from 1929 to 1940, when it battled a formidable political Right.

It was not the success of cardenismo that assured subsequent decades of rule by a corrupt, oligarchical regime employing revolutionary rhetoric even while vigorously suppressing popular agitation for basic human liberties. On the contrary, it was the its failure that set Mexico on its sad course into the present.

NOTES

1. For a collection of essays by leading scholars and Mexican political figures on periodization, change in the Revolution, and the importance of 1940, see Stanley Ross, ed., *Is the Mexican Revolution Dead?* (Philadelphia: Temple University Press, 1966).

2. Regarding the first interpretation, promoted especially by North Americans, see, among others, Townsend, *Lázaro Cárdenas, Mexican Democrat*; Weyl and Weyl, *Reconquest of Mexico*; and Tannenbaum, *Struggle for Peace and Bread*. For the revisionist interpretations, see Hernández Chávez, *La mecánica cardenista*, and Ianni, *El estado capitalista*, among others.

3. See Arturo Anguiano, *El estado y la política obrera del cardenismo* (Mexico City: Ediciones Era, 1975), pp. 46–74.

4. Campbell, *La derecha radical*; narrower monographs on different aspects of the Right include Jean Meyer, *Sinarquismo*; Sargoza, *The Monterrey Elite*; and Negrete's *Relaciones entre el estado y la Iglesia*.

5. Michaels, "Crisis of Cardenismo," pp. 52, 72.

6. Alan Knight, "Popular Culture and the Revolutionary State in Mexico, 1910–1940," *Hispanic American Historical Review* 74:3 (August 1994): 441.

7. Alan Knight, "Cardenismo: Juggernaut or Jalopy?" *Journal of Latin American Studies* 26 (February 1994): 79.

8. Lieuwen, *Mexican Militarism*, p. 125. By sectors: 1.25 million in labor (overwhelmingly in the CTM), 2.5 million in agriculture (mostly the CNC), 55,000 in the military, and 55,000 in "popular" (middle-class) organizations; Edgar Butler, Elizabeth Lanzer, and James Pick, *Atlas of Mexico* (Boulder, Colo.: Westview Press, 1989), p. 11. Nor did Cárdenas begin the longstanding precedent of corrupt elections.

9. Dana Markiewicz, *The Mexican Revolution and the Limits of Agrarian Reform, 1915–1946* (Boulder, Colo.: Lynne Rienner Publishers, 1993), pp. 3, 75, 106, 166.

10. Contreras, *Industrialización y crisis política*, pp. 153–82. The author points to PAN's limited endorsement of Almazán, and meetings between the opposition and PRM, to support his case.

11. A related point is the extent to which the ruling elite intentionally exercise control over the lower classes through the dissemination of conservative social and cultural ideas. Direct links between wealthy industrialists and the grassroots Right will likely disappoint Marxist analysts, the oft-quoted possible funding of the Dorados by the Monterrey elite notwithstanding.

12. Hamilton, *Limits of State Autonomy*, pp. 23, 140–41.

13. Francesca Miller, *Latin American Women and the Search for Social Justice* (Hanover, N.H.: University Press of New England, 1991), pp. 97–101; Contreras, *Industrialización y crisis política*, pp. 150–51. Women were enfranchised gradually in most of Latin America during the 1930s. Brazil extended women's suffrage by constitution in 1934, Argentina in 1949.

Bibliography

ARCHIVAL SOURCES

Mexico

Archivo de la Biblioteca Nacional de Antropología e Historia, Museo Nacional de Antropología e Historia, Mexico City.

Archivo General de la Nación, Ramo Presidentes, Fondos Abelardo Rodríguez and Lázaro Cárdenas, Mexico City.

Archivos de Plutarco Elías Calles y Fernando Torreblanca, Archivo Plutarco Elías Calles, Mexico City.

Hemeroteca Nacional, Centro Cultural Universitario, Universidad Nacional Autónoma de México, Mexico City.

Hemeroteca de la Universidad de Sonora, Hermosillo, Mexico.

United States

Herbert Hoover Presidential Library, Papers of Cabinet Offices, West Branch, Iowa.

National Archives, Records Relating to the Internal Affairs of Mexico, U.S. State Department, 1929–1940, Washington, D.C.

National Archives, War Department Military Intelligence Division, Reports on Mexico, 1919–1940 (microfilm), Washington, D.C.

CONTEMPORARY SOURCES

Periodicals

Spanish Newspapers
  Excelsior
  El Hombre Libre

El Nacional
Omega
La Prensa
El Pueblo (Hermosillo)
El Universal
Spanish Journals, Magazines, and Newsletters
Así
El Eco Revolucionario
Nuevo Régimen
La Palabra
La Reacción
Ultimas Noticias
La Voz de Sureste
English Newspapers
Douglas (Arizona) Daily Dispatch
El Paso Herald-Post
El Paso Times
The Laredo Times
New York Times
San Antonio Express

Printed Documents

Acción Católica Mexicana. *Estatutos Generales de la Acción Católica Mexicana.* Mexico City: Gráficos Michoacán, 1930. [Biblioteca Nacional, Mexico City.]

Almazán, Juan Andreu. *Memorias: Informe y documentos sobre la campaña política de 1940* Mexico City: E. Quintanar Impresor, 1941.

Anguiano Orozco, Arturo, Guadalupe Pacheco Méndez, and Rogelio Vizcaíno. *Cárdenas y la izquierda mexicana: Ensayo, testimonios, documentos.* Mexico City: Juan Pablos Editor, 1984.

Calles, Plutarco Elías. *Correspondencia personal, 1919–1945.* Mexico City: Fondo de Cultura Económica, 1993.

Fernández Boyolí, Manuel, Eustaquio Marrón de Angelis. *Lo que no se sabe de la rebelión cedillista.* Mexico City: P.S.I., 1938.

Mena Brito, Bernardo. *El P.R.U.N., Almazán, y el desastre final.* Mexico City: Ediciones Botas, 1941.

Vasconcelos, José. *Cartas políticas de José Vasconcelos.* Edited by Alfonso Taracena. Mexico City: Editora Librera, 1959.

Diaries, Interviews, and Literary Sources

Alessio Robles, Vito. *Mis andanzas con nuestro Ulises.* Mexico City: Editorial Botas, 1938.

Arbaiza, Genaro. "Are the Americas Safe?" *Current History* 47:12 (December 1937): 29–34.

Beals, Carlton. "Blacks Shirts in Latin America." *Current History* 49:3 (November 1938): 32–34.

———. *The Coming Struggle for Latin America.* New York: Halcyon House, 1938.

———. "Mexico Turns to Fascist Tactics." *The Nation* 82 (January 28, 1931): 110–12.

Beherendt, Richard. "Foreign Influence in Latin America." *Annals of the American Academy of Political and Social Science* 204 (July 1939): 1–8.

Cabrera, Luis. *Veinte años después.* Mexico City: Ediciones Botas, 1938.

Cantú Corro, José. *¿Qué es el Liberalismo? ¿Qué es el Socialismo? ¿Qué es el Comunismo? ¿Qué es el Anarquismo?* Mexico City: 1937. [Biblioteca Nacional.]

Cárdenas, Lázaro. *Obras: Apuntes, 1913–1940.* 2 vols. Mexico City: Universidad Nacional Autónoma de México, 1986.

Creel, George. "Can We Prevent Chaos in Mexico?" *Colliers* (July 23, 1938): 12–13, 49–50.

Daniels, Josephus. *Shirt-Sleeve Diplomat.* Chapel Hill: University of North Carolina Press, 1947.

Dr. Atl. *Oro, más Oro!.* Mexico City: Ediciones Botas, 1936.

Hackett, Charles. "Mexico's New War on the Church." *Current History* 35 (February 1932): 715–18.

———. "Mexico Reopens War on Church." *Current History* 37:2 (November 1932): 205–9.

Hanighen, Frank. "Mexico Moves to the Right." *The Commonweal* 14:11 (July 15, 1931): 280–82.

———. "The Law in Monterrey." *The Commonweal* 17:15 (February 8, 1933): 399–401.

Kelley, Francis. *Blood-Drenched Altars.* Milwaukee: Bruce Publishing Co., 1935.

Kirk, Betty. *Covering the Mexican Front.* Norman: University of Oklahoma Press, 1942.

Kluckhohn, Frank. *The Mexican Challenge.* New York: Doubleday, Duran & Co., 1939.

McCullagh, Francis. *Red Mexico: A Reign of Terror in America.* New York: Louis Carrier Co., 1928.

Portes Gil, Emilio. *Quince años de política mexicana.* Mexico City: Ediciones Botas, 1941.

Rodríguez, Abelardo. *Notas de mi viaje a Rusia.* Mexico City: Editorial Cultura, 1938.

Trejo, Blanca Lydia. *Lo que vi en España: Episodios de la Guerra.* Mexico City: Editorial Polis, 1940.

White, Owen. "Next Door to Communism." *Colliers* (October 3, 1936): 12–13, 53–54.

Wilkie, Edna, and James Wilkie, eds. *México visto en el siglo XX.* Mexico City: Instituto Mexicano de Investigaciones Económicas, 1969.

SECONDARY SOURCES

Adamson, Walter. *Hegemony and Revolution: A Study of Antonio Gramsci's Political and Cultural theory.* Berkeley: University of California Press, 1980.

Allardyce, Gilbert. "What Fascism is Not: Thoughts on the Deflation of a Concept." *American Historical Review* 85 (April 1979): 367–88.

Anderson, Benedict. *Imagined Communities: Reflections on the Origion and Spread of Nationalism.* London: Verso, 1991.

Anguiano, Arturo. *El estado y la política obrera del cardenismo.* Mexico City: Ediciones Era, 1975.

Ankerson, Dudley. *Agrarian Warlord: Saturnino Cedillo and the Mexican Revolution in San Luis Potosí.* DeKalb: Northern Illinois University Press, 1984.

Ashby, Joe. *Organized Labor and the Mexican Revolution under Lázaro Cárdenas.* Chapel Hill: University of North Carolina Press, 1963.

Azuela, Salvador. *La aventura vasconcelista, 1929.* Mexico City: Editorial Diana, 1980.

Bailey, David. *Viva Cristo Rey: The Cristero Rebellion and the Church-State Conflict in Mexico.* Austin: University of Texas Press, 1974.

Bantjes, Adrian. "Politics, Class and Culture in Post-Revolutionary Mexico: Cardenismo and Sonora, 1929–1940." Ph.D. dissertation, University of Texas, 1991.

Bazant, Jan. "From Independence to the Liberal Republic, 1821–1867." In *Mexico since Independence*, pp. 1–48. Edited by Leslie Bethell. Cambridge: Cambridge University Press, 1991.

Becker, Marjorie. "Torching La Purísima, Dancing at the Altar: The Construction of Revolutionary Hegemony in Michoacán, 1934–1940." In *Everyday Forms of State Formation: Revolution and the Negotiation of Rule in Modern Mexico*, pp. 247–64. Edited by Gilbert Joseph and Daniel Nugent. Durham: Duke University Press, 1994.

Bell, James Dunbar. "Attitudes of Selected Groups in the United States towards Mexico, 1930–1940," Ph.D. dissertation, University of Chicago, 1945.

Brachet-Márquez, Viviane. "Explaining Sociopolitical Change in Latin America: The Case of Mexico." *Latin American Research Review* 27:3 (Fall 1992): 91–122.

Brading, David. *Los orígenes del nacionalismo mexicano.* Translated by Soledad Loaeza Grave. Mexico City: Secretaría de Educación Pública, 1973.

Britton, John. *Educación y radicalismo en México: Los años de Bassols, 1931–1934.* Mexico City: Secretaría de Educación Pública, 1976.

———. *Educación y radicalismo en México: Los años de Cárdenas, 1934–1940.* Mexico City: Secretaría de Educación Pública, 1976.

Burke, Edmund. *Reflections on the Revolution in France.* Edited by Oskar Piest and Thomas H. D. Mahoney. New York: Liberal Arts Press, 1955.

Butler, Edgar, Elizabeth Lanzer, and James Pick. *Atlas of Mexico.* Boulder, Colo.: Westview Press, 1989.

Callcott, Wilfrid H. *Liberalism in Mexico, 1857–1929.* Hamden, Conn: Archon Books, 1965.

Camp, Roderic. *Memoirs of a Mexican Politician.* Albuquerque: University of New Mexico Press, 1988.

———. *Politics in Mexico.* New York: Oxford University Press, 1993.

Campbell, Hugh. "The Radical Right in Mexico, 1929–1949." Ph.D. dissertation, University of California at Los Angeles, 1967.

———. *La derecha radical en México, 1929–1949.* Translated by Pilar Martínez Negrete. Mexico City: Editorial Jus, 1976.

Carr, Barry. *Marxism and Communism in Twentieth-Century Mexico.* Lincoln: University of Nebraska Press, 1992.

Case, Robert. "Resurgimiento de los conservadores en México, 1876–1877." *Historia Mexicana* 25:5 (October–December 1975): 204–31.

Clark, Marjorie. *Organized Labor in Mexico.* Chapel Hill: University of North Carolina Press, 1934.

Contreras, Ariel José. *México 1940: Industrialización y crisis política.* Mexico City: Siglo Veintiuno Editores, 1977.

Córdova, Arnaldo. *La ideología de la revolución mexicana: La formación del nuevo régimen.* Mexico City: Ediciones Era, 1973.

————. *La política de masas del cardenismo*. Mexico City: Ediciones Era, 1974.

Correa, Eduardo J. *El balance del cardenismo*. Mexico City: Talleres Linotipográficos, 1941.

Cosío Villegas, Daniel. *La sucesión presidencial*. Mexico City: Cuadernos de Joaquín Mortiz, 1975.

Dantan, Javier Garciadiego. "Duelo de gigantes." *Boletín de Archivos Plutarco Calles y Fernando Torreblanca* 11 (September 1992): 1–15.

Deutsch, Sandra McGee. *Counterrevolution in Argentina, 1900–1932: The Argentine Patriotic League*. Lincoln: University of Nebraska Press, 1986.

————, and Ronald Dolkart, eds. *The Argentine Right: Its History and Intellectual Origins, 1910 to the Present*. Wilmington, Del.: Scholarly Resources, 1993.

Diccionario Porrúa: De historia, biografía, y geografía de México. 5th ed., vol. 1. Mexico City: Editorial Porrúa, 1986.

Dulles, John W. F. *Yesterday in Mexico: A Chronicle of the Revolution, 1919–1936*. Austin: University of Texas Press, 1961.

Dumas, Claude. "El discurso de oposición en la prensa clerical conservadora de México en la época de Porfirio Díaz, 1876–1910." *Historia Mexicana* 39 (July–September 1989): 243–56.

Fagen, Patricia. *Exiles and Citizens: Spanish Republicans in Mexico*. Austin: University of Texas Press, 1973.

Foulkes, Vera. *Los "niños de Morelia" y la escuela España-México: Consideraciones analíticas sobre un experimento social*. Mexico City: Universidad Nacional Autónoma de México, 1953.

Fowler Salamini, Heather. *Agrarian Radicalism in Veracruz, 1920–1938*. Lincoln: University of Nebraska Press, 1971.

García Gutiérrez, Jesús. *Acción anticatólica en México*. Mexico City: Editorial Campeador, 1956.

Gaxiola, Francisco, Jr. *El Presidente Rodríguez*. Mexico City: Editorial Cultura, 1938.

Gledhill, John. *Casi Nada: A Study of Agrarian Reform in the Homeland of Cardenismo*. Albany: State University of New York at Albany: Institute for Mesoamerican Studies, 1991.

Goddard, Adame. *El pensamiento político y social de los católicos mexicanos, 1867–1914*. Mexico City: Universidad Nacional Autónoma de México, Instituto de Investigaciones Historicas, 1981.

González, Luis. *Los artífices del cardenismo*. Mexico City: El Colegio de México, 1979.

————. *Los días del presidente Cárdenas*. Mexico City: El Colegio de México, 1981.

————. *Pueblo en vilo: Una microhistoria de San José de Gracia*. Mexico City: Colegio de México, 1968.

González Navarro, Moises. *La vida social. In Historia moderna de México. 7 vols.* Edited by Daniel Cosío Villegas. Mexico City: El Colegio de México, 1958.

Gramsci, Antonio. *A Gramsci Reader: Selected Writings, 1916–1935*. Edited by David Forgacs. London: Lawrence and Wishart, 1988.

Haglund, David. *Latin America and the Transformation of U.S. Strategic Thought, 1936–1940*. Albuquerque: University of New Mexico Press, 1984.

Hale, Charles. *Mexican Liberalism in the Age of Mora*. New Haven: Yale University Press, 1968.

Hamilton, Nora. *The Limits of State Autonomy: Post-Revolutionary Mexico*. Princeton: Princeton University Press, 1982.

Hernández Chávez, Alicia. *La mecánica cardenista*. Mexico City: El Colegio de México, 1979.

Ianni, Octavio. *El estado capitalista en la época de Cárdneas*. Mexico City: Ediciones Era, 1977.

Joseph, Gilbert, and Daniel Nugent. "Popular Culture and State Formation in Revolutionary Mexico." In *Everyday Forms of State Formation: Revolution and the Negotiation of Rule in Modern Mexico*. Edited by Gilbert Joseph and Daniel Nugent. Durham: Duke University Press, 1994.

Knight, Alan. *The Mexican Revolution*. 2 vols. Cambridge: Cambridge Unversity Press, 1986.

———. "Cardenismo: Juggernaut or Jalopy?" *Journal of Latin American Studies* 26 (February 1994): 73–107.

———. "Popular Culture and the Revolutionary State in Mexico, 1910–1940." *Hispanic American Historical Review* 74:3 (August 1994): 393–444.

———. "The Rise and Fall of Cardenismo, c. 1930–c. 1946." In *Mexico since Independence*, pp. 241–320. Edited by Leslie Bethell. Cambridge: Cambridge University Press, 1991.

———. "Weapons and Arches in the Mexican Revolutionary Landscape." In *Everyday Forms of State Formation: Revolution and the Negotiation of Rule in Modern Mexico*, pp. 35–51. Edited by Gilbert Joseph and Daniel Nugent. Durham: Duke University Press, 1994.

Krause, Corinne. *Los Judíos en Mexico*. Mexico City: Universidad Iberoamericana, 1987.

Laqueur, Walter, ed. *Fascism, a Reader's Guide: Analyses, Interpretations, Bibliography*. Berkeley: University of California Press, 1976.

León-Portilla, Ascensión. *España desde México: Vida y testimonio de transterrados*. Mexico City: Universidad Nacional Autónoma de México, 1978.

Lerner, Victoria. *La educación socialista*. Mexico City: El Colegio de México, 1979.

Lieuwen, Edwin. *Mexican Militarism: The Political Rise and Fall of the Revolutionary Army*. Albuquerque: University of New Mexico Press, 1968.

Lipset, Seymour Martin. *Political Man: The Social Bases of Politics*. Garden City, N.Y.: Doubleday, 1963.

Mabry, Donald. *The Mexican University and the State: Student Conflicts, 1910–1971*. College Station: Texas A & M University Press, 1982.

Magdaleno, Mauricio. *Las palabras perdidas*. Mexico City: Manuel Porrúa, 1956.

Markiewicz, Dana. *The Mexican Revolution and the Limits of Agrarian Reform, 1915–1946*. Boulder: Lynne Rienner Publishers, 1993.

Mayer, Arno J. *Dynamics of Counterrevolution in Europe, 1870–1956: An Analytic Framework*. New York: Harper & Row, 1971.

Medina, Luis. *Del cardenismo al avilacamachismo*. Mexico City: El Colegio de México, 1978.

Meyer, Jean. "Le catholicisme social au Mexique jusqu'en en 1913." *Revue historique* 260 (July–September 1978): 143–59.

———. *The Cristero Rebellion: The Mexican People between Church and State, 1926–1929*. Translated by Richard Southern. Cambridge: Cambridge University Press, 1976.

———. *La Cristiada: La guerra de los cristeros*. 3 vols. Mexico City: Siglo Veintiuno Editores, 1973–1974.

————. "Revolution and Reconstruction in the 1920s." In *Mexico since Independence*, pp. 201–40. Edited by Leslie Bethell. Cambridge: Cambridge University Press, 1991.

————. *Sinarquismo, un fascismo mexicano?* Mexico City: Editorial Joaquín Mortiz, 1979.

Meyer, Lorenzo. *El conflicto social y los gobiernos del Maximato, 1928–1934.* Mexico City: El Colegio de México, 1978.

————. *Los inicios de la institucionalización: La política del Maximato.* Mexico City: El Colegio de México, 1978.

————. *México y los Estados Unidos en el conflicto petrolero, 1917–1942.* Mexico City: El Colegio de México, 1968.

Meyer, Michael C. *Huerta: A Political Portrait.* Lincoln: University of Nebraska Press, 1972.

Michaels, Albert. "The Crisis of Cardenismo." *Journal of Latin American Studies* 2 (1970): 51–79.

————. "Las elecciones de 1940." *Historia Mexicana* 21:1 (July–September 1971): 80–134.

————. "Fascism and Sinarquismo: Popular Nacionalisms Against the Mexican Revolution." *Journal of Church and State* 8 (Spring 1966): 234–50.

Miller, Barbara. "The Role of Women in the Mexican Cristero Rebellion: Las Señoras y las Religiosas." *The Americas* 40:3 (January 1984): 303–23.

Miller, Francesca. *Latin American Women and the Search for Social Justice.* Hanover, N.H.: University Press of New England, 1991.

Monroy Huitrón, Guadalupe. *Política educativa de la revolución, 1910–1940.* Mexico City: Secretaría de Educación Pública, 1975.

Negrete, Martaelena. *Relaciones entre la iglesia y el estado en México, 1930–1940.* Mexico City: El Colegio de México y Universidad Iberoamericana, 1988.

Nolte, Ernst. *Three Faces of Fascism: Action Française, Italian Fascism, National Socialism.* Translated by Leila Vennewitz. New York: Holt, Rinehart & Winston, 1966.

Olivera Sedano, Alicia. *Aspectos del conflicto religioso de 1926 a 1929: Sus antecedentes y consecuencias.* Mexico City: Instituto Nacional de Antropología e Historia, 1966.

O'Malley, Illene. *The Myth of the Revolution: Hero Cults and the Institutionalization of the Mexican State, 1920–1940.* Westport, Conn: Greenwood Press, 1986.

Powell, T. G. *Mexico and the Spanish Civil War.* Albuquerque: University of New Mexico Press, 1981.

Quirk, Robert. *The Mexican Revolution and the Catholic Church, 1910–1929.* Bloomington: Indiana University Press, 1973.

Raat, W. Dirk. "The Antipositivist Movement in Pre-Revolutionary Mexico, 1892–1911." *Journal of Inter-American Studies and World Affairs* 19:1 (February 1977): 83–98.

————. *Mexico and the United States: Ambivalent Vistas.* Athens: University of Georgia Press, 1992.

Raby, David L. *Educación y revolución social en México, 1921–1940.* Translated by Roberto Gómez Ciriza. Mexico City: Secretaría de Educación Pública, 1974.

Reich, Peter Lester. *Mexico's Hidden Revolution: The Catholic Church in Law and Politics since 1929.* South Bend: University of Notre Dame Press, 1995.

Rius Facius, Antonio. *La juventud católica y la revolución mejicana 1910–1925.* Mexico City: Editorial Jus, 1963.

Rivas Mercado, Antonieta. *La campaña de Vasconcelos*. Mexico City: Editorial Oasis, 1981.

Rosenbaum, Walter. *Political Culture*. New York: Praeger, 1975.

Ross, Stanley, ed. *Is the Mexican Revolution Dead?* Philadelphia: Temple University Press, 1966.

Sargoza, Alex. *The Monterrey Elite and the Mexican State, 1880–1940*. Austin: University of Texas Press, 1988.

Sauer, Franz von. *The Alienated "Loyal" Opposition: Mexico's Partido Acción Nacional*. Albuquerque: University of New Mexico Press, 1974.

Sauer, Wolfgang. "National Socialism: Totalitarianism or Fascism?" *American Historical Review* 73 (December 1967): 404–24.

Schmitt, Karl. "Catholic Adjustment to the Secular State: The Case of Mexico, 1867–1911." *Catholic Historical Review* 18 (July 1962): 182–204.

Schuler, Friedrich. *Mexico between Hitler and Roosevelt: Mexican Foreign Policy in the Age of Lázaro Cárdenas*. Albuquerque: University of New Mexico Press, 1997.

Skirius, John. *José Vasconcelos y la cruzada de 1929*. Mexico City: Siglo Veintiuno Editores, 1978.

Soboul, Albert. *The French Revolution, 1787–1799: From the Storming of the Bastille to Napoleon*. Translated by Alan Forrest and Colin Jones. New York: Random House, 1974.

Sodi de Pallares, Elena. *Los Cristeros y José de León Toral*. Mexico City: Editorial Cultura, 1936.

Spencer, Allan A. "The Mexican Revolution under Lázaro Cárdenas: Strategies of Institutionalization." Ph.D. Dissertation, University of Pittsburgh, 1990.

Sutherland, D. M. G. *France 1789–1815: Revolution to Counterrevolution*. London: Fontana Paperbacks and William Collins, 1985.

Tannenbaum, Frank. *Mexico: The Struggle for Peace and Bread*. New York: Alfred A. Knopf, 1956.

Thomas, Hugh. *The Spanish Civil War*. New York: Harper & Row, 1961.

Townsend, William C. *Lázaro Cárdenas, Mexican Democrat*. Ann Arbor, Michigan: George Wahr, 1952.

Turner, Frederick C. *The Dynamic of Mexican Nationalism*. Chapel Hill: University of North Carolina Press, 1968.

Valadés, José C. *Historia general de la revolución mexicana*. 10 Vols. Mexico City: Editor Quesada Brandi, 1963–1967.

Vanderwood, Paul. *Disorder and Progress: Bandits, Police, and Mexican Development*. Lincoln: University of Nebraska Press, 1981.

Vasconcelos, José. *El Proconsulado*. Mexico City: Ediciones Botas, 1939.

Vaughan, Mary Kay. "The Construction of the Patriotic Festival in Tecamachalco, Puebla, 1900–1946." In *Rituals of Rule, Rituals of Resistance: Public Celebrations and Popular Culture in Mexico*, pp. 213–245. Edited by William Beezley, Cheryl English Martin, and William French. Wilmington, Del.: Scholarly Resources, 1994.

———. "The Educational Project of the Mexican Revolution: The Response of Local Societies (1934–1940)." In *Molding the Hearts and Minds: Education, Communications, and Social Change in Latin America*, pp. 106–18. Edited by John A. Britton. Wilmington, Del.: Scholarly Resources, 1994.

———. "Rural Women's Literacy and Education during the Mexican Revolution: Subverting a Patriarchal Event?" In *Women of the Mexican Countryside, 1850–1990*.

Edited by Heather Fowler Salamini and Mary Kay Vaughan. Tucson: University of Arizona Press, 1994.

Wasserman, Mark. "Strategies for Survival of the Porfirian Elite in Revolutionary Mexico: Chihuahua during the 1920s." *Hispanic American Historical Review* 67:1 (Winter 1987): 87–107.

Weber, Eugen. "The Right: An Introduction." In *The European Right: A Historical Profile*, pp. 1–16. Edited by Hans Rogger and Eugen Weber. Berkeley: University of California Press, 1965.

Weyl, Nathaniel, and Sylvia Weyl. *The Reconquest of Mexico Years of Lázaro Cárdenas*. New York: Oxford University Press, 1939.

Index

About the Author

JOHN W. SHERMAN is Assistant Professor of History at Wright State University.

ISBN 0-275-95736-5

90000>

9 780275 957360

HARDCOVER BAR CODE